Seeing the
Deep Sky

Other Wiley Science Editions

Seeing the Deep Sky

Telescopic Astronomy Projects Beyond the Solar System

FRED SCHAAF

with illustrations by Doug Myers

Wiley Science Editions

JOHN WILEY & SONS, INC.

New York • Chichester • Brisbane • Toronto • Singapore

Library of Congress Cataloging-in-Publication Data

Schaaf, Fred.
   Seeing the deep sky : telescopic astronomy projects beyond the solar system / by Fred Schaaf.
     p. cm. — (Wiley science editions)
   Includes bibliographical references and index.
   ISBN 0-471-53068-9. — ISBN 0-471-53069-7 (pbk.)
   1. Astronomy projects—Popular works. 2. Telescopes—Popular works. 3. Astronomy—Observers' manuals. I. Title. II. Series.
QB64.S426 1992
522'.2'078—dc20
                                      91-33119

Printed in the United States of America

10 9 8 7 6 5 4 3 2

Preface

This is the third book in a series devoted to projects in astronomy. Each book is independent of the others. But to capture anything close to the full range of what astronomy offers, you should take a look at all three.

The first book, *Seeing the Sky* (Wiley, 1990), covers naked-eye observations of everything from rainbows, twilights, and meteors out to various kinds of stars and the Milky Way. The second work, *Seeing the Solar System* (Wiley, 1991), is devoted to telescopic projects involving the Moon, Sun, planets, comets, and various minor members of our solar system. The third book—the one you are now reading—offers telescopic projects about the different kinds of stars, star clusters, nebulae, and galaxies that lie beyond our solar system—in what astronomers have come to call *the deep sky.*

This third book, like the previous books, is meant to be used by novice and veteran observers alike, by everyone from a bright junior high school student to an adult amateur astronomer. Like the second, it assumes only that the reader has access to a telescope, and not necessarily a large one (although in some of the activities there are special challenges posed for observers who do happen to have large telescopes). The vast array of additional projects that would be possible with the use of photographic, photoelectric, spectroscopic, and video equipment is outside the scope of this already full book.

There are, however, two possessions that are important, and occasionally critical, to have for carrying out some of the projects. They are: good star maps and access to a sky that is not too severely light-polluted.

First, let's consider the star maps. The complete novice in astronomy can use this book—I assume virtually no prior knowledge. I do assume, however, that even a novice is likely to have already acquired, or will now acquire, at least one basic astronomy handbook that offers star maps. Some of these activities demand, or at least strongly benefit from, the reader having more than basic star maps. Special finder charts for some of the variable stars, nebulae, and galaxies can be found in other books—but above all else in the three-volume *Burnham's Celestial Handbook.* This classic (though modern) and widely available work is indispensable to any serious or avid searcher of the heavens beyond our solar system. Whenever the activities here deal with an object that you do not find on naked-eye star maps, or on a chart of background star fields, the place to locate a photograph or finder chart is implicitly assumed to be in *Burnham's,* unless otherwise noted.

But what of general star maps—what are the best sources for these? Although some introductory astronomy book maps include stars down to near the naked-eye limit, and perhaps plot many fainter deep-sky objects of special interest, I do recommend that the reader obtain a good star atlas. For complete coverage of stars down to the standard naked-eye limit of magnitude 6.5 (and generous coverage of many of the deep-sky objects visible in small telescopes), the best book probably remains *Norton's Star Atlas* (recently revised and published as *Norton's 2000.0 Star Atlas and Reference Handbook*). The more experienced observer who wishes a much fainter limiting magnitude (hence vastly more stars) is probably best served by *Sky Atlas 2000.0,* which has the additional virtue of having had a two-volume *Sky Catalogue 2000.0* produced in conjunction with it. A still fainter limiting magnitude, and conveniently large scale, can be found in the two-volume star atlas *Uranometria 2000.0.* Information on all these star atlases, plus *Burnham's Celestial Handbook,* and many other useful books, periodicals, video- and audiotapes, and astronomical organizations, can be found in the Sources of Information at the back of this book. But the beginner could do well with every activity in this book with no more than *Burnham's* and *Norton's* in his or her possession.

The second important possession is access to a sky that is free from severe light pollution. Light pollution is society's excessive or misdirected outdoor lighting. Double stars and variable stars that are not too faint may be observed fairly well or very well in the telescope even in the midst of strong light pollution. But the majority of sights in this book benefit immensely from a dark sky. Check the Telescopes, Observing Conditions, and Observing Techniques section for advice on how best to minimize or escape from the light pollution that you probably have to deal with at home—and advice on how to work, as all of us who love the stars should, on actually reducing light pollution in our municipality, county, and state. Nothing is a greater threat to the study and enjoyment of the heavens than light pollution.

As with the previous books in this series, my deepest hope is that *Seeing Beyond the Deep Sky* will be used. Reading these activities should be elucidating. In its roots, "elucidating" means "to draw light from," and that is the real goal of the book—to get you outside drawing starlight from the heavens through your telescope and into your eyes. I urge readers to try these activities and to report the results—to local and national amateur astronomical organizations, but also to me (send your letters in care of Wiley Science Editions, John Wiley & Sons, Inc., 605 Third Avenue, New York, NY 10158).

Speaking of Wiley, I want to thank my editors there, Kate C. Bradford and David Sobel. Once again, I've also been glad to work with Laura Cleveland, my production editor at Word Crafters. Personal thanks go to my excellent illustrator Doug Myers, and to Jeff Page, for his invaluable computer work with the diagrams.

Along with surveying a selection of deep-sky objects of the kinds much discussed in books and magazines in recent years—nebulae, star clusters, and galaxies—I hope readers will enjoy the projects in this book on objects less often appreciated (but equally deserving): double stars, colorful stars, and stars that are representative of the various spectral types and classes. A large portion of the book is devoted to learning about the nature of stars themselves (rather than clusters or galaxies of them, or nebulae). And that is as it should be.

Expressed most passionately, this book is about just-touching twin suns of gold and blue (or "crocus yellow" and "light apple green," and "cherry red"); stars of different chemical or atomic brew, ancient or newborn, tiny and dense or vast and tenuous, speeding, spiraling, flaring, hiding and being hid, pulsing, exploding, even behaving in ways for which we do not yet really have convincing explanations; stars pouring in endless varieties of patterning from gases lit and dust clouds silhouetted, as they, and these nebulosities that they both derive from and give rise to, all follow their courses about our great galaxy whose countless relatives swarm like fireflies on a summer night.

That's a bit of what this book is about, expressed most passionately. But whether or not you express the passion, I am sure you will find it if you take yourself out to sift through the shining splendors of a starry night.

Fred Schaaf
Cumberland, NJ

Fundamental Measurements in Astronomy

The following concepts are not necessary to know for many activities in this book; for some activities, however, they are very important.

Time. Universal Time (UT) is 24-hour time, essentially the same as Greenwich mean time (GMT). The day in UT begins at midnight in the time zone of England's Greenwich meridian. In the United States, local standard time is 5 (eastern standard time [EST]), 6 (central standard time [CST]), 7 (mountain standard time [MST]), and 8 (Pacific standard time [PST]) hours behind UT. Thus, 10h UT on January 18 would be 5:00 A.M. EST and 4h UT on January 18 would be 11:00 P.M. EST on January 17.

Position. The system of celestial coordinates sometimes referred to in this book is that of *right ascension* (RA) and *declination*. On the celestial sphere of the heavens, with its equator and poles directly over those of Earth, RA and declination are similar to longitude and latitude, respectively, on Earth. RA is not measured in degrees west or east of the Greenwich meridian, however, but in 24 "hours" (containing "minutes" and "seconds" of angular measure), which run east from the 0^h line of RA. That line goes through the vernal equinox point in the sky (where the Sun is located in the heavens as spring begins). Declination is measured in degrees, minutes, and seconds, like latitude, but declinations north of the celestial equator are preceded by a plus sign ($+$) and those south of the celestial equator are preceded by a minus sign ($-$).

FUNDAMENTAL MEASUREMENTS IN ASTRONOMY

Angular Distance. From horizon to zenith is 90° (of the 360° around the entire heavens above and below the horizon). The Moon and Sun appear about 0.5° wide. Your fist at arm's length is about 10° wide. Your hand at arm's length, with the forefinger and little finger extended fully, is about 15° wide.

Distance in Space. The most famous unit of measure for interstellar and intergalactic distances is the light-year. It is the distance that light (or any form of electromagnetic radiation), the fastest thing in the universe (speed about 186,300 miles per second or about 300,000 km/s) can travel in one year. A light-year is about 6 trillion (that is, 6 million million) miles or about 63,000 AU (AU is *astronomical unit*—the average distance between the Sun and Earth). Another unit of measure for great distances is the *parsec* (short for "parallax second"), the distance at which an object's *parallax* (its change of position due to a change of our viewing angle—in this case the change from one side of Earth's orbit to the other) is one arc-second. One parsec equals 3.2616 light-years.

Brightness. In astronomy, brightness is measured by magnitude. Originally, all naked-eye stars were categorized in six classes of brightness, from first magnitude (brightest) to sixth magnitude (faintest). In modern times, the scale has been extended to zero and to negative magnitudes for very bright objects and to much higher numbers for objects so faint that they require optical aid to see. Decimals are used between two magnitudes: A star midway in brightness between magnitude 1.0 and 2.0 is 1.5 (the magnitude 1.5 star is dimmer than the magnitude 1.0 star—the lower the magnitude, the brighter the object). A difference of 1 magnitude means one object is about 2.512 times brighter than another. This is because it was considered useful to set a 5-magnitude difference equal to 100 times—2.512 (actually 2.5118 . . .) multiplied by itself 5 times is 100.

There are various kinds of magnitude. Best known is *apparent magnitude,* which is simply the magnitude that an object appears to have in our sky (we can further specify *apparent visual magnitude* or *apparent photographic magnitude*). Apparent magnitude is contrasted with *absolute magnitude,* the brightness that an object would appear to have if it were located at a standard distance from us—a distance of 10 parsecs (thus 32.616 light-years). *Bolometric magnitude* is the brightness of an object measured not just in visible light but in all wavelengths of electromagnetic radiation (Betelgeuse is not the star of best apparent visual magnitude in our sky, but it radiates so much in the invisible infrared wavelengths that it is the star of best apparent bolometric magnitude).

Metric Conversions. This book uses both miles and kilometers. To convert from kilometers to miles, multiply the figure by 0.6214. To convert from miles to kilometers, multiply the figure by 1.609.

Telescopes, Observing Conditions, and Observing Techniques

Telescopes. This book is not a guide to telescope selection, use, or care. The reader is directed to the Sources of Information for suggested reading on these topics. But a few elementary points on telescopes may be mentioned here.

The three most important types of telescopes are the *reflector,* the *refractor,* and the *catadioptric.* The reflector uses mirrors and the refractor uses lenses, while the catadioptric employs both reflective and refractive elements. The most popular type of reflector is the *Newtonian;* the most popular catadioptric is the *Schmidt–Cassegrain.* The two most important types of telescope mountings are the *equatorial* and the *altazimuth.* A special form of the latter, the *Dobsonian mounting,* has become popular in the past decade for observing many of the kinds of deep-sky objects discussed in this book. The idea is to use a telescope with as large an *aperture* (diameter of primary mirror) as possible on an inexpensive Dobsonian mounting to gather as much light as possible from these mostly faint objects. A large-aperture but small-*focal-ratio* (ratio of mirror focal length to width) Newtonian or Schmidt–Cassegrain will generally not give as sharp an image as a large-focal-ratio Newtonian or refractor (which are thus good for splitting double stars). But a small-focal-ratio ("fast") Newtonian or Schmidt–Cassegrain will give adequately sharp images of deep-sky objects if these telescopes are in proper *collimation* (alignment of optical elements).

The quality of the eyepieces, or *oculars,* used with a telescope can be nearly as important as proper collimation.

While large aperture is generally highly desirable in observing most objects beyond our solar system, there are views of widely spread star clusters and star fields that are best seen with the very low magnification and wide fields of view of binoculars or an *RFT* (rich-field telescope).

Transparency and "Seeing." There is more to good observing conditions than a cloud-free sky. The atmosphere's degree of freedom from moisture and dust is called *transparency;* its degree of freedom from turbulence is called *"seeing."*

Some kinds of astronomical observations demand good transparency; others, good "seeing." Any observation that requires glimpsing faint objects is best tried when the transparency is good, because the light from celestial objects is scattered away by moisture and dust in the air. Any observation that requires sharp images is best tried when the "seeing" is good, because the steadier the atmosphere is (the less turbulent) the sharper your view should be. Double star observations require excellent "seeing." But most other observations of stars, clusters, nebulae, and galaxies benefit more from good transparency.

Light Pollution. This is the greatest threat to astronomy, to our direct view of our universe. Light pollution is excessive or misdirected artificial outdoor lighting. It results from inferior lighting fixtures and practices that do more than rob us of our view of the stars. Light pollution costs all of us money (several billion dollars a year in the United States alone) and wastes energy, as millions of unnecessary tons of coal and barrels of oil are burned each year—a significant contribution to air pollution, acid rain, and greenhouse warming. The glare from poor lighting fixtures greatly reduces traffic safety and certainly does not provide greater security against crime.

Light pollution is so damaging to our view of most objects beyond our solar system that we need to educate ourselves about how best to minimize and escape it. Larger-aperture telescopes, light pollution filters, and even a dark cloth placed over the head while observing to block off stray light are all means by which to improve the view. The fact remains, however, that traveling to a darker site is usually the best expedient. When trying to select a prime site, bear in mind *Walker's law,* which indicates that if you have two cities with the same population—and thus roughly the same amount of urban skyglow (light pollution shining up and out from them), and one city is at half the distance of the other, the closer city has 6 times more effect on the sky. Thus, it is worse to have a moderate-sized city a few miles away than a very large city a few dozen miles away. For more on the Walker's law formula, refer to pages 116 and 117 in the first volume of this series, *Seeing the Sky.*

Comparing the actual intensity of skyglows to that predicted by

Walker's law can produce some very important data (a city with a glow that exceeds the Walker's law prediction must be producing more than the law's assumed average of about 500 to 1,000 lumens of light per person). And such data can now be sent to a central clearinghouse of information and advice about light pollution and how we can reduce it.

For, of course, we must reduce it. The spread of light pollution in recent years has been so great that no increase in your telescopic aperture, no use of filter, no running ever farther away from cities can suffice in ultimately saving your view of a truly dark sky (these expedients become quite expensive, too, threatening to make astronomy's cost beyond the means of the average person). I urge every reader of this book to help restore our generation's view of the heavens, and to save the next generation's, by learning more about the problem and its solutions and by sharing that information with others. The essential way to begin is to consult the International Dark-Sky Association (IDA), the central clearinghouse for light pollution information and advice. For information, write to:

IDA
3545 North Stewart
Tucson, AZ 85716

Observing Techniques. There are a number of pointers that can be given to improve your observational abilities. Here, I will mention only a few of the basics.

One basic technique that most observers soon learn is to give the eyes about 15 to 30 minutes to adjust to darkness until they reach something close to their maximum sensitivity to faint light. This is *dark adaptation.* Equally important is the technique of using *averted vision.* If you direct your gaze just to the side of a faint celestial object, you will find it becomes easier to see. This is due to the fact that the retinas of our eyes are most sensitive to light that is somewhat away from their centers.

Many other observing techniques are just plain common sense. Resting the eyes frequently makes obvious sense, but it is also important to move the eyes around somewhat while observing, due to a strange trait of the visual system called the *Troxler phenomenon:* An image kept at the same point on the retina after awhile is ignored and seems to disappear from view! For more on the various abilities and limitations of our vision with regard to astronomy, see the chapter, The Powers of Vision, in my earlier book *The Starry Room* (Wiley, 1988). For additional information on observing with glasses and contact lenses, understanding exit pupils and eye relief, and more, refer to articles on these topics in the major astronomy magazines and treatment of the subject in books on telescopes and their use.

Note on Nomenclature

There are various names and designations that are given to stars and deep-sky objects.

Many of the naked-eye stars receive a scientific name using a letter of the Greek alphabet and the genitive form of the constellation in which they are located. The *Bayer letters* (because they were originally applied to the stars by Johannes Bayer) often work in order of brightness (the first letter of the alphabet—alpha (α)—is given to the brightest star in the constellation, and so on). But Bayer was mistaken about the relative order of brightness in many cases and in others deliberately followed another criterion for assigning letters to stars. The letters of the Greek alphabet and genitive forms of the constellations' names are given in the Appendixes of this book.

After the Bayer letters are used up in a constellation, the next fainter stars may be given only a *Flamsteed* number within the constellation. In John Flamsteed's catalog, stars were numbered in order of increasing right ascension within their constellation. This method is also used for star clusters, nebulae, and galaxies in the New General Catalogue (NGC), except that there the numbering is in order of increasing right ascension *within the entire heavens.* For more on the NGC and the Messier Catalogue (the latter is listed in its own appendix at the back of this book), see the text itself.

One final kind of star designation especially deserves explanation here, because it is not explained fully in the text (unlike the system of designations for variable stars, which *is*). In double star systems, the brighter star is generally given the added designation *A* (Sirius A and B, etc.). But sometimes the capital letters are applied in order of discovery or of increasing right ascension. When a superscript number is added to the Greek letter—such as Alpha[1] Capricorni and Alpha[2] Capricorni—the numbering is generally in order of increasing right ascension, rather than decreasing brightness.

Contents

CONTENTS

STARS

1.

The Brightest Stars—1 (Autumn Stars)

Observe each of the first-magnitude stars of autumn, noting their color through the telescope. Identify the quasi-companion of Fomalhaut. Ponder the true nature of each of these suns and how it differs from that of our own Sun, and from that of other stars.

The easiest way to start learning about the nature of the stars is to observe and learn about the physical realities of the most familiar stars—those that appear brightest in our sky.

You may have already seen all of the very brightest stars visible from your latitude—with the naked eye. But how about through a telescope? Even many veteran observers have not done so—or don't have any idea whether they've done so!

A look through the telescope at a bright star is impressive because of the increased power of the radiance. The star Sirius shines as brightly as a concentrated half-Moon in a 6-inch telescope. But there is more to see. The view is especially interesting because you can see the star's color better than you could with the naked eye (if the star is fairly high up on a night when the atmosphere is fairly calm). And maybe even more interesting is trying to split, or see a lesser companion star of, those bright stars that are *double stars*.

But whether or not the bright star you see is colorful, or a double star, there is a more basic reason for observing it: Doing so helps you appreciate it as both an example of several general classes of stars and as an individual star.

In activities later in this book, we will define and learn more about the differences between red giant and white dwarf stars, spectral class O and G stars, luminosity class I and V stars, various kinds of double stars, and sundry kinds of variable stars. But in our first four activities, we will merely note some of these classifications and properties briefly as they apply to each of the apparently brightest stars. A simple listing of the most important statistics about the brightness and distance of these stars is given in Table 1. A much more complete listing appears as Appendix 2.

Notice that I refer to these objects in the first four activities as the

Table 1
Some Basic Data on the Brightest Stars

Star	Constellation	App. Mag.	Abs. Mag.	Distance light-years
Sirius	Canis Major	−1.46	1.4	8.6
Canopus	Carina	−0.72	−2.5	74
Alpha Centauri	Centaurus	−0.27	4.1	4.3
Arcturus	Bootes	−0.04	0.2	34
Vega	Lyra	0.03	0.6	25
Capella	Auriga	0.08	0.4	41
Rigel	Orion	0.12	−7.1	910
Procyon	Canis Minor	0.38	2.6	11.4
Achernar	Eridanus	0.46	−1.3	69
Betelgeuse	Orion	0.50v	−5.6	540
Beta Centauri	Centaurus	0.61v	−4.4	320
Alpha Crucis	Crux	0.76	−4.6	510
Altair	Aquila	0.77	2.3	16
Aldebaran	Taurus	0.85v	−0.3	60
Antares	Scorpius	0.96v	−4.7	440
Spica	Virgo	0.98v	−3.2	220
Pollux	Gemini	1.14	0.7	40
Fomalhaut	Piscis Austrinus	1.16	2.0	22
Beta Crucis	Crux	1.25v	−4.7	460
Deneb	Cygnus	1.25	−7.2	1,500
Regulus	Leo	1.35	−0.3	69
Adhara	Canis Major	1.50	−4.8	570
Castor	Gemini	1.57	0.5	49

The letter v indicates that the star is variable (of these stars, only Betelgeuse and Antares vary markedly). The magnitudes for double stars are the combined brightnesses.

"apparently" brightest stars. A basic lesson about stars is this: Their apparent brightness is the product of both their true brightness and their distance from us. The stars we see, seemingly all equally far, are actually at many different distances. Veteran amateur astronomers think they are well aware of this fact. But how often do they actually ponder it when they look at a constellation with the naked eye, or a smaller star field through the telescope? Doesn't the fact usually remain a mere idea, completely divorced from actual observation?

It shouldn't. When looking at stars we should always bear in mind not only their appearance, but the physical reality which underlies that appearance. Doing so enriches the experience, making the sight more beautiful because it is more meaningful.

Before we start our telescopic tour of the brightest stars, you need to know the basic facts about astronomers' measures of brightness, position, and distance. If you don't already know the basics about *magnitude, right ascension* (RA), and *declination,* or what and how far a *light-year* is, refer now to the note on Fundamental Measurements in Astronomy at the beginning of this book. Here, I will reiterate only a few of the definitions. *Absolute magnitude* is the magnitude (brightness) a star would have if placed at a standard distance from the Earth—a distance of about 32½ light-years (actually 10 *parsecs,* the parsec being a special unit of distance we discuss in Activity 12). Besides absolute magnitude, another measure of the true brightness of stars is *luminosity.* In this book the word *luminosity* will always refer to the true brightness of a star or other object. Luminosity is usually given in units of the Sun's luminosity (Sun's luminosity = 1).

Now let's proceed with our season-by-season tour of the stars of greatest apparent brightness (lowest apparent magnitude). We'll start with the season that has the fewest first-magnitude stars—autumn (autumn in Earth's Northern Hemisphere, that is). If you are currently in another season, you may wish to simply read about these autumn stars; but in one of the next three activities, you can read about *and* actually observe the stars of the season you are currently in. Remember, however, that when we say "autumn stars" or "summer stars" we really mean just those visible in the mid-evening hours for that season. That time of night is the most convenient for a majority of people. But if you are willing to go out later in the night, you can check out the stars of the next season (maybe even two seasons ahead if you get up before a winter dawn to observe). So you have no excuse for putting off actually doing (not just reading about) most of these first four activities!

There are only two traditional first-magnitude stars in the quarter of the heavens that is best seen while Earth's Northern Hemisphere is experiencing autumn.

Achernar is a lonely star of the far south, well below the horizon of viewers at 40°N latitude. It is located at the south end of long Eridanus the River. This star is one of the very few bright ones which earns the lowercase letter designation "p" for "peculiar spectrum." In the past few decades, estimates of this star's distance (and therefore of its true brightness) have lessened (see Table 1). But there's surely no doubt that its true brightness is much greater than that of Vega (summer's star of greatest apparent brightness), which is the star of greatest true brightness within 30 light-years of Earth.

Fomalhaut is the lone bright beacon in Piscis Austrinus (the Southern Fish), or indeed in a whole vast, dim section of the heavens. Fomalhaut beats Antares for the title of the most southerly first-magnitude star visible from 40°N latitude (whereas Vega passes nearly overhead for the United States, Fomalhaut holds that distinction for Australia). The true brightness of Fomalhaut seems to be a bit greater than that of the summer star Altair, but it is somewhat farther (Yet Fomalhaut lies only 22 light-years away, one of the closer bright stars).

Fomalhaut is distinctive in having a companion star too far from it to be bound to it by gravity, yet lying at the same distance from us and moving through space with a motion similar to Fomalhaut's. The best guess is that Fomalhaut and the star (which I propose we might call its "quasi-companion") are the final survivors of what used to be a *star cluster* or *star association,* the other members having long since drifted off on their own. The quasi-companion is nearly 1 light-year away from Fomalhaut and can be found almost 2° south of Fomalhaut in the sky (see Figure 1). It is an orangish star with an apparent magnitude of 6.5, so that its true brightness is only about 10 percent that of the sun.

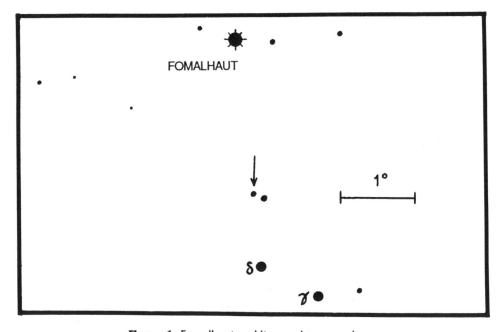

Figure 1 Fomalhaut and its quasi-companion.

Questions

1. Are you located far enough south to be able to spot Achernar? If so, what do you note about its appearance? (Is its supposedly white color affected by its appearing at low angular altitude in your sky?)

2. What hue does Fomalhaut possess at different angular altitudes on different nights?

3. Can you find the "quasi-companion" of Fomalhaut?

2.

The Brightest Stars—2 (Winter Stars)

> *Observe each of the first-magnitude stars of winter, noting their color through the telescope and identifying any true or false companion stars they may have. Ponder the true nature of each of these suns and how it differs from that of our own Sun, and from that of other stars.*

Whereas (Northern Hemisphere) autumn constellations have the fewest first-magnitude stars, the winter constellations have the most. We continue with our tour.

Sirius appears far brighter than any star seen in the night sky. In fact, its magnitude is −1.46, reminding us that calling it a "first-magnitude" star is not strictly accurate, merely a throwback to earlier history when all stars in the first class of brightness were lumped together as "first magnitude."

Sirius is the only star bright enough to show obviously and frequently even to the naked eye the color changes caused by turbulence in our atmosphere. The show of these colors in the telescope is all the more amazing.

But when you learn more about the nature of Sirius, its impressive appearance becomes still more interesting.

Sirius is the closest bright star visible from 40°N, and the sixth-closest star system known in all the heavens (excluding our own Sun).

Sirius is 8.6 light-years away. We say Sirius is "near" for a star—yet light, the fastest thing in the universe, traveling at 186,000 miles per second, takes over 8 years to reach us from Sirius. Sirius is over 500,000 times farther from our Earth than the Sun is. And yet, Sirius is, compared to most stars, "near"—only one of the other dozen or so apparently brightest stars in its constellation Canis Major is less than 200 light-years from Earth! These other, more distant suns of Canis Major are all of greater true brightness than Sirius. Sirius is, however, the star of greatest true brightness in our "neighborhood" until we get out to Vega.

For comments and questions on the true color of Sirius, see the entry on Vega in Activity 4.

Sirius has a famous white dwarf companion star, a true companion in that it really does orbit Sirius (or rather the two stars orbit around a common center of gravity). This star is only magnitude 8 and close enough to Sirius itself to be extremely difficult to observe. In the early 1990s, the companion star—called Sirius B or, playfully, "the Pup"—moves into its least apparent separation from Sirius. For an orbital chart showing the position of this star relative to Sirius, see Figure 12 and Activity 17.

Moving your telescope about 4°S from Sirius brings you to the relatively bright, attractive star cluster M41 (see Activity 24).

Canopus appears as the second brightest star in the heavens, but is too far south to appear at all for viewers north of 37°N latitude. Viewers at this latitude and slightly farther south will have to point their telescopes due south when Canopus culminates (crosses the meridian, the line running from due north through the zenith to due south) and is at its highest. Culmination at midnight occurs about December 27 for Canopus, only about 20 minutes before Sirius culminates (thus, Sirius is not exactly, but roughly due north of Canopus). When even a star as bright as Canopus is peeking just above the horizon, the dimming effect of a longer pathway of air down low—*atmospheric extinction*—renders it too dim to see with the naked eye. If you observe from a latitude where Canopus rises fairly high in the sky, check its color.

Only a few decades ago, astronomers thought Canopus was a superluminous star as much as 600 light-years distant. Now there has been enough study of Canopus to indicate its distance may be as little as 70 light-years. But that would still make this star over 700 times more luminous than the Sun!

Capella, in Auriga the Charioteer, passes high in the sky for midnorthern latitude viewers, and at 40°N is almost a *north circumpolar star* (a star whose apparent circling around the north celestial pole is never cut off by the horizon, and so never appears to set). The spectroscope proves that the point of light we see is actually produced by a close-together pair of stars, both of which are a number of times larger than the Sun, but rather similar to the Sun in spectral type. The two stars are too close together to see separately in the telescope, but can you detect a slight (and Sunlike) yellowish hue in their combined radiance? There is still considerable mystery about these suns, which are thought to revolve around each other in a nearly circular orbit and about 70 million miles (roughly the Sun–Venus distance) apart. One of the stars may have very turbulent motion in its atmosphere. Another point of light which is part of this system is a tenth-magnitude red dwarf star, situated about 12 arc-minutes southeast of the primary star (it is at about PA 137° from the primary—"PA" being the position angle, which runs from 0° = North to 90° = East and so on around the compass 360° back to North). This red dwarf is itself a close (but splittable) double, so there are at least four stars in the Capella system.

Rigel appears imperceptibly fainter than Capella, but is tremen-dously farther away and thus tremendously greater in true brightness. Rigel is in fact a blue giant star, and one of the most luminous suns in our part of the galaxy. Of the first-magnitude stars, only Deneb rivals it in true brightness. Its blueness ought to be more prominent than that of Sirius, though in a glance at the two together with the naked eye the better apparent brilliance of Sirius is an advantage in making any color vivid. See what you think of the color of Rigel when you look at it through your telescope. If you have a 6-inch telescope, or even a slightly smaller telescope on an excellent night, you should be able to detect the companion of Rigel, about magnitude 6.7 and about 9 arc-seconds from Rigel at about PA 202°. This star is itself at least a spectroscopic double (in other words, too close together to be split in the telescope). Both members of this pair that form the companion are themselves about 75 times brighter than our meager Sun. The primary star, Rigel A, seems to be losing some material, puffing it off (though some falls back) with a period of about 21.9 days. After the occurrence of Supernova 1987A, astronomers now believe that some blue giants could go directly to the explosive supernova stage (rather than first becoming a red giant). Rigel may be a prime candidate for such an explosion.

Procyon is the *lucida* (star of greatest apparent brightness in a constellation) in Canis Minor the Little Dog. It is, appropriately, consid-erably less bright in our sky than Sirius, the *lucida* of Canis Major the Big Dog. What is surprising is that Procyon happens to be not much farther from us than Sirius; thus, it is considerably less bright in reality. Procyon has a white dwarf companion like that of Sirius except even smaller and dimmer. Amateur telescopes have not revealed the companion. But see whether you think your telescope shows a tinge of any color other than white in the main star.

Betelgeuse shines brighter in our sky than any other red giant, and may be as large as any sun known. While its luminosity is far less than Rigel's, there have been rare occasions when its apparent brightness rivaled or surpassed Rigel's, for Betelgeuse is a *variable star* with a large possible range of brightness variation (see my earlier book *Seeing the Sky* for more on Betelgeuse's variations). The brightness changes are thought to be associated with radical pulsations in size. We can conjecture that the average diameter of the star could be as "small" as the orbit of Mars or even larger than the orbit of Jupiter. Betelgeuse probably has at least two companions, both much too close to the star to see in the telescope—in fact, one is so close that it may orbit within the dimly glowing and incredibly tenuous outer layers of Betelgeuse (a star within a star!). Betelgeuse was the first star to have features—corresponding to sunspots on our own Sun, but vastly larger—identified on its surface (by special electronic imaging and computer techniques). Through your own telescope, however small, you can study the color of Betelgeuse and how that color may vary with its changes in brightness.

Aldebaran appears to be the brightest star in the Hyades star cluster, but is actually about twice as close as the cluster members and unrelated to them in space. Aldebaran (eye of Taurus the Bull) is almost exactly as distant and as luminous as the spring star Regulus (heart of Leo the Lion). But Aldebaran is a far cooler star (note the orangish hue of Aldebaran in the telescope) and thus tremendously larger than Regulus and the Sun—it is in fact about 20 times wider than the Sun. The only true companion star of Aldebaran is an exceedingly faint and difficult one. Aldebaran has a large space velocity and almost all of it is directed away from us (it is the first-magnitude star receding from us most rapidly).

Pollux and *Castor* lie about 4° apart, the twin bright lights of Gemini the Twins. Their true brightnesses seem to be almost identical, but Castor is a little farther and thus appears somewhat dimmer. Castor just misses being on the bright side of the traditional cutoff between first- and second-magnitude stars (in fact, the far less famous Canis Major star Adhara is marginally brighter than Castor). Compare the colors of Castor and Pollux in the telescope, noting that Pollux is the ruddier, cooler, and thus (considering that their true brightnesses are similar) considerably larger (see Figure 2). A profound difference between Pollux and Castor, moreover, is that Pollux seems to be a single star, whereas the Castor system contains at least six stars! A small telescope at a fairly high power shows Castor as two bright and beautiful points. A redder dim compan-

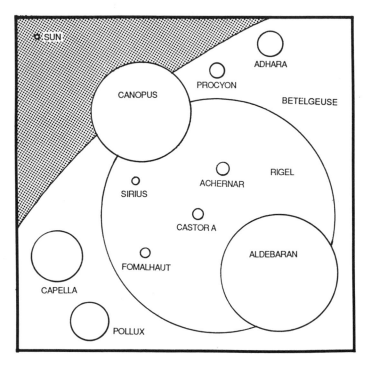

Figure 2 Sizes of the brightest autumn and winter stars.

ion is at a considerable distance away. For statistics on the component stars of Castor, see Table 6 in Activity 16.

Adhara, located in southern Canis Major, is (like Castor) just a bit too faint to have been considered a first-magnitude star. It actually appears a little brighter than the far more famous Castor. It is a B-type star and its luminosity is very great.

Questions

1. What is the true color of Sirius? How good must "seeing" (the measure of image quality as a function of atmospheric turbulence) be in order for you not to see a variety of colors fluctuating in the rays of Sirius? Can you rise to the very difficult challenge of finding the companion of Sirius?

2. Does Canopus get above the horizon at all as seen from your latitude? If you are able to see it, what color does it display and how is this affected by its angular altitude on different nights? Can you detect any yellow in Capella? In Procyon?

3. How much blue do you detect in Rigel? How small a telescope suffices to reveal the companion of Rigel? How reddish does Betelgeuse appear? How much does this color vary with changes in the star's brightness?

4. What color is Aldebaran exactly? Can you picture it as an object in the foreground of the Hyades cluster? What colors are Castor and Pollux? How small a telescope suffices to split Castor?

3.

The Brightest Stars—3 (Spring Stars)

Observe each of the first-magnitude stars of spring, noting their color through the telescope and identifying any true or false companion stars they may have. Ponder the true nature of each of these suns and how it differs from that of our own Sun, and from that of other stars.

We continue the tour of the previous two activities, this time with the first-magnitude stars of spring.

Alpha Centauri (sometimes called Rigel Kentaurus) is too far south to be seen from 40°N, but is famous for being the closest star to Earth, less than 4.4 light-years distant. We will deal with it in our activity on observing the nearest stars. Actually, Alpha Centauri is a triple star system, the light of the two bright, close-together members making a combined radiance that looks slightly brighter than Arcturus to the naked eye. Even a small telescope splits the point of light into a spectacular pair, and can be used to locate the third star, a red dwarf called Proxima Centauri, almost 2° away from the main pair (see Table 2 in Activity 12 and Table 7 in Activity 17 for statistics on the components of the system). One of the pair of bright stars is very Sunlike, and the whole system shows a great *proper motion* (apparent motion in relation to a fixed background—see Activity 13). Beings on a planet in the Alpha Centauri system would see our Sun as a first-magnitude star a few degrees from the Perseus Double Cluster.

Arcturus is the brightest star north of the celestial equator, the brightest orange star, and the first-magnitude star with the most unusual motion and destination. Arcturus is the only bright star we see that is not traveling pretty much in the equatorial plane of the Milky Way galaxy, but instead is circling the galactic center in an orbit highly inclined to that plane. Arcturus is swooping down through the equatorial plane, having been too far north of the plane to be visible to the naked eye from Earth about half a million years ago. Its future path brings us a little closer to it in the next few thousand years, but then its dive south of the equatorial plane takes it away from unaided vision again in about half a million years. The *space velocity* (true velocity through space) of this "gypsy star" is twice as great as any other first-magnitude star, about 3 to 10 times greater than most. Little of this swift motion is in *radial velocity* (the component of its motion directed away from or toward—in this case, still a little toward—us). Thus, although it is about 35 light-years away, its proper motion is much greater than that of any first-magnitude star except our nearest neighbor Alpha Centauri. Arcturus is heading at the rate of 2.28 arc-seconds per year toward the territory of the constellation Virgo. Arcturus appears to have no true companion star or notable false companion, but its color—variously described as "topaz," "golden-orange," and "champagne-colored"—deserves careful study. This gypsy is a great object, up to 15 times larger and 100 times more luminous than our Sun (see Figure 3).

Beta Centauri (also called Hadar) is only about 4½° from Alpha Centauri in our sky (thus too far south to be seen from 40°N), but lies roughly 100 times farther away. Thus, it is a profoundly different star than Alpha, its luminosity perhaps almost 10,000 times greater than the Sun. Does it show color other than white? It is a rather difficult double star, even though its companion is magnitude 4.1, because the fainter star is only 1.3 arc-seconds from the primary.

Alpha Crucis (also called Acrux) is a splendid double star, whose components are stars of similar size and luminosity, separated by about 4½ arc-seconds. Though only a few times larger than the Sun, each of these stars is several thousand times more luminous. Acrux is part of the small but striking Crux—the Southern Cross, not visible from 40°N.

Spica is quite similar to Alpha[1] and Alpha[2] Crucis in size, luminosity, and spectral type, all three stars resembling lesser versions of Beta Centauri. But Spica has been shown to be a spectroscopic double with the companion star very close, slightly eclipsing the main star—and the main star itself subject to regular pulsations. The brightness changes associated with these slight eclipses and small pulsations are too minute to notice visually. Look for blue in the glow of Spica.

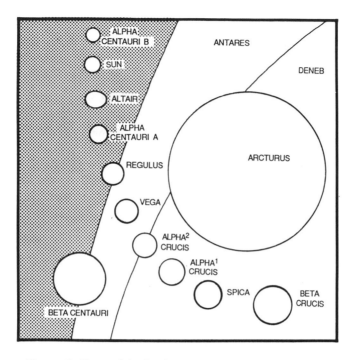

Figure 3 Sizes of the brightest spring and summer stars.

Beta Crucis (sometimes called Becrux or Mimosa) is yet another star similar in spectral type to Spica and the two Alpha Crucis stars, but somewhat larger and more luminous (almost as large and bright as Beta Centauri). Like Acrux, this star is too far south to see from most of the United States. Like Spica, Becrux pulses with only a slight change of magnitude. A companion star, probably not physically related, is only eleventh magnitude and only 44 arc-seconds away from the main star.

Regulus marks the heart of Leo the Lion and is the first-magnitude star closest to the ecliptic (thus a frequent target of Sun, Moon, and planets). It is about as far as Canopus and Aldebaran, and about as luminous as Aldebaran—but far smaller than those other two stars. Its spectral class is close to that of Rigel (but Rigel is immensely more luminous and big)—so look for a tinge of blue in it. Look for a companion of Regulus about 180″ from the main star, with a PA of about 307°.

Questions

1. If you live (or visit) far enough south, can you judge the colors of Alpha Centauri A and B, and locate the third star, Proxima Centauri (see Activity 12 for finding information)? Can you split Acrux, and find the faint and probably false companion of Becrux?

2. What are the colors of Arcturus and Spica? Can you detect the large proper motion of the former in comparison to its position on an old star chart, or even to its position you observed last year? Can you contemplate the unusual motion and physical nature of Arcturus while observing it?

3. Can you detect blue in Regulus? Can you find its companion (what color is it)? If you have a large telescope can you split the companion of Regulus?

4.

The Brightest Stars—4 (Summer Stars)

Observe each of the first-magnitude stars of summer, noting their color through the telescope and identifying any true or false companion stars they may have. Ponder the true nature of each of these suns and how it differs from that of our own Sun, and from that of other stars.

Let us continue our tour of the brightest stars, this time by observing those that are best seen in (Northern Hemisphere) summer.

Vega is the brightest star of northern summer, and a look at Table 1 shows that it deserves to be called "the Sirius of Summer" for more reasons than just this. Vega's true brightness (as measured in absolute magnitude or in luminosity) and its true size are not too much greater than those of winter's beacon, that most brilliant star in all the heavens, Sirius. Vega appears much less bright than Sirius only because Vega is about 3 times more distant from us. The most basic similarity between the two stars is their composition, as revealed to us by their spectral class—to which the color and surface temperature correspond closely. Many naked-eye observers detect a tinge of blue in the otherwise whitish light of both Sirius and Vega, but you should see what you think of their color through a telescope (several different ones, if possible) on various nights. Astronomer Robert Burnham, Jr., says in *Burnham's Celestial Handbook* that (with both naked eye and telescope?) "Vega has always seemed distinctly bluer than Sirius" to him.

Vega differs significantly from Sirius in having no known true companion star—but it does have a physically unrelated star (in fact, two) which happen to lie along almost the same line of sight and make a pretty view with it for amateur observers. Both of these false companions are about magnitude 9½, one of them about 1 arc-minute south of Vega, the other about 2 arc-minutes northeast of Vega. On one fine night, my 10-inch f/7.5 reflector revealed both stars clearly, while a friend's 8-inch f/4.5 showed only one of them, and not so plainly. By the way, Vega's little constellation Lyra has several other stars that are fascinating doubles, plus several important variable stars and a major nebula.

Altair, located in Aquila the Eagle, is connected with Vega in the giant star pattern known as the summer Triangle. This star is "only" 16.5 light-years away, the fourth closest of the first-magnitude stars. It happens to be approaching us slightly more quickly than any of those other stars. And, of all the first-magnitude stars, only one is more similar in size and true brightness to our Sun. But Altair is still a much brighter and hotter star. Furthermore, a feature of its spectrum indicates that it must be the fastest-spinning of the brightest stars. Whereas our Sun's mean rotation period is about 25 days, the equatorial rotation period of the larger Altair is estimated to be just 6½ hours! This fast rotation is thought to deform the shape of Altair into a flattened ellipsoid, with the equatorial diameter being nearly twice the polar diameter. Whenever observing Altair, consider this amazing fact. Also, note the star's color on various nights in various optical instruments—is it entirely white, or do you notice any hint of yellow? Finally, you may wish to note that Altair has a tenth-magnitude star, physically unrelated to it, glinting a little less than 3 arc-minutes to the northwest of it.

Antares is one of the two first-magnitude stars that is a red giant. Although inferior to winter's Betelgeuse in brightness, size, and variability, this star marking the heart of Scorpius the Scorpion is prodigious nonetheless. Even if Antares is 440 light-years away (it may be farther), its true brightness would be about 6,000 times as great as our Sun's and its diameter almost 200 times as great (about enough to fill the solar system out to the orbit of Earth). Also fascinating about Antares is its companion star, which looks vividly green in contrast to Antares itself. This companion can be seen in 6-inch and even smaller telescopes, but only when "seeing" is excellent. For statistics on the components of this system, see Table 7 in Activity 17.

Deneb, the final member of the Summer Triangle, may have the greatest true brightness of any first-magnitude star, but is also almost certainly the most distant. If Deneb is 1,800 light-years away, then its light output is 80,000 times the Sun's! Although not one of the O or B class stars of very high temperature and typically great luminosity, Deneb is a prodigious object, containing perhaps 25 times the mass of our Sun and having a diameter of 60 to perhaps more than 100 times that of our Sun. Deneb and Altair form a striking example of the extremes of star distance and star brightness among the first-magnitude class: Deneb appears fainter, but only because it is about a thousand times farther away. Indeed, an intelligent being on a planet near Deneb would need at least a 6-inch telescope just to barely glimpse our Sun as a thirteenth-magnitude star.

Questions

1. Do you detect any blue in the tint of Vega? Does it seem bluer than Sirius, under similar conditions? Can you find one or both of the faint stars near Vega which are not true companions of it? How large a telescope is needed to see the false companions?

2. Can you think about the profoundly different distance and size and shape and true brightness of Deneb and Altair as you observe them? Do they both look completely white? Can you find Altair's false companion?

3. How would you characterize the color of Antares (both verbally and on a scale of 0 to 10 [see Activity 19 for an explanation of the scale])? Does its color change with its brightness? Can you detect the companion of Antares and decide on this companion's color?

5.

The Spectral Types of Stars

Learn the basics of stellar spectra and the classification of stars by spectral type. Observe stars that are examples of the standard spectral types, considering the physical properties of each type as you are observing.

We now turn to a series of activities (through Activity 11) involving spectral types, luminosities, and the Hertzsprung–Russell diagram of stars.

Why this series before double and variable star observations, or other projects? Because without it, our observations suffer from a basic lack of comprehension about what stars are. And that has serious ramifications for our understanding of specific matters like why we can have different colors to compare in double stars and why certain kinds of variable stars behave as they do. Even in our friendly and basic introductory tour of the brightest stars (Activities 1–4), we had to encounter such terms as *red giant* and *white dwarf* which cried out for explanation. And that explanation begins with a discussion of *spectral types*.

Even up through the early nineteenth century, many astronomers believed that we would never learn anything about the composition of stars. How, after all, could we sample the ingredients of objects so hopelessly, incredibly distant? Little did they know that all we needed was a device called a *spectroscope*.

A spectroscope is an instrument that uses a slit and prism to obtain the spectrum of a star's (or other glowing celestial object's) light. The *continuous spectrum* is the basic display of the component colors—the different wavelengths—of light coming from glowing gas under high pressure (such as inside a star). The *emission spectrum* is the additional bright lines produced at certain wavelengths by various substances (elements or compounds) in a glowing gas under low pressure (such as in the outer parts of a star). The *absorption spectrum* is the dark lines produced at certain wavelengths by various substances in a tenuous gas that is cooler than the light source (such as in the atmosphere of a star). The pattern of positions for the bright lines and dark lines is a unique signature for each element and compound. After identifying the spectral lines caused by elements and compounds in laboratories here on Earth, we can look for the lines in the spectra (plural of "spectrum") of stars and learn the chemical composition of those distant suns. Displacements, broadenings, and other alterations of the expected appearance of the lines can reveal much more about the size and motions of a star, and what kind of companion star it may have. Simple observations of the brightness of stars and study of their spectra can together permit us to figure out—at least roughly—almost all the basic properties of the stars and their lives!

The first step is the establishment of *spectral types*. These spectral types relate closely to the surface temperatures (and colors) of different kinds of stars. The spectral types are normally listed in order from the hottest to the coolest stars. A capital letter is used to designate each spectral type, and although once alphabetically arranged the letters now run (in order from hottest to coolest): O, B, A, F, G, K, and M. (The traditional mnemonic for remembering this order is "Oh, Be a Fine Girl, Kiss Me"—but this will hardly do in today's world where we are striving for equality between the sexes.)

After these standard types were established, R, N, and S types were added at the right (cool) end. But actually these overlap M (the stars of R, N, and S being judged distinctive by virtue of just a few compositional pecularities), and now R and N have been combined into spectral type C (the carbon stars). The Wolf–Rayet stars, rare and very hot (left of O), have been designated W (with subclasses WC and WN). White dwarf stars are designated as spectral type D. The temporarily exploding stars called novae are sometimes given a spectral type designation (Q), and even gaseous nebulae, clouds of gas in space, have been given one (type P).

Let us here, however, concentrate on the traditional seven types—O, B, A, F, G, K, M—into which over 95 percent of all stars can be placed. Stars of each type have a characteristic color, the color corresponding to a surface temperature. When a substance is at its hottest, it radiates at short wavelengths—blue-white (it is white hot, like metal on the verge of melting). When a substance is only just barely hot enough to glow, it radiates at long wavelengths (it is red hot, like an ember). This is what we find with stars, the hottest of which shine blue–white and the coolest of which shine reddish.

A note on temperature is required here. In astronomy, temperatures are usually given on the Kelvin (K) scale, in which the degrees are of the same size as Centigrade (Celsius) but begin at absolute zero rather than at the freezing point of water. Since absolute zero (the temperature at which all atomic and molecular motion is at rest) is $-273°C$, temperatures on the Kelvin scale are 273° lower than those on the Centigrade scale—hardly a significant difference when we are discussing stars with surface temperatures in the thousands and tens of thousands of degrees.

(To figure out what Fahrenheit temperatures correspond to temperatures on the Kelvin scale, use the formula $T(K) = T(F°)/1.8 + 255.37$. T stands for temperature, of course.)

Type O stars (see Figure 4) are blue–white and extremely hot (temperatures of around 35,000 K and much higher). These very massive stars are very luminous, and the most short-lived of stars. Their spectra show lines from ionized helium, nitrogen, and oxygen.

Type B stars are blue–white and hot (temperatures of around 20,000 K). They are massive and quite luminous. Their spectra display strong helium lines.

Type A stars are white, with temperatures of around 10,000 K. Their luminosities are usually about 50 to 100 times that of the Sun (much less than most type O or B stars). There are no helium lines, but strong hydrogen lines in these stars' spectra.

Type F stars are yellow–white, with temperatures of about 7,000 K. Their spectra show weaker hydrogen lines, but strong calcium.

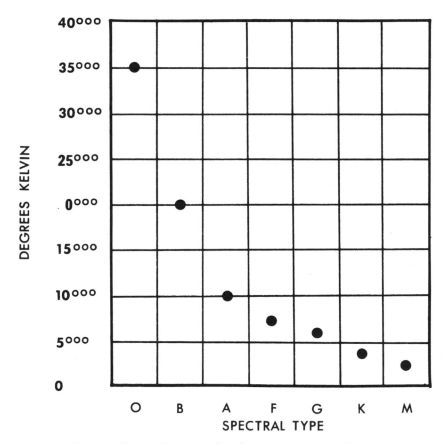

Figure 4 Spectral types and surface temperatures of stars.

Type G stars are yellow, with temperatures of about 6,000 K. Their spectra show weaker hydrogen lines, but stronger lines of many metals. (The Sun is a type G star.)

Type K stars are orange, with temperatures of about 4,000 to 4,700 K. They have faint hydrogen lines, strong metal lines, and hydrocarbon bands in their spectra.

Type M stars are red, with temperatures of about 2,500 to 3,000 K. They have many strong metallic lines and wide titanium oxide bands in their spectra.

To read a general description of these spectral types is one thing, to observe examples of the stars of each type is another. The goal of our current activity is to go out and view examples of each type, bearing in mind the physical features and composition of the stars in question. Here are the examples:

Type O. Iota Orionis and Zeta Puppis in winter, Zeta Ophiuchi in summer.

Type B. Often called "Orion stars," because there are so many in Orion. Rigel is the preeminent example, but two of spring's brightest stars—Spica and Regulus—are type B stars, as are Achernar, Beta Centauri, and Beta Crucis.

Type A. Often called "Sirian stars," because Sirius is the classic example. Examples in summer are Vega and Altair.

Type F. Canopus and Procyon are brilliant examples.

Type G. Called "solar type" stars because the Sun is one. Other famous examples are Alpha Centauri and Capella.

Type M. Includes red dwarfs and red giants. The most famous representatives of this type are the giants Betelgeuse and Antares.

Most of the stars listed above are bright, easy-to-find examples. But the true brightness and size of stars in the same spectral type may be tremendously different. Both the brightness and size of a star depend on two things: how massive the star is and what stage of life the star is in. In the activities ahead, we'll see how mass and luminosity are related, and how plotting stars on the *H–R diagram* provides the key for understanding the entire life cycle of stars.

In the next two activities, we will look at the more detailed divisions of spectral types called spectral classes.

Questions

1. Is there any visible color difference between type O and type B stars? What about between them and stars of type A (take into account the great apparent brightness of Sirius and Vega—perhaps by looking at these two stars with a somewhat smaller telescope than used on the O and B stars)?

2. Can you detect the color difference between A and F stars? F and G? G and M? Can you compare stars of the same spectral type which look somewhat similar but have tremendous differences in true brightness (for instance, Canopus and Procyon)?

6.

The Spectral Classes of Stars—1

Observe the stars of the O spectral classes, trying to identify their associated nebulae and star clusters, and pondering their nature as young, extremely luminous stars radiating much energy in the ultraviolet. Observe the stars of the B spectral classes, comparing their colors and noting what peculiarities of particular stars may result in any differences.

Each spectral type of star can be further divided into at least ten spectral classes. The numbering begins with 0, 1, 2 . . . and progresses up to 9, followed by the 0 of the next spectral type (in order of decreasing surface temperature—thus, B9 is followed by A0, and so on).

When examination of a star's spectrum places it on the borderline between two spectral classes, further decimal division can be used: For instance, the star Xi Persei is classified as O7.5, Beta Crucis as B0.5. Arcturus is sometimes given as K2, sometimes K1.5. And this raises another important point: There is still considerable controversy over exactly what spectral class many stars should be assigned to (bear this in mind when trying the present activity).

Various prefixes and suffixes are sometimes added to the spectral class designation. Suffixes that are often encountered include: "e" for "emission lines"; "m" for "metallic lines"; "n" for "nebulous lines"; "p" for "peculiar spectrum"; "q" for lines that indicate both approach and recession of material in an expanding shell of gas or dust around the star; and "v" for "variable spectrum."

(These suffixes are added not directly after the spectral class designation, but after the luminosity class designation which we will study in the next activity. The full designation for Sirius would be A1Vm— spectral class A1, luminosity class V, and prominent "m" or metallic lines.)

In this activity and the next, we will concentrate on just the basic spectral classes. Our goal is to observe examples of stars of spectral classes all the way from the hot to the cool end of the range. Remember that the presence of strong hydrogen or helium or whatever lines does not necessarily indicate that there is more of that gas in a particular star, only that the star's temperature is the one at which that element is best at absorbing light and producing the characteristic dark lines in the spectrum. Not until we plot the spectral types and their classes with the luminosities of stars in the H–R diagram will we see patterns emerge which teach us the nature of stars and how they evolve through their lives depending on their mass.

By the way, we don't have examples for every single spectral class here, for several reasons. One is that not all the classes are even used (others are sparsely represented)!

The first-magnitude stars described in our first four activities are given in capital letters in this activity.

In the present activity, we consider just the O and B stars, which is appropriate, considering their similarities, which extend to many of them being related in *O–B associations,* a subject of Activity 27.

O6. Theta-C Orionis, one of the members of the multiple star system called the Trapezium, located in the Great Orion Nebula. This star system is so young it may only have emerged into visibility from out of the nebula gases mere thousands of years ago. Much of any such O6 star's energy is radiated at ultraviolet wavelengths, too short for the eye to perceive.

O7. 15 Monocerotis is a fourth-magnitude (slightly variable) star in the star cluster NGC 2264 (NGC stands for the New General Catalog), which is surrounded by a glowing nebula that silhouettes the dark form of the Cone Nebula.

O8. Plaskett's Star, in Monoceros (2000 position: $6^h37^m24.0^s$, $+6°08'$). A magnitude 6.1 star which is actually composed of two large O stars (too close to separate visually), which together form possibly the most massive star system known—about 100 times the Sun's mass. This star is probably an outer member of the cluster NGC 2244 (which is associated with the nebula NGC 2237), whose central grouping is about 2° away from Plaskett's Star.

O9. Iota Orionis. Actually a fine triple star system (see Activity 17), this is the brightest star of Orion's sword, and is located just south of the Great Orion nebula. Like our other O stars, it is associated with a nebula (NGC 1980), is extremely luminous in both the blue–white and ultraviolet, and must be young.

B0. Gamma Cassiopeiae. Middle star in the famous M or W shape of Cassiopeia's main pattern. This star has its own peculiarities, being an odd variable (see Activity 22) with bright hydrogen emission lines, associated nebula, and probable ejections of shells of material.

B1. SPICA, BETA CENTAURI, Beta Canis Majoris (this star is the standard example of a special type of pulsating variable).

B2. Gamma Pegasi. It is at B2 that spectral lines of neutral helium are strongest. Gamma Pegasi happens to be one of the Beta Canis Majoris-type variables.

B3. ACHERNAR.

B4. Lambda Canis Majoris.

B5. Eta Canis Majoris.

B6. Several of the brightest Pleiades cluster stars (Electra, Merope, Taygeta).

B7. REGULUS, Beta Tauri, more of the bright Pleiads (including the brightest, Alcyone).

B8. The bright Pleiads which are not B6 or B7, Beta² Cygni (part of the beautiful Albireo double star system—see Activities 16 and 18), Beta Librae (controversial for being called a green star by some observers, also for possible major brightness changes).

B9. By about B9 the lines of neutral helium have almost vanished (while hydrogen lines are now much stronger than in the previous B classes).

Our tour continues with the A, F, G, K, and M stars in the next activity.

Questions

1. Can you observe the hot young stars of the O spectral classes? Can you identify the formative nebula and/or cluster with which they are associated?

2. Can you observe the stars of the B spectral classes, noting any difference in color and pondering to what extent a star's apparent or true brightness, the color of a companion, or pulsations or ejected shells may affect our perception of its color?

7.

The Spectral Classes of Stars—2

Observe the stars of spectral classes in types A, F, G, K, and M, noting at what class various colors first become apparent. Try to account for any colors that appear to be unexplained by spectral class (such as by color contrast with a companion star's hue). Ponder the physical differences exhibited by the stars of the different classes.

We continue our tour of the stars of the different spectral classes, resuming our journey toward cooler surfaces and redder color with the A stars.

As we continue, however, look ahead to Figure 5 which shows that all the stars of a given spectral type within any one of the three most important *luminosity classes* (I, III, and V) have very similar luminosity (or absolute magnitude), also mass and diameter. Thus, all *main sequence* (luminosity class V) stars of spectral class A0 are roughly 80 times more luminous, 2.5 times wider, 3.2 times more massive than the Sun—and indeed the main sequence A0 star Vega is listed by various authorities as 50 or 58 times more luminous, 2 or a bit over 3 times wider, and about 3 times more massive than the Sun. But a class I star of spectral class A0 should be about 20,000 times more luminous, 40 times wider, and 16 times more massive than the Sun.

In the next activities, we will study the luminosity classes and the role that mass plays in determining the luminosity and the whole life story of stars.

A0. VEGA, Gamma Centauri, Alpha Piscium.

A1. SIRIUS.

A2. At A2, hydrogen lines are at their strongest. DENEB, Beta Aurigae.

A3. FOMALHAUT, Beta Leonis, Alpha^2 Librae (the brighter of the famous double star pair), Delta Herculis (the primary of this famous *optical double*).

A4. Nu^1 Draconis. See A6 for the identically bright companion of this supposedly white star.

A5. Alpha Ophiuchi.

A6. Nu^2 Draconis. Part of the famous double star pair (see A4).

A7. ALTAIR, Alpha Cephei. Both of these stars are noted for their rapid rotation—but so are many other stars of other spectral classes.

A9. Gamma Herculis. Has a dim companion which forms an optical double with it, but Delta Herculis (see A3) is more famous for this.

F0. CANOPUS.

F2. Pi Sagittarii (magnitude 2.9).

F4. Alpha^1 Librae (dimmer member of the famous double star— see A3.

F5. Metallic lines increase throughout the F classes, with the Fraunhofer H and K lines of ionized calcium especially notable. PROCYON and Alpha Persei—same spectral class, but incredibly different stars, with Alpha Persei maybe 500 times more luminous and the chief member of a loose star cluster or a star association. But both Procyon and Alpha Persei are judged to have a little yellow in their hue by some observers—what about hotter stars of slightly "earlier" (farther toward the O-class end) spectral class?

F7. Polaris.

F8. Beta Virginis.

G0. Metallic lines still increasing. Beta Aquarii (by an amazing coincidence, about the same apparent and true brightness, and almost the same spectral class, as Alpha Aquarii—G2).

G2. The Sun, ALPHA CENTAURI A, Alpha Aquarii.

G5. Alpha² Herculis—or rather this is the spectral class of the primary star of this spectroscopic double (inseparable in any telescope)—a close duo themselves paired with fascinating Alpha¹ Herculis (see M5) to form one of the heavens' most beautifully colored doubles. The close companion of the G5 star is probably F2— together many observers see them as bluish-green when observed with the ruddy Alpha¹.

G7. Gamma² Leonis. The fainter member of one of the most beautiful double star systems. The brighter member is K0 (see below), and although many observers think both members look yellow, some regard this G7 star as greenish (compare this case with that of Alpha Herculis—see the note to G5). And there are many other opinions (see Activity 18 for more on the colors of double stars).

G8. CAPELLA, Beta Herculis.

G9. Beta Leo Minoris.

K0. In K stars the metallic lines become stronger than the hydrogen lines, and the bands of molecules—like cyanogen—become noticeable. Gamma¹ Leonis. The brighter member of the famous double (see G7 for discussion); Beta Ceti, Gamma Librae.

K1. Beta Volantis (magnitude 3.8 in Volans the Flying Fish, for southerners).

K2. ARCTURUS, Alpha Arietis, Epsilon Pegasi.

K3. Gamma Andromedae A. The brightest star of a famous and lovely double star system. The companion is a very close double (too close for amateur telescopes) with both its components being "late" B (say B8 or B9) or "early" A (say A0 or A1). The companion looks greenish-blue compared to the gold or slightly orange color of the A star (as opposed to Gamma Leonis and Alpha Herculis, this is a case where the dimmer star really is hot enough to perhaps truly show blue even if it weren't contrasting with the color of the cooler primary).

K4. Beta Ursae Minoris (compare with color of F7 star Polaris).

K5. ALDEBARAN, Gamma Sagittae.

M0. Bands of titanium oxide strengthening. Beta Andromedae.

M1. BETELGEUSE, ANTARES.

M2. Alpha Ceti (this star is neither a red dwarf nor a variable), Beta Pegasi.

M3. Eta Persei.

M4. Gamma Crucis (magnitude 1.67—not as bright as Antares or Betelgeuse in apparent magnitude, but impressive).

M5. Alpha Herculis A (see G5 for comments on the color of this star and its companion)—like Betelgeuse and Antares, an especially huge red giant whose variable brightness and size are due to actual pulsations.

M6. Mira (Omicron Ceti)—most famous and brightest of the long-period variables (see Activity 20)—at maximum brightness, with surface temperature of about 2,500 K. (See also M9.)

M7. Maximum strength of titanium oxide bands. Theta Apodis.

M9. Mira at minimum light, with surface temperature only about 1,900 K (see Activity 20 for more details on this star and observing it).

Questions

1. How much does the presence of a fairly bright companion star of different color alter the apparent color of a star compared to what you would expect from its (the primary star's) spectral class?

2. What is the "latest" spectral class in which you detect any blue in a single star? What is the "earliest" in which you detect yellow? Orange? Red? In what star systems, if any, do you detect a green star—and what are the circumstances (including spectral class of the star)?

3. Can you compare stars of the same spectral class which are in other ways strikingly different? (Deneb is in almost the same spectral class as Sirius, Fomalhaut, and Castor yet has an immensely greater true brightness—because, as we will see in the next activity, it is in a much brighter *luminosity class* . . . and, as we will see in the activity after that, this in turn is because of the much greater mass that Deneb was born with.)

8.

The Hertzsprung–Russell Diagram and the Luminosity Classes

Study the Hertzsprung–Russell diagram and the position of the luminosity classes upon it. Then, observe stars from as many of the classes as possible among the ranks of the brightest stars and plot these stars' positions on your copy of the diagram with the help of the data from Appendix 1. Also try observing stars from as many of the luminosity classes as possible in a single constellation, as detailed for Canis Major and Scorpius below.

It sounds incredible but it is true: In a few sciences, a single graphic representation of reality, simple enough for anyone to understand in principle, has proved a cornerstone of the entire science. A drawing on a piece of paper itself becomes one of the great tools for not just organizing existing knowledge, but actually generating new information otherwise unobtainable. In chemistry (and to some extent, physics), there is the periodic table of the elements. And in astronomy, there is the Hertzsprung–Russell diagram.

The H–R diagram was discovered independently by Ejnar Hertzsprung and Henry Norris Russell in 1913. But the diagram would not have been possible without the cataloging and ideas of three female astronomers at Harvard, particularly Annie Jump Cannon.

The H–R diagram uses a vertical axis and a horizontal axis. The most typical version of the diagram has true brightness plotted (upward in order of increasing brightness) on the vertical axis and spectral type plotted (left to right in order of increasingly "late" or cool spectral type) on the horizontal axis.

In what terms do we plot the brightness? The brightness can be plotted in terms of *luminosity,* with the Sun's luminosity being 1. Or the brightness can be plotted in terms of *absolute magnitude*—the apparent magnitude that a star would have if placed about 32½ light-years or 10 parsecs away—or *bolometric* absolute magnitude (bolometric magnitude is the brightness in all wavelengths, not just those of visible light the eye can see—for more on the various kinds of magnitude and on distance terms like parsec, see Fundamental Measurements in Astronomy).

In what terms do we plot the spectral type? The spectra-type can be divided, as usual, into spectral classes 0 to 9 working left to right. But the horizontal axis of the H–R diagram can also be used to plot properties which, though not quite the same as spectral class, are nevertheless intimately related to it. We can plot the temperature (strictly speaking, the *effective temperature*—the temperature of the star's light-producing layer as revealed by study of the spectrum). Or we can plot the color, as measured by the *color index* (the difference between the brightness of the star through a blue filter and a visual filter—for more on this, see Activity 19).

For our present purposes, we should study a standard form of the diagram. Figure 5 shows such an H–R diagram—one with absolute magnitude and luminosity plotted against spectral class and type.

The first thing you notice about the diagram is that the dots representing individual stars are by no means scattered randomly across the whole diagram. The majority of stars—including our own Sun—can be found to lie somewhere along a diagonal strip that stretches from the upper left to the lower right. This is called *the main sequence*.

Other patterns, other concentrations of stars, are found on the H–R diagram. Early researchers learned that although many M-type stars are located on the main sequence (lower right end), some of them are very luminous and thus are grouped in the upper right corner. For these stars to have such low surface temperature (and thus low surface brightness) and still be so bright must mean that they have an enormous amount of surface area—hence, that they are very large stars. Consequently, these stars were called *red giants*. Calculations showed that the dim M-type stars at the lower right end must be quite small stars (typically quite a bit smaller than the Sun)—and so were called *red dwarfs*.

Well to the left of the red dwarfs and far below the main sequence, another patch of stars is located. These have absolute magnitude or luminosity virtually as dim as the red dwarfs but they are very much hotter, ranging up through B-type, even into O-type. For stars to have such high surface temperature (and thus high surface brightness) but still be so faint must mean that they have an extremely small amount of surface area—hence, that they are very small stars. These stars are called *white dwarfs*. And, indeed, calculations show that many of them are no larger than planets, some even smaller than our Earth (which is, remember, not even 1/100 as wide as the Sun).

There are several other interesting groupings of stars—for instance, of particular types of variable stars—in certain places on the H–R

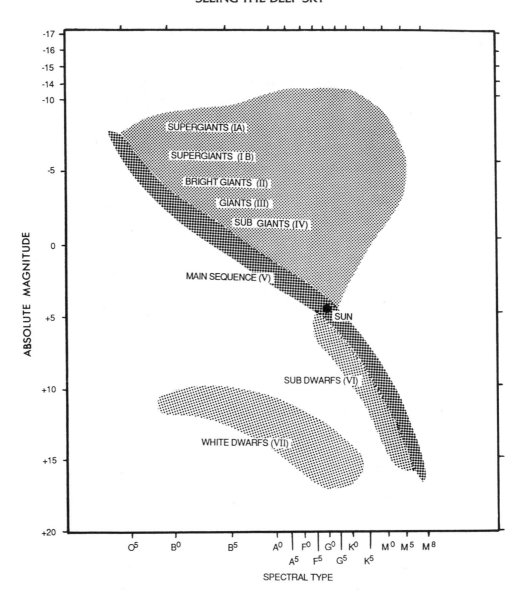

Figure 5 Hertzsprung–Russell diagram showing luminosity classes.

diagram. But we will deal with this in the next three activities when we study what the H–R diagram tells us about the life cycles of stars from birth to death.

For our present activity, we will observe examples from the seven different luminosity classes of stars which the H–R diagram reveals.

In the most popular system of nomenclature, the classes are designated with Roman numerals ranging from I for the most luminous stars (that is, those of lowest absolute magnitude) down to VI and VII for the two groups that vie for the distinction of being the least luminous (highest absolute magnitude).

Here are the luminosity classes:

I—Supergiants (divided into Ia and Ib, with Ia the brightest)
II—Bright giants
III—Giants
IV—Subgiants
V—Dwarfs
VI—Subdwarfs
VII—White dwarfs

Designations II and IV are not much used, compared to I, III, and V. Class VI, the subdwarfs, is a very small class of poorly understood stars which lie between the main sequence and the white dwarfs. But it is in the names for classes V and VI that this system leaves most to be desired. Class V are called dwarfs yet are the main sequence stars—many of which are much larger and brighter than the Sun, which itself is a lot bigger than many red dwarfs (which are also in class V) and immensely bigger than the white dwarfs. The terms *red dwarf* and *white dwarf* are usages that were coined independently from (and earlier than) the names in this system of luminosity classes. But now we end up hearing of the Sun being a yellow dwarf and subdwarfs (class VI) being much larger than white dwarfs.

In this system, the Roman numerals are suffixes to the spectral designation: As I mentioned previously, Sirius would be A1V or A1Vm (the "m" indicating "metallic lines"). But another system adds mostly lowercase letters to represent some of the classes, and adds them as prefixes to the spectral designation: c is for supergiant, g is for giant, sg for subgiant, d for dwarf, and sd for subdwarf, with white dwarfs getting a capital D—so that Sirius would in this system be dA1, and Sirius B (its white dwarf companion) would be DA5. Note that in this system there are no "bright giants" (class II in the other system).

Bearing in mind these potentially confusing aspects of the nomenclature, let's set out a program of examples from each luminosity class to observe.

One program would be to observe some of our already familiar stars grouped by luminosity class. Thus, class Ia stars would include Deneb, Rigel, Betelgeuse (sometimes classed Iab), and Delta and Eta Canis Majoris. Class Ib would include Antares (sometimes classed Iab), Polaris, and Epsilon Pegasi. Class II has few stars, and many of those are sometimes placed in Ib—for instance, Canopus and Epsilon Canis Majoris. Class III features Arcturus, Aldebaran, Capella, Beta Centauri, Pollux, and Beta and Gamma Crucis. Class IV is not much used, but among the apparently brightest stars Lambda Scorpii (magnitude 1.6) is still listed as one. Class V accounts for all the other first-magnitude stars, including Sirius and our own Sun. No class VI star I know is by itself an easy target for amateur astronomers (one example is the companion of Mira). The easiest class VII star—white dwarf—to observe is Omicron Eridani B, part of an amazing triple star system, even though Sirius B is the brightest white dwarf.

A more challenging program is to observe stars of every luminosity class in one constellation. In Canis Major, we have Delta, Eta, and Omicron² as Ia; Tau (and sometimes Iota) as Ib; Gamma and Epsilon as II; many stars, including Theta and Xi, as III; Omega sometimes listed as IV; several stars listed as V—including Sirius; no VI for observers; and Sirius B as a very difficult VII. For the summer, if we're willing to do without a white dwarf or a subdwarf, we could choose Scorpius and observe: Zeta-1 for Ia and Iota-2 for Ib (and Antares for either subclass of I); Theta, which is sometimes classed in II; many stars, including Epsilon, for III; a number of stars, including very bright Lambda, for IV; many stars, including Delta and both components of Beta as V.

What we haven't determined here is: Why do stars of these few different luminosity classes bunch together in certain parts of the H–R diagram, leaving other areas vacant? In addition, if you plot a lot of stars of the same spectral class that are all main sequence (luminosity class V) stars, why do you find that they all have about the same luminosity, thus the same position on the diagram? A red giant of that spectral class will have a greater luminosity—but why are some stars red giants and others blue giants or white dwarfs, and so on? The answers to these questions, and the key that they provide to understanding the lives of the stars, is the subject of our next activity.

Questions

1. Can you observe stars from each of the luminosity classes Ia through VII? Can you place all the brightest stars on an H–R diagram with the aid of the data from Appendix 1 (the brightest stars)—then observe each of these stars visible from your latitude while studying the meaning of its position on the diagram?

2. Can you observe stars from most of the luminosity classes in either Canis Major (winter half of the year) or Scorpius (summer half of the

year), as detailed above? What conclusions do you draw from your observations and your knowledge of the classes to which these stars belong?

9.

The Hertzsprung–Russell Diagram and the Life of the Sun—1

Consider the physics of stellar evolution in the context of following the Sun's development from a nebula to its current main sequence position. Then, to help envision the Sun's future, observe the prominent stars that most resemble the Sun in the future stages of its life until it reaches its maximum luminosity, size, and redness as a red giant.

In the previous activity, we saw how each star of a given spectral class would typically have about the same luminosity, mass, and diameter as all the other stars in the same spectral class and luminosity class. But there were the different luminosity classes, occupying their different positions on the H–R diagram.

Through the previous four activities, we have become better acquainted with the spectra and luminosities of stars and how these are classified and how we can display them on the H–R diagram. It does not require much thought to realize how useful it is to be able to determine the spectral class of a star whose spectrum you observe and then, even if you have only a rough idea of how far and thus how luminous the star is (just know what luminosity class it must belong to), being able to figure out almost everything else about the star. Almost everything? With the H–R diagram and some basic physics formulas, you can take the spectral class and luminosity class and read from the diagram or perform simple calculations to determine what the star's mass, diameter, temperature, and almost exactly what its luminosity and distance should be.

But we still haven't answered the deeper questions: Why are there different luminosity classes? Why do we find some stars at one spectral class and temperature and some stars at others? Why are there patterns on the H–R diagram, places where many stars are plotted and other places where none are plotted?

The answers all lie in realizing that we must be seeing stars at different stages of life, and that the route a star takes across the H–R diagram during its life is determined by its initial mass.

Astronomers have found that there is a mass–luminosity relation (it can, in fact, be precisely quantified). The more material there is to a star, the more pressure is exerted on its center, and the more energy is produced. Thus, the more massive a star, the more luminous it will be— at each stage of its life. But the luminosity of a star changes as it goes through its life. Thus, less massive stars at their most luminous stage can outshine more massive ones at the latter's less luminous stages. For instance, the Sun will have a greater luminosity when it eventually becomes a red giant than Sirius or even Achernar now have.

But the best way to explain the role of mass in a star's life, and answer our other deep questions about the stars and the H–R diagram, is to follow the life story of the Sun (and also the stories of stars of different masses) as we believe they would transpire in space (and, representationally, across the H–R diagram).

Stars begin as gas and dust in space. Various disturbances (such as density waves) can push this tenuous material into a *nebula* (cloud) of sufficient density for gravity to take over and cause further contraction and condensing. A small nebula might eventually produce one star, or have several condensing areas and produce a double or multiple star system. A larger nebula might develop many denser, contracting areas and eventually give rise to an entire *star cluster*. Whatever the case may be, it is at first just the energy of the inward-falling matter which produces heat in the center of the protostar. At an advanced stage this can lead to a dimly glowing *T Tauri star*. Only when the contraction has built tremendous pressure in the center is it sufficient to begin nuclear fusion: atoms of the universe's most common and simplest element, hydrogen, fusing to produce the next most complex element, helium. This is the power by which all stars at first shine, and at whose ignition they reach the main sequence on the H–R diagram.

From the start it was the amount of mass involved in the contracting protostar which determined how long the contraction would take before fusion would begin (the more mass, the quicker the contraction). It was also the amount of mass which determined how hot and luminous—how high up and how far left on the H–R diagram—the star would be when it joined the main sequence (again, the more mass, the hotter and brighter it would become). But at least up until now, all the objects—regardless of their mass—were heading leftward (becoming hotter, infrared radiation being joined by the glow of visible red light) on the diagram (see Figure 6). After reaching the main sequence, the life histories of stars of different mass take very different courses.

First, in this activity and the next, we will consider the Sun's life history.

Our Sun probably took a billion years to contract to the point where it reached the main sequence. Roughly four and one-half billion years (perhaps more) have passed since then. Maybe more than four and one-half billion years are left before the Sun starts moving off the main sequence. What happens is that more and more of the hydrogen "fuel" in its core is used up, converted to helium. There is still plenty of hydrogen in the rest of the star, however, and fusion proceeds in a shell surrounding the core. As the core runs out of hydrogen, the outward radiational pressure of its fusion weakens and gravity (the weight of the rest of the star) presses harder, so that the core contracts. The greater heat from this contraction speeds up the fusion in the shell and causes the outer layers of the star—of our Sun!—to start expanding immensely. The surface becomes so vast it cools and reddens, and the outer layers become very tenuous. But even with the lower surface temperature, the total amount of light—the luminosity—coming from the Sun increases greatly. The Sun has become a red giant!

Exactly what will the Sun look like on its way to becoming a red giant, and then as a red giant? We can—at least approximately, and still uncertainly—see what the future appearance of our Sun will be by observing a series of stars of similar mass which are further down the evolutionary track of their lives. This is the main goal of our current activity.

Phase 1. First, the Sun may look like Eta Cassiopeiae A. This star is part of a beautiful double star system. It is G0 and slightly brighter than the Sun, and actually a bit smaller, not to mention a bit more massive. (I'm not sure why the Sun initially becomes a bit hotter and presumably a bit smaller but that seems to be what the experts' plot of the Sun's future course on the diagram shows.)

Phase 2. Next, it is like Beta Hydri (unfortunately for most of this book's readers, a star at $-77°$, thus too south to see). Beta Hydri (Beta star of the constellation Hydrus) is a G1 or G2 subgiant (luminosity class IV) several times more luminous than the Sun, and about 1½ times larger.

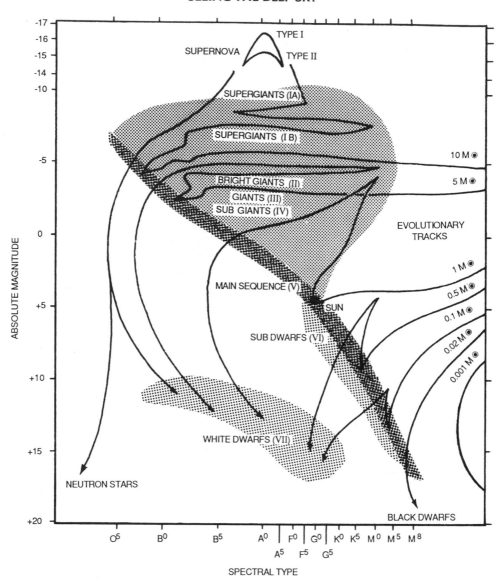

Figure 6 Hertzsprung–Russell diagram with stellar evolutionary tracks (symbol *M* means "solar masses"—1 *M* is mass the same as the Sun's).

Phase 3. The Sun swells and brightens tremendously and turns distinctly orange. As it grows out to 20 times its current diameter, it becomes in rapid succession a star in appearance much like today's Atria (Alpha Trianguli Australis), Alphard (Alpha Hydrae), Eltanin (Gamma Draconis), and finally like today's Aldebaran. It has become a giant (luminosity class III) and emits well over 100 times as much light as it does today. Its surface temperature has declined to about 3,800 K—but that surface has expanded to reach part of the way out to Mercury, and the Sun appears as an orb something like 8° wide (16 times its present size) in Earth's sky.

Phase 4. But even after this, the Sun still grows and brightens. It swells and consumes Mercury, and expands still further to devour Venus. Whether it will ever grow quite large enough for its visible surface to reach the Earth is uncertain. But at this time, billions of years in the future, life on Earth will have long since ceased to be possible (unless humanity has moved the home planet). How red and how bright will the Sun be at this, the reddest and brightest it will ever become? Maybe not quite as red as Antares or Betelgeuse, perhaps more like Beta Andromedae, an M0 giant. But the Sun will be far more luminous than Beta Andromedae. Its greatest luminosity may rival that of Spica or Lambda Scorpii, stars that are several thousand times brighter than today's Sun! In checking the spectra and luminosities of all the stars easily visible to the naked eye, I find none that is very close to what the Sun will be during this stage in its development. Eta Persei is too bright, far too large, and too cool. As for the comparison of our someday-Sun to our most familiar red supergiants of today, Betelgeuse and Antares, the best the Sun can ever hope to be is several to many times smaller and much less luminous than either of those stars.

In our next activities, we will follow the further development of the Sun, and compare the Sun's evolution with that of less massive and more massive stars.

Questions

1. Can you observe Eta Cassiopeiae A or Beta Hydri, bearing in mind that these may resemble what the Sun will look like in its next stages of development?

2. Can you observe Atria, Alphard, Kochab, Eltanin, and Aldebaran, imagining that these are the Sun in its future stage of development as an orange giant or subgiant?

3. Can you observe Spica and Beta Andromedae, and contemplate the Sun as a red giant as luminous as the former and about the same spectral class as the latter? Or can you view Antares or Betelgeuse, thinking about the true nature of these vast brilliant suns, and

thinking of our maximum-red-giant Sun as a several to many times smaller and dimmer version of these?

10.

The Hertzsprung–Russell Diagram and the Life of the Sun—2

Consider the physics of stellar evolution in the context of following the Sun's development from its future stage as a red giant until its final stage as a white dwarf fading into darkness. Then, to help envision the Sun's future, observe the prominent stars that appear most like what the Sun will be in those final eons of its passage from red giant to white dwarf.

In the previous activity, we saw that when the Sun's core, turned completely to helium, began contracting under gravitational pressure, the heat from this contraction sped up the fusion in the shell of hydrogen around the core, making the outer layers expand to become a red giant.

But what stopped the core's contraction? The answer is that, when heat and pressure became high enough, a new type of fusion in the core occurred, the fusion of helium atoms into a yet heavier element, carbon. Such a measure only postpones the star's eventual collapse, however. Soon, the carbon core faces the same problem the helium core did, and is eventually contracted enough to fuse into an even heavier element. Shell after shell surrounds the core. The star's (our Sun's) various contractions and expansions may lead to it becoming distinctly variable in brightness (and size). Finally, no further fusion is possible—the mass of the Sun is not great enough. Some of the material of the star is (more or less peacefully) lost, but the remainder (no longer supported by the outward pressure from the energy of fusion) collapses steadily until it is no larger than a planet.

The contraction is stopped when the star becomes crushed into a substance in which the electrons of the atoms are stripped and mingle, but still cushion the atomic nuclei from each other. This substance, or rather state of matter, is called *degenerate matter*. And the star made of it has contracted so much that its remaining heat is released from a tiny surface which therefore becomes white hot. The star—in this case, our Sun—has gone from being a red giant to being a white dwarf.

Now there is more to this transition than an immediate change from red giant to white dwarf. Once again, we can compare the Sun's appearance at different stages to that of stars we can observe in today's sky. We continue the previous activity's program, picking up from where the Sun was at its maximum luminosity, size, and redness as a red giant.

Phase 5. The Sun's size dwindles, its luminosity fades—but so far only back to roughly that of Aldebaran. Only now, instead of having about a K5 spectrum, the Sun is about K0—a more golden orange than that of Aldebaran. It appears much like today's star Dubhe (Alpha Ursae Majoris). Dubhe is the pointer star in the Big Dipper that is closest to Polaris.

Phase 6. The Sun shrinks to no more than a few times the size it has today, but is still far more luminous, because its surface temperature has become much higher. It resembles Rasalhague (Alpha Ophiuchi) and Zosma (Delta Leonis)—spectral class about A4 or A5.

Phase 7. The Sun's surface temperature rises to bring it to spectral class A0 or A1—the same as Sirius and Vega. It is now more luminous than the former, less luminous than the latter.

Phase 8. Now the Sun's shrinking must be very swift, for we see virtually no stars well to the left of the moderately bright section of the main sequence. The most leftward (on the diagram) spectral class that the Sun achieves is maybe about B5—similar to Achernar or Eta Canis Majoris, but now the shrinking Sun is immensely less luminous than those stars. In fact, it maintains about the same spectral class until it has become dimmer than it is in our day. Around the time its fading makes it again as bright as it is today, it will have dwindled to less than the size of Jupiter. Its disk would be just big enough to the naked eye to see as a dot at sunset from Earth—if there was a burnt cinder remnant of our planet left to observe it from (not to mention a thick enough atmosphere to dim its fierce radiance to safe levels).

Phase 9. The Sun becomes a white dwarf, reaching its minimum size—perhaps smaller than Sirius B and thus only about twice as large as

Earth. Its spectral type is probably F, its luminosity something like ⅟₅₀₀ that which it has today.

Phase 10. The Sun becomes a black dwarf. After an enormously long period as a white dwarf, the Sun's heat and light are at last exhausted, leaving it a dark body.

Questions

1. Can you observe Alpha Ursae Majoris (Dubhe), Alpha Ophiuchi (Rasalhague), and Delta Leonis (Zosma) and contemplate the Sun looking like them as it first shrinks, heats up, and whitens (but fades somewhat because the shrinking is so great) after having been a red giant?

2. Can you observe Vega and Sirius and imagine the far-future Sun being of the same spectral class as them, with luminosity intermediate between them? Can you observe Achernar or Eta Canis Majoris and imagine the very old Sun shining with this color but no more brightly than its present self and already at a size hardly large enough for its globe to be detected with the naked eye from Earth—if any Earth is left?

3. Can you observe Sirius B or another white dwarf and meditate upon this being the last luminous form that our Sun will ever take?

11.

The Hertzsprung–Russell Diagram and the Lives of Other Stars

Consider the physics of stellar evolution in the context of following the development of stars less massive and more massive than the Sun. Then, to help envision these stars' lives, observe prominent stars that are examples of different stages in the lives of such stars.

How do the fates of stars less massive and more massive than the Sun differ from the Sun's?

The stars much less massive than the Sun lead quiet but very long lives. They reach the main sequence lower and farther to the right than the Sun—that is, they are dimmer and cooler (redder). Then, their fusion proceeds less strongly, so the eventual contraction of their helium cores does not produce enough heat to expand the outer layers to red giant status. The core may not become hot enough to initiate the fusion of helium atoms into carbon. After moving only slightly upward and rightward off the main sequence, such a star runs out of usable "fuel" and shrinks to a white dwarf—but a cooler and somewhat less luminous one than that which results from a star as massive as our Sun.

An example of such a star still on the main sequence is Eta Cassiopeiae B—the other member of the lovely double star system whose brighter member the Sun may resemble in the future. Observe this system knowing that the Sun is already much like the brighter star, but that if it had formed with only half its mass it would look like Eta Cassiopeiae B.

A star with far less than a tenth the mass of the Sun probably cannot become hot enough to fuse even helium in its core. It will never surge up from the main sequence at all; it will never be anything but a red dwarf. Proxima Centauri and the two stars of the UV Ceti system are classic examples to observe (see the next activity, on the nearest stars).

Now we turn to the stars more massive than the Sun. These stars join the main sequence much higher and hotter, but they are profligate and their intense shining must be fueled by the fusion of ever heavier elements in their cores. They soon bloat to become the most enormous of stars, the red supergiants, of which Betelgeuse and Antares are the most famous examples. But the many shells of different elements undergoing fusion in these stars cause them to undergo various pulsations, changes in both size and brightness. These pulsations may be rather rapid and regular, or they may take years and be quite irregular and be complicated by various losses of material—these factors giving us many different kinds of variable stars. A very massive star may zigzag back and forth across the top of the diagram, its color ranging from red to white over a relatively short period of time (perhaps no more than a few million years, compared to the Sun's steady billions of years on the main sequence).

Such massive stars cannot die peacefully. We used to think the prime candidate for explosion was red giants. Now we believe that very massive stars may also undergo this cataclysm while they are blue supergiants—Orion's star Rigel could explode before its star Betelgeuse.

What happens is that the core of the star becomes iron, an element too heavy to undergo fusion without some incredibly great increase in pressure and temperature. The increase comes when the core of the star literally collapses—from perhaps as much as a million miles wide down to a few thousand or even a few dozen miles wide in about one second! This implosion creates a wave of energy which hurls the outer part of the star—something like 90 percent of it—into space at speeds of tens of millions of miles per hour. For a few months, the explosion may shine as bright as a billion stars like our Sun. Such an event is called a *supernova*, and we will touch upon how amateur astronomers can look for one in distant galaxies, or for the remnants of great past ones that lit up our own galaxy, later in this book.

What concerns us here is what happens to the collapsed core. If the star began life only a few times more massive than the Sun, it might be able to lose enough mass during its variable star stage to avoid blowing up. But if it started out 5, or even 3, times more massive than the Sun, it is doomed to go supernova. After the supernova, the fate of the core depends on how much mass is left.

If less than about 1.4 solar masses (where the mass of the Sun = 1) is left, the collapse leaves the core a white dwarf—a body of degenerate matter so dense that a teaspoonful would weigh at least several tons. But if the core is more than 1.4 solar masses—a figure known as the *Chandrasekhar limit*—then the collapse must be even greater. The cushion between the nuclei provided by the "fluid" of intermingled electrons cannot hold. The electromagnetic repulsion of the negatively charged electrons and the positively charged protons in the nuclei is overcome. Each electron is driven into a proton to produce a neutron. These neutrons combine with those already in the nuclei to form a mass of nothing but neutrons—the entire star is now composed entirely of the state of matter called *neutronium*. It has become a *neutron star*. And that star's diameter is not a few thousand miles as in the case of a white dwarf. The neutron star is an object roughly 10 to 20 miles wide—yet containing more mass than our Sun! A teaspoonful of neutronium would weigh something like hundreds of millions of tons!

Perhaps as amazing is the fact that this 10-mile-wide object can be spinning at the rate of hundreds of revolutions per second. How do we know that neutron stars can spin this fast? Because we have observed as many as hundreds of regular pulses of radio waves (and even visible light) per second from objects which we believe to be neutron stars and which are called *pulsars*. All neutron stars may be pulsars but we can only detect those in which the magnetic poles—from which the outpouring of radio and/or other wavelengths escapes—point our way. The pulsars are like lighthouses or radio beacons in which the beam rotates around to hit us at regular (but incredibly brief) intervals. The older a pulsar, the slower it seems to rotate—which gives us a good way to determine the length of time since a supernova occurred in that location.

Even the visible light of the Crab pulsar—the most famous—is extremely faint. But in our later activity on supernova remnants, we'll see how even a small telescope can show us the Crab nebula supernova remnant—the gas and dust blown out of this peculiar star.

Is a neutron star the final word in collapse and mind-boggling density? No. If the mass of the supernova's core is greater than about 3 times the Sun's, even the force that keeps neutrons from collapsing into one another is not strong enough to resist the gravitational force. The core becomes a *black hole:* a mass with infinitely great density, infinitely small size, and a gravity so powerful that nothing within the hole's *Schwarzschild radius* could escape—not even the fastest thing in the universe, light.

Our prime hope of detecting black holes is by their effect on surrounding objects. Much speculation exists on whether their presence has been detected, whether they lurk in the hearts of many a bright galaxy, whether they may be connected by a *wormhole* to other parts of the universe where intense radiation issues forth from *white holes*.

Questions

1. Can you observe Eta Cassiopeiae B as an example of a star half the mass of the Sun which is still on the main sequence? Can you observe even less massive stars like Proxima Centauri or the UV Ceti pair, realizing that these—alone of all stars except the most massive—will never become white dwarfs, merely fading versions of their red dwarf selves?

2. Can you observe supergiants like Rigel and Betelgeuse, imagining the fate of going supernova which awaits them? Can you observe the Crab nebula or Veil nebula (see Activity 31) and picture them as something like what will surround the next supergiant as massive as Rigel or Betelgeuse a few hundred (Crab) or many thousand (Veil) years after it goes supernova? Can you picture in this nebula the incredibly fast-spinning, tiny, ultra-dense pulsar which is the neutron star left at the end of a very massive star's life?

12.

The Nearest Stars

Observe as many of the nearest stars as possible, appreciating how the distance to them has been determined by measurements of their parallax. Look for outbursts from those that are flare stars. Ponder the immense distance to even these closest stars, as well as their physical nature and the kind of planetary system they might possess.

We have seen in Activities 7 through 11 how knowing the luminosity and the type of spectrum a star shows can enable us to figure out most of its other properties.

But how do you discover the distances to the stars? What clue do we have that one speck of light in the telescope is any closer or any farther than another (their relative distances), let alone their distances in light-years (their absolute distances)?

There are several methods that astronomers use to determine the distances to the stars. One is to study the spectrum of a star's light to find certain clues about what the star's luminosity is. Another method, which can be used with some double stars, involves applying a certain relationship that exists between the period of revolution of the secondary star and the true size of its orbit. In an upcoming activity, we will see how certain kinds of variable stars are the "standard candles" of the universe for distance estimation.

However, of the various methods, the one which interests us here is the one used on the nearest stars—the observational objects of our current activity.

The best method for determining the distance of one of the nearest stars is measuring its *parallax*. Parallax is the apparent shift in an object's position that is actually caused by a shift in the observer's vantage point or viewing position.

An easy example of this is provided by your finger and a wall or any background considerably farther from you than your finger. Hold your finger up fairly close in front of your face. Now look at the finger with just one eye open. Quickly close that eye and open the other. Did you see your finger seem to change position? If you didn't, try this procedure again, noting the apparent position of your finger in relation to the background wall or scenery behind it. If you try the experiment with your finger held as far from you as possible, you'll notice that its apparent change in position—its parallax—is less. If you hold your finger very close to your eyes, the parallax is greater. Obviously the parallax depends on how great the distance of the object is in comparison to your two different vantage points (in this case, the vantage points being just a few inches apart, on either side of your nose).

Figure 7 shows how by measuring the angle of apparent change and knowing the distance between the two viewing positions we can compute the distance of an object.

If the most distant stars are our background, a near star is like our finger—seeming to change its position in relation to the background when we change our viewing position. But the problem is that even the nearest stars are so much farther than any change in position we can make: The angles involved are so tiny they are difficult to measure. In fact, the only way to make the angles large enough to measure is to use the longest baseline, the greatest distance between viewing points that we can make. The distance between one side of the Earth and the other is great enough to show parallax for the Moon or planets, but not great enough to permit us to see a parallax for the stars. Instead, we must use the diameter of the Earth's orbit. In other words, we measure a star's position among the background stars at one time of our year, and then again six months later—when our observing platform Earth is at the opposite side of its orbit.

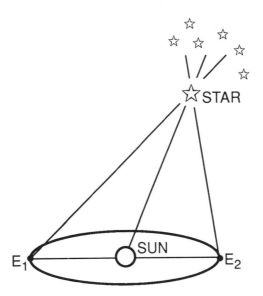

Figure 7 Parallax—a nearby star changes its apparent position against the background of more distant stars when viewed from opposite sides of the Earth's orbit (E_1 and E_2).

45

How large is the parallax of the nearest stars? Astonishingly small. An arc-second is a very tiny unit of angular measure. It takes a fairly large telescope on a night when the "seeing" is good (that is, when the atmosphere is calm) to split the combined image of a pair of stars much less than 1 arc-second apart. It is only about ¼₀ the average apparent diameter of Jupiter in the telescope. The distance at which a star would show a parallax of 1 arc-second when observed from opposite sides of Earth's orbit is a distance called a *parsec* (short for *parallax-second*). A parsec is equal to 3.2616 light-years. The light-year is a more familiar unit to most of us, it being the enormous distance which light, the fastest thing in the universe, can travel in one year. Light, traveling at 186,000 mps (300,000 km/sec), can reach us from the Moon in less than 1½ seconds, from the Sun in about 8 minutes, from the most distant known planets of our solar system in a few hours. But it takes years for light from the stars to reach us—even the closest stars are a few light-years away. The parsec is a considerably larger unit of distance, however. How many stars are close enough to show at least a parallax of 1 tiny arc-second? None. There are no known stars as near as 1 parsec away.

The Alpha Centauri system is the closest star system to us. The closest of its three stars, Proxima Centauri, has a parallax of 0.772" (" being the symbol for arc-seconds, not inches, in this case). By the time we are out to Procyon, the sixteenth-nearest star system, the parallax is down to little more than a quarter of an arc-second.

Most of us don't properly appreciate just how remote the stars are even after hearing about these tiny parallax angles, or the long travel time it takes light to reach us from even the nearest stars. A better way to envision this is by means of a model. Guy Ottewell has published his remarkable 1,000-Yard Model of the solar system (see Sources of Information). On his scale, our Sun is a soccer ball, with tiny nuts and grains of salt (representing planets) in a very large field—with the nearest star system represented by a few more balls (and perhaps scattering of tiny planet rubble) in another large field . . . thousands of miles away!

Now let's study not just the distance of the stars, but the neighborhood of stars in which the Sun lives, with the main goal of this activity—observing as many as possible of the nearest stars.

Table 2' gives information on all the stars now known out to a distance of 11.5 light-years or 3.5 parsecs. The column listing these stars' absolute magnitude confirms what we might have guessed: There are far more dim stars than bright stars in this possibly somewhat typical volume of space. Our neighborhood out to 3.5 parsecs is populated mostly with very dim M-type red dwarf stars, with only five K-type, two G-type, one F-type, and one A-type star—and the latter two stars (Procyon and Sirius)

Table 2
The Nearest Stars, out to 3.5 Parsecs

Star	RA h	m	Dec. °	′	App. Mag.	Abs. Mag.	Distance light-years
Sun	—		—		−26.72	4.8	—
Proxima Centauri	14	29.7	−62	41	11.05v	15.5	4.2
Alpha Centauri A	14	39.6	−60	50	−0.01	4.4	4.3
Alpha Centauri B					1.33	5.7	
Barnard's Star	17	57.8	+04	34	9.54	13.2	6.0
Wolf 359	10	56.5	+07	01	13.53v	16.7	7.7
Lalande 21185	11	03.3	+35	58	7.50	10.5	8.2
UV Ceti A	01	38.8	−17	57	12.52v	15.5	8.4
UV Ceti B					13.02v	16.0	
Sirius A	06	45.1	−16	43	−1.46	1.4	8.6
Sirius B					8.3	11.2	
Ross 154	18	49.8	−23	50	10.45	13.1	9.4
Ross 248	23	41.9	+44	10	12.29	14.8	10.4
Epsilon Eridani	03	32.9	−09	28	3.73	6.1	10.8
Ross 128	11	47.8	+00	48	11.10	13.5	10.9
61 Cygni A	21	06.9	+38	45	5.22v	7.6	11.1
61 Cygni B					6.03	8.4	
Epsilon Indi	22	03.4	−56	47	4.68	7.0	11.2
BD +43°44 A	00	18.5	+44	01	8.08	10.4	11.2
BD +43°44 B					11.06	13.4	
L789-6	22	38.5	−15	19	12.18	14.5	11.2
Procyon A	07	39.3	+05	13	0.38	2.6	11.4
Procyon B					10.7	13.0	

each having its own white dwarf. There are no O-type or B-type stars, no red giants.

The dim apparent magnitude of many of these stars makes them difficult targets for identification. In addition to the RA and declination figures provided, you will need an excellent star atlas or special finder chart to locate these objects. Finder charts are provided for some of them in the invaluable *Burnham's Celestial Handbook* (see Sources of Information), which are marked in the notes below with an asterisk (*).

See how many of our neighbors you can locate. Here are a few notes on some of the more interesting stars (you can learn more about some of them in other activities in this book).

Proxima Centauri. This dim star may be orbiting Alpha A and B in an orbit which takes, about a half a million years to complete, or it may be merely moving through space with them. It appears about 1°51′S and 9.9^{m}W of the Alpha A–B pair, while the true distance between it and them is several hundred times greater than the separation between the Sun and Pluto (in fact, it is about ⅙ of a light-year). The diameter is estimated to be only about 40,000 miles, slightly larger than Uranus or Neptune. Proxima is a *flare star,* in which a suddenly hotter area may increase the star's brightness greatly for a matter of mere minutes. In Proxima's case these flares are frequent (you might detect the star at least half a magnitude brighter than normal something like one out of every 10 or 12 times you observe Proxima).

Barnard's Star.* The star with the greatest proper motion (see the next activity).

Wolf 359* (CN Leonis). A flare star, somewhat larger and somewhat less dim than Proxima Centauri.

Lalande 21185* (BD + 36°2147). An easy target even in binoculars, suspected of having a planetary companion (period about 8 years, mass about 1/100 that of the Sun).

UV Ceti A and B* (L726-8). Previously thought to be more distant than Sirius. The combined mass of this system is only 0.08 the Sun's mass, so the components are among the very few least massive stars known. The fainter star is a flare star which on one occasion brightened from magnitude 12.3 to about 6.8 in seconds!

Epsilon Eridani. The third-nearest naked-eye star. Its motion through space shows signs of its having a planetary companion, and its fairly Sunlike nature has long placed its system high on the list of ones that might be a home to extraterrestrial life.

61 Cygni. The fourth-nearest naked-eye star. It is a beautiful double star (see Activity 16), with the A star possessing an unseen companion which may have only 8 times the mass of Jupiter—thus possibly a planet.

Questions

1. How many of the nearest stars can you observe? Can you ponder, while observing, the immense distance and true nature of these objects? What kind of planetary system might these stars possess?

2. Can you detect any of the outbursts of the nearby flare stars? How bright are the flares, and how long do they last?

13.

Proper Motion and Other Motions of the Stars

Learn about the proper motion of stars by observing as many as possible of the stars with largest proper motion, especially Barnard's Star. Then, try to see proper motion for yourself by sketching the position of Barnard's Star against background stars a second time, a year after—or even mere months after!—the first time. Observe a sample of stars with high space velocity, understanding how radial motion and tangential motion are the components from which we can derive space velocity. View the runaway stars AE Aurigae, 53 Arietis, and Mu Columbae. Try to record the variability of AE, and observe the Flaming Star Nebula it is lighting as it passes through. Observe the star field around the solar apex (in Hercules) and around the apex of the Local Group of stars' collective motion (in Cygnus).

The stars are so distant as to appear fixed in the same positions relative to each other year after year—or so people thought until modern times. When comparisons could be made with ancient star charts and current positional measurements could be made very accurately through the telescope, it was found that a few of the stars seemed to have changed their positions slightly. We now know that all of the stars are in motion in one form or another around our Milky Way galaxy, and have motion relative to that of our own Sun and solar system (themselves circling the galaxy).

Unless it is a member of a very wide double or multiple star system, of a star cluster, or of a star association, each star has a movement somewhat different than that of other stars. We can define two components of that movement which when considered together can give us the true velocity and direction of the star through space.

Here's how it works.

Each star has a transverse (sideways) component of its motion, which we see as a change in its position in relation to the background grid of celestial coordinates we have made. This is called its *proper motion*. In addition, if we know the distance to the star, the angular value for the proper motion can give us the *tangential velocity*—the real transverse component of the star's motion through space, measured in kilometers (or miles) per second.

Each star also has a component of its motion which is either toward or away from us, approaching or receding from us. This is called the *radial velocity*. The velocity of approach or recession may be figured out by studying the spectrum of a star. If the lines in the spectrum are displaced toward the blue end of the spectrum, we say they are *blue-shifted*, if toward the red end we say *red-shifted*. What we are witnessing is an example of the *Doppler effect*. Just as the pitch of sound from an approaching car is shifted toward a lower pitch, and a receding car to a higher pitch, so too is the pitch of an approaching star's light shifted toward a lower (shorter) wavelength—the blue end of the spectrum—and a receding star toward a higher (longer) wavelength—the red end of the spectrum. The amount of the blue shift or red shift of course tells us how fast the approach or recession is.

If we know the velocity and direction of the tangential motion (based on the proper motion), and we know the velocity and direction of the radial motion (approach or recession), these two vectors give us the true direction of the star's motion and the true or *space velocity* of the star.

Proper motion is bound to be very large for some nearby stars (see Table 3). But although the nearest star has the largest parallax (see the previous activity), it turns out not to have the largest proper motion.

Proxima Centauri and the other members of the Alpha Centauri system happen to have an only moderately fast space velocity, and quite a bit of this is in radial velocity. There are at least 13 star systems that show larger proper motion than any member of the Alpha Centauri system!

The first recordholder for greatest proper motion was Arcturus. It was one of three stars which Edmund Halley in 1718 announced had slightly different positions than those noted for them in ancient catalogs. He was discovering proper motion. He had several other lines of evidence and argument supporting his idea that these stars truly had changed their position, however slightly. The three stars were Arcturus, Sirius, and Aldebaran which we now know would in 2000 years have a proper

Table 3
Selected Stars of Very Large Proper Motion

Star	RA h	m	s	Dec. °	'	"	Mag.	Dist. light-years	PA °	Proper Motion "
Barnard's Star	17	57	50.4	+04	38	19	9.54	6.0	360	10.31
Kapteyn's Star	05	11	17.8	−44	59	04	8.84	12.7	131	8.72
Groombridge 1830	11	52	58.7	+37	43	08	6.45	30	327	7.05
Lacaille 9352	23	05	32.2	−35	51	52	7.44	11.7	79	6.90
61 Cygni A	21	06	53.7	+38	44	57	5.22v	11.1	52	5.26
61 Cygni B	21	06	55.2	+38	44	30	6.04	11.1	53	5.17
Lalande 21185	11	03	20.2	+35	58	13	7.50	8.2	187	4.78
Epsilon Indi	22	03	21.3	−56	47	10	4.68	11.2	123	4.70

Fainter stars of very large proper motion include: Cordoba 32416 (6.11″), Ross 619 (5.40″), and Wolf 359 (4.71″). See *Burnham's Celestial Handbook*, Page 1257, for further information on these and other stars of large proper motion.

The RA and declination are in year 2000.0 coordinates; the magnitude is apparent visual magnitude (the photographic magnitudes of some of these stars are much dimmer); the PA is prediction for year 2000.0; the proper motion is annual proper motion.

motion of 1°16′ (Arcturus), 41′ (Sirius), and 7′ (Aldebaran). In 1792, Giuseppe Piazzi found what he called "the Flying Star"—61 Cygni, with a proper motion of 5.22″ annually. In 1842, Friedrich Wilhelm Argelander found that the star we now call Groombridge 1830 had an annual proper motion of 7.04″. In 1897, Jacobus Cornelis Kapteyn found a star with an annual proper motion of 8.70″. Finally, in 1916, Edward Emerson Barnard proved that a ninth-magnitude red dwarf in Ophiuchus had by far the greatest proper motion of any known star—10.29″ a year.

Barnard's "Runaway Star" changes its position by an apparent Moon's width about every 175 years at present. But its proper motion is increasing as it nears us at the very rapid rate of 87 miles per second, so that in 8,000 years its distance from us will have shrunk from 6.0 light-years (second-closest star system) down to less than 4 light-years. This remarkable star is thought to have only about 16 percent as much mass as the Sun and to be about 140,000 miles in diameter. And a wobble in its motion indicates that it has a companion only about 1½ times more massive than Jupiter—thus presumably a planet.

The *space velocity* of some stars is many times greater than others. Such stars are usually the ones that are not orbiting pretty much in the equatorial plane of our Milky Way galaxy, the plane in which the Sun revolves around the galaxy. Stars with high space velocity—like Arcturus—have orbits substantially inclined to the galaxy's equatorial plane. If we see them—especially if we see them bright like Arcturus—they must just happen to be dropping through or rising through the equatorial plane. Velocities greater than 100 kps (kilometers per second) are fairly unusual. A few of the brightest stars that apparently have space velocities even higher than Arcturus' 118 kps are Kappa Cephei, Alpha and Beta Columbae, and Iota and Rho Cygni. Presumably all are stars which, like Arcturus, are merely passing through this equatorial plane of heaviest galactic traffic our Sun is always in. Observe them with this thought in mind.

Three stars with much lower space velocities than Arcturus, and much lower proper motions than Barnard's Star are nevertheless popularly called *runaway stars*. These are 53 Arietis, AE Aurigae, and Mu Columbae. Their space velocities are 35 kps, 80 kps, and 75 kps, respectively. They may be stars that truly are running away (or flying away, if you prefer) from something: The paths of all three can be traced back to roughly the same region, the very general vicinity of the Great Orion Nebula or, at any rate, the midst of the Orion Association of stars (see Figure 8). This region is filled with hot and massive new stars, including many prime candidates for supernova-hood. Each of the three runaway stars may have been the close companion of an Orion Association sun that went supernova. That at least is the theory—no one is certain how or even whether such a thing could really happen.

If their space velocities have remained fairly constant, then the three stars would have been back in the Orion Association region 5 million years (53 Arietis), 2.7 million years (AE Aurigae), and 2.0 million years (Mu Columbae) ago. Whatever the explanation of their flight, these three runaway stars should be observed. The magnitude of 53 Arietis is 6.09, AE Aurigae's varies from 5.4 to 6.1, and Mu Columbae's is 5.16. AE Aurigae is presently racing through a region of nebulosity called IC 405, which it is lighting up and thereby inspiring us also to call it the "Flaming Star Nebula."

A final important aspect of stellar motion should be considered here. We know that all the stars that we easily see are part of the Milky Way galaxy and are revolving around this vast system (our own Sun may take roughly 200 to 250 million years to make one orbit of the galaxy). We also know that most stars we see are not like Arcturus but instead are orbiting more or less like our Sun (and solar system) is, which is to say roughly within the equatorial plane of the galaxy. Now, if all of this is the case, we should expect to be able to determine a point in the sky from which our Sun has departed and another point in our sky to which it is headed. And we can. The former is the *solar antapex* or *Antapex of the*

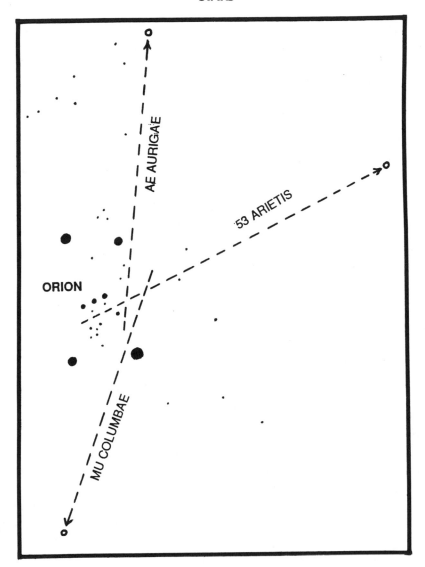

Figure 8 Three runaway stars.

Sun's Way (or "the Sun's Quit"—a beautiful old term). The latter is the *solar apex* or the *Apex of the Sun's Way*.

The solar apex is located at about 18^h4^m, $+30°$. This is near the stars Nu and Xi Herculis, which are near the border of Lyra. But we are not sure enough to really be so precise. It is worthwhile to look at the calculated apex point and these stars, but bear in mind that this is merely an estimate. We are roughly heading toward the bright star Vega. Likewise, though the solar antapex is calculated to be in Columba, near the

Canis Major border, we might do better to merely say that Sirius marks the region of the sky from which we are departing.

Now do note that all this does not mean that we will be passing very close to Vega in the future, or that we went right by Sirius in the past. Those stars are themselves moving, so when we arrive in what is now the region of space that Vega is in, Vega will long since be gone. Quite independent of any of these considerations, both the distance between us and Vega and us and Sirius happens to be lessening somewhat now.

There is a more difficult concept here, however. It is the idea that the direction and velocity of an object in space is relative—that is, we must relate it to some frame of reference. The standard can be the Sun's own velocity and direction—what is a star's velocity and direction relative to the Sun's, as if the Sun itself were at rest. The standard frame of reference can also be the average direction and velocity of a larger number of local stars. When we speak of "space velocity" as "true velocity," we mean true in the frame of reference in which the Sun is imagined to be at rest. If our frame of reference is the galaxy and the throng of stars we are in, circling the center of the galaxy at an approximate distance of 30,000 light-years, then we find the average speed of the Sun and other stars is about 250 kps. And the direction of the collective motion of the throng is not quite the same as the Sun's. The apex of the throng's motion is about 21^h10^m, $+48°$, which is near the star 63 Cygni, a faint planetary nebula, and a star which went "nova" very brightly not so many years ago (Nova Cygni 1975).

So how do we conceive of the Sun's motion relative to this throng orbiting the galaxy? In his invaluable book *The Astronomical Companion* (see Sources of Information), Guy Ottewell finds a beautiful analogy: "We are like a leaf carried along on a broad stream of which we cannot see the sides; we are at this moment sliding slightly across the current toward another leaf (Vega) and this movement we can discern by reference to surrounding leaves; it is small compared to the total rush, but of this we are less directly aware."

Questions

1. How many of the stars of greater proper motion can you observe? Using the finder chart in *Burnham's Celestial Handbook*, can you observe Barnard's Star? Can you check and sketch its position next year (or even a few months from now!) and detect its proper motion?

2. How many of our selected stars of high space velocity can you observe?

3. Can you view 53 Arietis, Mu Columbae, and AE Aurigae—the runaway stars which may have been blasted out of the Orion Association by companion stars of theirs which went supernova? Can you make magnitude estimates of AE Aurigae at different times, noting its variability? Can you detect the Flaming Star Nebula that is being lit by AE Aurigae?

4. Can you observe the stars and other objects around the solar apex and antapex, and around the apex and antapex of the local group of stars' motion?

14.

Double Stars—General Observations

Learn the basics about the different kinds of double stars, partly by observing examples of each. View a naked-eye and a telescopic double, an optical double, a true binary, and a star which shares a common proper motion with its primary. Also view star systems which include three, six, or more members. Observe stars which, though not splittable visually, have been determined to be a spectroscopic binary and an eclipsing binary.

In stellar astronomy, there is a type of observing that does not require perfectly haze-free and dark skies but does require steady (nonturbulent) atmosphere. This type of observing brings to us the most vivid perceptions of color beyond our solar system—some very vivid indeed—and sights of exquisite precision. I refer to the viewing of *double stars*.

A double star is a star that upon closer examination or further study turns out to be really two or more stars. The two stars may just happen to lie along nearly the same line of sight for us, with one star actually being very much farther than the other. This is called an *optical double*. On the other hand, the stars may be near (or fairly near) each other in space and bound together by gravitational attraction. This is called a *physical double*. Some physical doubles involve stars far enough apart for them to be merely traveling forward through space together. But many physical doubles actually do feature one star orbiting around another or, really, both stars orbiting around a common center of gravity (a *barycenter*). Such a double star is called a *binary*.

It is unfortunate that the words *double star* and *binary*—both of which imply that no more than two stars are involved—have come to be applied more generally to include star systems in which there are three or even more stars (*multiple stars*). There is also a little uncertainty as to when there are enough stars together for us to cease calling the group a multiple star system and start calling it a *star cluster*.

We can further categorize types of double stars by the method of their discovery. A *visual double star* (not to be confused with an *optical* double) is one in which the members can be seen separated, the single point of light split, by an observer using some sort of optical instrument. Since the unaided eye is itself an optical instrument, we can speak of *naked-eye doubles* and *telescopic doubles* as subcategories of the class visual double stars. A *spectroscopic binary* is a double star or binary in which the presence of two stars can only be detected by the spectrum of the starlight. An *astrometric binary* is one in which the *duplicity* (the physical doubleness, not moral doubleness or dishonesty!) is detected by noting a wiggle in the plot of the star's proper motion (proof that an unseen companion star must be pulling on it, preventing it from moving in a perfectly straight line). Finally, an *eclipsing binary* is one in which the point of light we see fades at regular intervals, and clearly not from any instability in a single star—rather from one of two component stars eclipsing the other during the course of their orbiting each other.

There are also some important terms to describe the relationship of the component stars of a double star system. The brighter star of a pair—which is not always the more massive—is called the *primary*. The dimmer star is called the *secondary*, or the *companion*, or the *comes* (Latin for "companion"—the plural is *comites*).

There are limits as to how close (that is, how close together) a pair of stars a telecope of a certain size can separate enough for a viewer to distinguish. We investigate these limits in our next activity. But in the current one, let us present some examples of the different kinds of double stars to observe.

Naked-Eye Double. There are not too many of these, unfortunately. A list of some good ones appears in my earlier book *Seeing the Sky*. But the most famous example is the Mizar–Alcor system. Mizar is the bright star which marks the bend in the handle of the Big Dipper (or the bend in the improbably long tail of Ursa Major). Under good sky conditions, a person with good eyesight does not need optical aid to see the companion star Alcor nearby.

Telescopic Double. There are thousands of double stars that can be split with amateur telescopes. Mizar itself is one of them. Very low magnification shows just Mizar and Alcor (along with background stars). But increase the magnification to a mere $40\times$ and Mizar splits into a beautiful pair. The primary (Mizar A) shines at magnitude 2.4, the secondary (Mizar B) shines at 4.0 (which is, by an odd coincidence, also the magnitude of Alcor).

Optical Double. One of the most interesting is Delta Herculis (sometimes called Sarin). The brighter star is third magnitude, the fainter eighth (by the way, the colors are intriguing—see Activity 16). The separation was 25.8″ in 1830, but by 1960 had decreased to a minimum of 9″. Is the fainter star orbiting the brighter? No indeed. The proper motion of the fainter star is almost perpendicular to that of the brighter! They just happen to be passing each other.

Spectroscopic Binary. A fascinating example is brilliant Capella. Of course, by definition you cannot split this spectroscopic binary with a telescope—but you can still observe it again and ponder its duplicity. A spectroscope is required to show that the familiar bright star consists of two suns, a G-type and an F-type, separated by about 70 million miles. It also shows that the red companion traveling through space at a great distance from the bright pair is a double star.

Multiple Star. There are many examples but some people would say the most beautiful of all triple stars is Beta Monocerotis. Unlike most triple stars, which feature two bright stars and a dim companion, Beta Monocerotis consists of magnitude 4.50, 5.22, and 5.60 stars. To deepen the feeling that these stars are near-identical triplets, it would be desirable for all the stars to be of the same color—and they are, white. But what is really remarkable is that all three are even of the same spectral class, B3! And if we wish to see as many stars as possible in a system? One of the leading candidates would be Theta[1] Orionis, whose four brightest components form the famous Trapezium in the brightest part of the splendid Great Orion nebula. Two more stars are well within the range of amateur telescopes. A seventh and eighth may be past the range of even today's amateur giants.

Astrometric Binary. The brightest star is an example: Before its white dwarf companion was ever seen, astronomers noticed that the proper motion of Sirius was not in a straight line.

Eclipsing Binary. The brightest example is Algol (see Activity 20). But we never see the companion of an eclipsing binary: If eclipses happen often enough to be noticed, the two stars must be too close together for any telescope to split them.

What other kinds of double stars are there? If we seek a variety of brightness and color combinations, and of separations, we can find an almost endless offering. An introduction to this variety is the purpose of Activities 16 and 17.

Questions

1. Can you observe examples of the various major types of double star? How high a magnification do you need to split each?

2. What magnification splits Mizar but keeps Alcor in the same field of view with a given telescope? What are the colors of the components of Delta Herculis? How many of the stars of Theta[1] Orionis can you detect with your telescope?

15.

Closest Double Stars for Your Telescope

Learn the basics about double star orbits and double star position angles and separations. Then, test how much of an apparent separation you need to achieve in order to split various doubles—those of different true angular separations and different brightnesses. Also find the closest star you can split with any and all telescopes you have and compare your result to that expected from the Dawes limit. See how the colors of the stars, their brightness, or the differences in their brightness affect your results.

One of the exciting aspects of double star observation is that of revealing a truly hidden sight: two stars where there seemed to be just one. But beyond the thrill of doing this, with some double star systems there remains the possibility of greater challenge—and, more importantly, the satisfaction of testing the worth of your telescope, your sky, and your ability as an observer. The greater challenge is to see what are the closest (that is, closest together) doubles you can split. The result you find will be different on different nights, with different relative brightnesses of the component stars, with different telescopes and different magnifications.

First, we need some background on double star orbits, position angles, and apparent separations.

The *true orbits* of a double star system are the ones that actually exist in space: two ellipses that share a common focus. Obviously, the more massive star has the smaller orbit (far less obvious is what we call *precession* of the orbits, so that they actually form rosettes, not just ellipses—see Figure 9).

To simplify matters, we plot the orbit of just the secondary, and plot it in a frame of reference in which the primary star is kept still. This *relative orbit* is an ellipse always larger than the true one.

On the relative orbit we can determine the points of *periastron* and *apastron*—the places where the secondary star is, respectively, nearest to and farthest from the primary. These are also the places where the secondary travels fastest (at periastron) and slowest (at apastron). The *line of the apsides* runs from apastron to periastron, and is the major axis of the ellipse.

But there is a further complication: We may see such an ellipse from any angle. If we just happen to see it face-on from Earth, it really is as if we are staring straight down or up at a plan or blueprint. But if our viewpoint from Earth gives us an edge-on view, the orbit would appear to be so narrow an ellipse it would become a line. Of course, most of the orbits are tilted somewhere between these two extremes. But the point is this: This *apparent orbit* (which should perhaps more precisely be called the apparent relative orbit) will almost always differ considerably from the relative orbit. Periastron and apastron will no longer correspond with the points of apparent minimum and maximum separation of the two stars. There will in fact usually be two minimum and two maximum separations on the apparent orbit. The line of the apsides will no longer necessarily coincide with the major axis.

A diagram of the apparent orbit is helpful and enjoyable to have no matter what the setup of the double star system may be. But such a diagram really only becomes extremely valuable for systems in which the secondary is going around the orbit rather rapidly, so that the appearance the two stars present to us changes from year to year or decade to

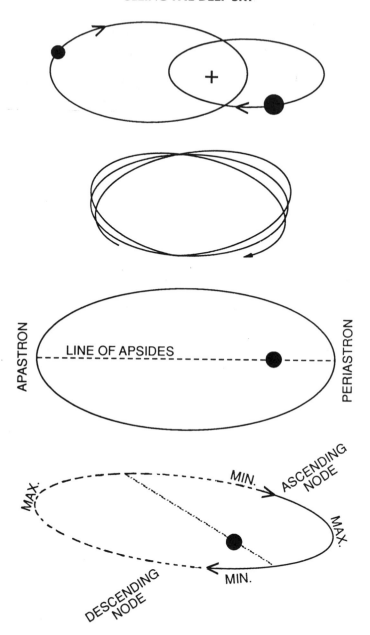

Figure 9 Anatomy of double star orbits (adapted from Guy Ottewell's *Astronomical Companion*). The true orbits are actually orbits around a common center of gravity (marked by a cross here); over time, each true orbit precesses, tracing out a rosette pattern; simplified version of true orbits represents one star as fixed point with lesser star orbiting, and the system seen from a plan view (from overhead or face-on); apparent orbit is the simplified version tilted and foreshortened as it appears when seen from our angle of view.

decade, sometimes the pair becoming closer together and requiring more magnification to split.

The double stars which by this consideration need to have their positions shown least are those that are *relfixes*. The term is short for "relatively fixed": The two stars appear to have a fixed position relative to each other. Of course, we can also suitably take the word *relatively* in another sense here, too: The positions of the two stars are not really or completely fixed—in other words, over long enough periods of time (perhaps far longer than the brief spans of human lifetimes), we would see some change in their apparent distance from each other and direction to each other.

The often quite satisfactory alternative to orbit diagrams is just a listing of two figures: the *separation* and the *position angle*. The separation is just what it sounds like, the angular distance between the two stars—usually measured in seconds of arc. The position angle is the angle at which the secondary lies from the primary if we consider 0° to be due north, 90° due east, and so on through the 360° of a circle until we return to due north.

Now, onward to the question of how close a double star you should be able to split at various magnifications, how close with telescopes of various sizes.

First, we need to define exactly what constitutes a "split." The custom is to say that when you see not merely an elongated star image but an actual narrowing—a waist of light—between two larger areas of light, you have split the double star. A little more magnification would be needed to separate the stars enough to see nothing but dark sky between the two.

How much magnification, then, is needed to "split" different double stars? Table 4 lists the magnifications needed to enlarge the actual angular separation of two stars to an apparent separation of 4' (arc-minutes), 8', and 20'. In practice, 8' ought to be enough of an apparent separation for normal eyesight under good conditions—as long as one star is not greatly (say 5 or more magnitudes) brighter than the other.

But how much magnification can be used on a telescope of a certain size and still produce a reasonably sharp image? This depends greatly on the "seeing" (level of turbulence in the atmosphere). If we assume excellent "seeing," a good and properly collimated telescope should provide a good enough image for splitting a double up to a magnification of about $40\times$ to $60\times$ per inch of aperture (that is, per inch of the main mirror or lens diameter). Thus, a 3-inch telescope can work at powers as high as $120\times$ to $180\times$, a 6-inch as high as $240\times$ to $360\times$, and so on.

Table 4
Magnifications Needed To Give Certain Apparent Separations

True Angular Separation "	Magnification Needed for Apparent Separations of		
	4'	8'	20'
1	240	480	1,200
1.5	160	320	800
2	120	240	600
2.5	96	192	480
3	80	160	400
3.5	68	136	343
4	60	120	300
4.5	54	108	266
5	48	96	240
6	40	80	200
7	34	68	171
8	30	60	150
9	27	54	133
10	24	48	120
15	16	32	80
20	12	24	60
25	10	20	48
30	8	16	40
35	7	14	34
40	6	12	30
45	6	12	27
50	5	10	24
55	5	10	22
60	4	8	20

Remember that on most nights the "seeing" where you live may not be good enough to permit such high powers.

Another approach to the question of what should be the closest double star a certain size telescope can split is provided by the calculation of the *Dawes limit*.

The nineteenth-century astronomer W. R. Dawes made many observations of double stars and came up with an empirical formula for determining how close a double star a telescope should split. The formula is 4.56 arc-seconds divided by the telescope's aperture in inches. The separation splittable by different telescopes would therefore be as follows:

1-inch telescope	4.56″
2-inch	2.28″
3-inch	1.52″
4-inch	1.14″
6-inch	0.76″
8-inch	0.57″
10-inch	0.46″
12½-inch	0.36″
16-inch	0.29″

Unfortunately, the figures for the larger telescopes are rarely approached. The reason is that in most climates a night with "seeing" of 0.5″ or less is unusual (even less than 1″ may be relatively rare in some regions). The greater resolving power of a 10-inch or 16-inch is rarely used; a good 6-inch can do as much (in this respect) on most nights.

There are further qualifications to the Dawes limit figures which must be made. First of all, the telescopes of Dawes' day were generally much inferior to today's. On the other hand, Dawes was an experienced observer, so today's novices shouldn't necessarily assume they are immediately going to better or even equal his figures—even though today's veteran observers do indeed see stars closer together than the Dawes limit. Another qualification is that the shorter-wavelength light of blue stars makes them easier to split. Then there are adjustments which must be made in consideration of how bright the stars are—both absolutely and in comparison to each other. The brighter a star (or brighter the image of it due to its being seen through a larger telescope), the more it spreads out on our retinas—an unfavorable factor for those who would split a double star. Also, the greater the difference in brightness between the two stars, the more difficult it is to perceive the dimmer close in.

Clearly, the Dawes limit is only a useful guideline for roughly how well you can expect to do. There is plenty of room for your own experimentation. Table 5 suggests some stars that are good test objects for various size telescopes. Try these with any and all telescopes you have on a variety of nights and under a variety of conditions.

Questions

1. Using the magnification figures in Table 4, how large an apparent

Table 5
Test Double Stars for Different Size Telescopes

Star	RA h	m	Dec. °	'	Magnitudes		PA °	Dist. "	Aperture inches
Epsilon Bootis	14	45.0	+27	04	2.5,	4.9	339	2.8	2
Zeta Aquarii	22	28.8	−00	02	4.4,	4.6	191	2.1	2
Omicron Cephei	23	18.6	+68	07	4.9,	7.1	223	2.8	2
20 Persei	02	53.7	+38	20	5.3,	10.1	237	14.1	3
Epsilon Arietis	02	59.2	+21	20	5.2,	5.5	203	1.4	3
Zeta Orionis	05	40.8	−01	57	1.9,	4.0	165	2.3	3
Theta Virginis	13	09.9	−05	32	4.4,	9.4	343	7.1	3
Epsilon-1 Lyrae	18	44.3	+39	40	5.0,	6.1	350	2.6	3
Epsilon-2 Lyrae					5.2,	5.5	82	2.3	3
Eta Orionis	05	24.5	−02	24	3.8,	4.8	80	1.5	4
Delta Cygni	19	45.0	+45	08	2.9,	6.3	221	2.5	4
7 Tauri	03	34.4	+24	28	6.6,	6.7	360	0.8	6
Zeta Bootis	14	41.1	+13	44	4.5,	4.6	299	0.8	6
Alpha-2 Capricorni	20	18.1	−12	33	3.6,	10.4	172	6.6	6
Lambda Cassiopeiae	00	31.8	+54	31	5.5,	5.8	191	0.6	8
Gamma Sextantis	09	52.5	−08	06	5.6,	6.1	56	0.6	8
Iota Leonis	11	23.9	+10	32	4.0,	6.7	116	1.7	8
Chi Aquilae	19	42.6	+11	50	5.6,	6.8	77	0.5	10
72 Pegasi	23	34.0	+31	20	5.7,	5.8	97	0.5	10
Hu 445 Tauri	05	01.7	+20	49	8.6,	8.9	300	0.4	12½
Phi Ursae Majoris	09	52.1	+54	04	5.3,	5.4	264	0.3	16

angular separation (4′ or 8′ or 20′) do you find you need to "split" various stars? To completely separate them? How much does your answer depend on your "seeing"? How much on the brightness of the component stars, or the difference in their brightness?

2. On a night of excellent "seeing," can you and your telescope perform up to the Dawes limit? How much are your results influenced by the color of the stars? By their brightness? By the difference in the component stars' brightness?

16.

Selected Double Stars—1

Observe some of the most interesting double stars north of the celestial equator. Judge how much magnification and what size telescope you need to split each in good (and less-than-good) "seeing." Name the colors you see and compare them with the estimates of some famous observers.

Now, armed with the knowledge gained from the previous two activities, we are ready to survey a selection of some of the more interesting double star systems. We will require two activities. The first deals with double stars north of the celestial equator, and is presented in order of RA. Remember that the following is only a selection, intended to present a variety of different views but by no means intended as a list of all the very "best" doubles.

Table 6 gives the basic observational data on the selected doubles in the north celestial hemisphere. A few first-magnitude stars with interesting companions are omitted because they are dealt with sufficiently in Activities 1 through 4, and elsewhere in this book. Reference is made in the text below to authors of several of the books listed in the Sources of Information in the back of this book. The text includes some additional notes.

Eta Cassiopeiae. Controversial colors (see Activity 18). Only 18 light-years away. Large proper motion. Apparent orbit nearly circular, period around 500 years. See Activities 9 and 11 for some comments about the A and B stars' positions on the H–R diagram.

Gamma Arietis. A remarkable optical double. Discovered to be a double by Robert Hooke in 1664 while he was following a comet. Spectra B9V and A0p. Note the exact north–south alignment (PA 0°).

Alpha Piscium (see Figure 10). Controversial colors (see Activity 18). Duplicity first noted by William Herschel in 1779. Closing. Companion has peculiar spectrum with strong metallic lines.

Gamma Andromedae. One of the most beautiful of all doubles. Primary is called golden or a bit orange, the secondary is greenish-

Table 6
Selected Double Stars in the North Celestial Hemisphere

Star	RA h m	Dec. ° '	Magnitudes	PA °	Dist. "
Eta Cassiopeiae	00 49.1	+57 49	3.5, 7.5	317	12.9
Gamma Arietis	01 53.5	+19 18	4.8, 4.8	0	7.8
Alpha Piscium	02 02.0	+02 46	4.2, 5.2	272	1.8
Gamma Andromedae	02 03.9	+42 20	2.3, 5.1	63	9.8
Iota Trianguli	02 12.4	+30 18	5.3, 6.9	71	3.9
Iota Cassiopeiae	02 29.1	+67 24	4.6, 6.9	230	2.5
Alpha Ursae Majoris	02 31.8	+89 16	2.0, 9.0	218	18.4
Gamma Ceti	02 43.3	+03 14	3.5, 7.3	294	2.8
Epsilon Arietis	02 59.2	+21 20	5.2, 5.5	203	1.4
Lambda Orionis	05 35.1	+09 56	3.6, 5.5	43	4.4
12 Lyncis	06 46.2	+59 27	5.4, 6.0	69	1.7
Alpha Geminorum[a]	07 34.6	+31 53	1.9, 2.9	65	3.9
Zeta Cancri[b]	08 12.2	+17 39	5.1, 6.2	72	6.0
Iota Cancri	08 46.7	+28 46	4.2, 6.6	307	30.5
Gamma Leonis	10 20.0	+19 51	2.2, 3.5	125	4.4
Xi Ursae Majoris	11 18.2	+31 32	4.3, 4.8	273	1.8
Alpha Canum Venaticorum	12 56.0	+38 19	2.9, 5.5	229	19.4
Zeta Ursae Majoris	13 23.9	+54 56	2.3, 4.0	152	14.4
Kappa Bootis	14 13.5	+51 47	4.6, 6.6	236	13.4
Zeta Bootis	14 41.1	+13 44	4.5, 4.6	299	0.8
Epsilon Bootis	14 45.0	+27 04	2.5, 4.9	339	2.8
Xi Bootis	14 51.4	+19 06	4.7, 6.9	318	6.6
Eta Coronae Borealis	15 23.2	+30 17	5.6, 5.9	63	0.8
Mu Bootis[c]	15 24.5	+37 23	4.3, 6.5	171	108.3
Zeta Herculis	16 41.3	+31 36	2.9, 5.5	12	0.8
Mu Draconis	17 05.3	+54 28	5.7, 5.7	8	1.9
Alpha Herculis	17 14.6	+14 23	var., 5.4	104	4.6
Delta Herculis	17 15.0	+24 50	3.1, 8.2	236	8.9
Nu Draconis	17 32.2	+55 11	4.9, 4.9	312	61.9
70 Ophiuchi	18 05.5	+02 30	4.2, 6.0	164	4.5
Epsilon Lyrae[d]	18 44.3	+39 40	4.7, 4.6	173	207.7
Theta Serpentis	18 56.2	+04 12	4.5, 5.4	104	22.3
Beta Cygni	19 30.7	+27 58	3.1, 5.1	54	34.4
Epsilon Draconis	19 48.2	+70 16	3.8, 7.4	15	3.1
Gamma Delphini	20 46.7	+16 07	4.5, 5.5	268	9.6
61 Cygni	21 06.9	+38 45	5.2, 6.0	150	30.3
Xi Cephei	22 03.8	+64 38	4.4, 6.5	274	8.2

[a]Alpha Geminorum. Castor C is the eclipsing binary YY Gemini (varies from visual magnitude 9.1 to 9.6) and is fixed at PA 163°, 70″ from the A–B pair.

[b]Zeta Cancri. A is itself a double of magnitudes 5.6 and 6.0, PA 86°, 0.8″ (prediction for 2000.0).

[c]Mu Bootis. Mu² Bootis is a double of magnitudes 7.0 and 7.6, PA 8°, 2.3″ (prediction for 2000.0).

[d]Epsilon Lyrae. Each star is a double: Epsilon¹ is 5.0, 6.1, PA 350°, 2.6″; Epsilon² is 5.2, 5.5, 82°, 2.3″ (prediction for 2000.0).

For all stars in the table: The RA and declination are in year 2000.0 coordinates; the PA and distance (separation) are predictions for year 2000.0.

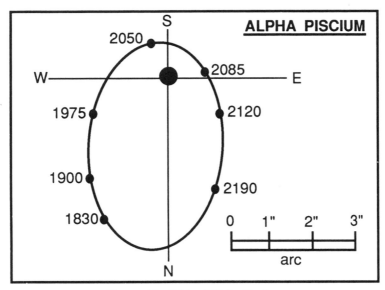

Figure 10 Orbit of Alpha Piscium.

blue. Easy to split in almost any telescope. PA and separation seem to be unchanging. The secondary has a companion which is nearly at its greatest separation in the 1990s (though closing) but is less than 0.5″ (0.4″ in PA 103 by the year 2000). This close pair making up the 5.1 magnitude secondary are magnitude 5.5 and 6.3. The primary star is a spectroscopic binary so this is at least a quadruple star system.

Iota Trianguli. Controversial colors (see Activity 18). Duplicity first noted by Herschel in 1781. Spectra G5III and F6V. Both stars are themselves spectroscopic binaries.

Iota Cassiopeiae. James Muirden says, "A glorious triple . . . yellow–white, bluish, and deeper blue." Despite this being the common color appraisal, the spectra are A5, F5, and G4—so the primary should be bluer! Resolvable in a good 3-inch. The C star is slowly closing, PA increasing.

Alpha Ursae Minoris. In good conditions, the companion to the North Star can be seen with a 60-mm refractor, but in bad conditions is very much harder to see. Companion usually said to look bluish. Orbit must take thousands of years. Primary is a spectroscopic binary.

Gamma Ceti. Usually called yellow and blue, but spectra are A2 and F3 (so companion should not really look blue). Some observers have called the companion "tawny" or "dusky." Should be easy in a 4-inch. Duplicity found by F. G. W. Struve in 1836.

Lambda Orionis. Controversial color (see Activity 18). First measured by F. G. W. Struve in 1830. Primary is one of hottest stars. Faint nebulosity photographed all around this field. The naked-eye triangle formed by Lambda and Phi-1 and Phi-2 Orionis seems minute but the Moon could be wedged in it.

12 Lyncis. A fine triple. PA decreasing, orbit about 700 years. Muirden says A is slightly yellowish compared to B. Good sight for a 4-inch. The C star is thought to be a physical part of the system, too.

Alpha Geminorum (Castor). See Activity 2.

Zeta Cancri. The A–B pair's 60-year orbit has its separation varying between 0.54″ (which it is in 1991) and about 1.2″. A and B both golden-yellow, and C "unusually white." C is a spectroscopic binary, and there could be as many as five or six stars in this system. Orbit of A and B inclined only 8° from face-on. Distance to system about 70 light-years, distance between A and B about same as Sun to Uranus. Duplicity discovered by T. Mayer in 1756, third star found by Herschel in 1781.

Iota Cancri. Controversial color (see Activity 18). Can be divided by as little as 12×. Spectra G8 and A3. John Sanford says it resembles Albireo (Beta Cygni).

Gamma Leonis. Muirden calls the colors "fine crocus yellow and greenish-yellow," but many observers see only yellow and yellow. Sanford calls them both "orange–yellow" and says this color helps him see them more easily against blue sky in daylight. Spectra K0III and G7III. Photoelectrically determined magnitudes of 2.14 and 3.39. Distance is about 90 light-years. Will be widest (about 5″) in about 2100. Orbit may take about six centuries, and is very elongated. Duplicity found by Herschel in 1782.

Xi Ursae Majoris. Both stars are Sunlike in spectrum, size, and brightness. Distance is only 26 light-years. Robert Burnham, Jr., says no color contrast to most observers, who see both as "a clear pale yellow." But R. H. Allen calls them "subdued white and grayish-white," and Muirden says they are "cream-colored." The system's most notable attribute is the fast positional changes. The maximum separation of 3.1″ occurred in 1974, the minimum separation of 0.84″ will occur in 1993. Sixty-year orbit. First double to have its orbit determined (by M. Savary in 1828).

Alpha Canum Venaticorum (Cor Caroli). Named not for Charles II, but rather for Charles I, and only reputedly (not necessarily really) by Edmund Halley. Much color controversy: Burnham says little if any contrast, but Allen saw "flushed white and pale lilac," Agnes Clerke saw "pale yellow and fawn." Dembowski called the fainter star "pale olive blue" (!), Webb called it "pale copper"—the latter, Burnham says, agreeing with the spectral type, F0V. Muirden sees them as white and "warm white." The primary is the standard example of a magnetic spectrum variable (Iota Cassiopeiae—see above—is another example). No change in position since first measured in 1830, but definitely a physical pair.

Zeta Ursae Majoris (Mizar). Controversial color. Muirden and Sanford see the two stars as white, but some see them yellow, and Allen says "brilliant white and pale emerald." The duplicity of Mizar was first noted by Riccioli in 1650—first telescopic double found. The system is 88 light-years away.

Kappa Bootis. Yellow and blue—but spectra A7 and F2. The primary is a Delta Scuti variable (very small range of variation).

Zeta Bootis. Separation varies from 1.16″ (in 1959) to only 0.03″ (in 2021). A and B are both A2.

Epsilon Bootis. Controversial color (see Activity 18). F. G. W. Struve's "Pulcherrima" ("most beautiful"). K0 or K1 and A2. Difficult for 3-inch, not easy sometimes even for larger telescope. Webb says Buffham resolved it with a 9-inch mirror stopped down to 1⅞ inches.

Xi Bootis. Controversial color (see Activity 18). Only 22 light-years away. Herschel found its duplicity in 1780. At nearly widest separation.

Eta Coronae Borealis. Both stars nearly twins of the Sun in size, mass, and luminosity. Needs about a 6-inch. Has completed more than three orbits since duplicity discovered by Struve in 1826. Period is 41½ years. At widest, about 1.0″—for instance, in 1993. Distance about 50 light-years.

Mu Bootis. Mu¹ and Mu² can be shown divided by binoculars. Specra F0 and G1. The fainter star is a binary, both components resembling the Sun in spectrum and luminosity. About 95 light-years away.

Zeta Herculis. Only 30 light-years away. Period about 34 years. Widest, at about 1.58″ in 1991. Closest, at only 0.49″, in 2001. Burnham calls this "the classical case of a subgiant in a visual binary system."

Mu Draconis. A and B are both dF6. Both yellowish, equally bright. In the 1990s is closest, but still should be splittable with 3-inch at high power. 100 light-years away. A third star is present, and maybe a fourth.

Alpha Herculis. Controversial color (see Activity 18). Remarkable primary—one of largest stars, and interesting variable. Spectra G5III and F2. Gases from primary extend to companion (at least 700 AU).

Delta Herculis. Some controversy about the colors. Remarkable optical double (see Activity 14).

Nu Draconis. So wide that binoculars can split it (even a claim of naked-eye splitting exists!). Identical brightness and similar spectral class—and both stars with unusually strong metallic lines in spectrum. Distance 120 light-years, true separation about 2,300 AU. Both about 11 times as luminous as the Sun.

70 Ophiuchi. Controversial color (see Activity 18). One of four stars that formed the V-shaped pattern of the obsolete constellation Taurus Poniatowski. Only 16½ light-years away. Much more open by year 2000. May possess an unseen companion with mass only 10 times that of Jupiter (thus possibly a planet).

Epsilon Lyrae (see Figure 11). The famous "Double Double," apparently first noticed as such by Herschel in August 1779. Sharp naked eyes can split Epsilon[1] from Epsilon[2]. A 3-inch can resolve the closer pairs. Most observers see all the stars as white, and indeed their spectral classes are A2 and A4 (Epsilon[1]), and A3 and A5 (Epsilon[2]).

Theta Serpentis. Both yellow or both white. A5 and A5, or A5 and A7. Binoculars or 1-inch telescope can split.

Beta Cygni (Albireo). Controversial color. Sometimes called the most beautiful of all doubles. Even good, steadily held binoculars can split it. Best view may be at about $30\times$ on a 6-inch. In recent years there has been evidence that Albireo might be an optical pair.

Epsilon Draconis. Muirden says that the "off-white primary gives companion a pleasing blue." G8 and F6V. Not too easy with a 4-inch.

Gamma Delphini. Yellow and white to Muirden, but much disagreement over tint of companion among various observers (one claim: "reddish-yellow and greyish-lilac"). Burnham says that most of to-

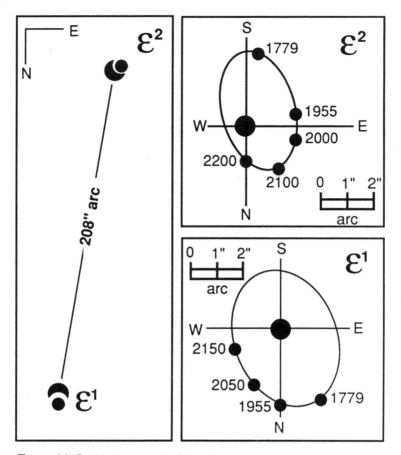

Figure 11 Positionings and orbits of stars in the Epsilon Lyrae system.

day's observers judge both are yellow, sometimes fainter star called green. K2 and F8.

61 Cygni. Both orange, both dwarfs. See Activity 12 for more on this fascinating and near star.

Xi Cephei. Slight color contrast, some call dimmer star ruddy or "tawny," Muirden says "pale yellow and blue–green." A3 and F7V. May be an outlying member of the Taurus Stream associated with the Hyades.

Questions

1. What magnifications and telescopes do you require to split the many north celestial hemisphere doubles listed above? What are your impressions of their colors?

2. What other doubles do you notice near, or even in the same field as, these stars?

17.

Selected Double Stars—2

Observe some of the most interesting double stars south of the celestial equator. Judge how much magnification and what size telescope you need to split each in good (and less-than-good) "seeing." Name the colors you see and compare them with the estimates of famous observers.

We continue the tour of double stars started in the previous activity. This time, the stars are those south of the celestial equator. All the comments regarding how Table 6 is arranged, and what it does and does not include, also apply to our current one, Table 7.

Let's continue the tour.

Theta Eridani. A3 and A2. Distance is about 115 light-years, luminosity about 50 and 20 Suns. Ptolemy rated this star as first magnitude, but now it is 2.9. The brighter star is a spectroscopic binary.

Beta Orionis (Rigel). See Activity 2.

Eta Orionis. Close and rather difficult. Most observers think both are white, but Webb thought companion was slightly purplish. Eta A is a spectroscopic binary, and a fourth star is present, too.

Theta¹ Orionis. Superb multiple star in the stellar birthing place called the Great Orion Nebula. The four brightest stars of the system form the Trapezium. Admiral Smyth thought the colors of these were pale white, faint lilac, garnet, and reddish, but Burnham attributes these to contrast with the surrounding bright and green nebula. The stars are lettered in order of RA, so C is the true primary, D next in brightness, A next, B last. B is an eclipsing binary. A wasn't known

Table 7
Selected Double Stars in the South Celestial Hemisphere

Star	RA h	m	Dec. °	'	Magnitudes		PA °	Dist. "
Theta Eridani	02	58.3	−40	18	3.4,	4.5	88	4.5
Beta Orionis	05	14.5	−08	12	0.1,	6.8	202	9.5
Eta Orionis	05	24.5	−02	24	3.8,	4.8	80	1.5
Iota Orionis	05	35.4	−05	55	2.8,	6.9	141	11.3
Sigma Orionis	05	38.7	−02	36	4.0,	6.0	115	0.2
Zeta Orionis	05	40.8	−01	57	1.9,	4.0	165	2.3
Beta Monocerotis	06	28.8	−07	02	4.7,	4.8	132	7.3
k Puppis	07	38.8	−26	48	4.5,	4.7	318	9.9
Gamma Velorum	08	09.5	−47	20	1.9,	4.2	220	41.2
Upsilon Carinae	09	47.1	−65	04	3.1,	6.1	127	5.0
Alpha Crucis	12	26.6	−63	06	1.3,	1.7	115	4.4
Gamma Centauri	12	41.5	−48	58	2.9,	2.9	347	1.0
Gamma Virginis	12	41.7	−01	27	3.5,	3.5	267	1.8
Beta Centauri	14	03.8	−60	22	0.7,	3.9	251	1.3
Alpha Centauri	14	39.6	−60	50	0.0,	1.3	222	14.1
Xi Scorpii[a]	16	04.4	−11	22	4.9,	4.9	308	0.4
Beta Scorpii	16	05.4	−19	48	2.6,	4.9	21	13.6
Nu Scorpii[b]	16	12.0	−19	28	4.2,	6.1	337	41.1
Alpha Scorpii	16	29.4	−26	26	var.,	5.4	273	2.6
Zeta Scorpii[c]	16	54.3	−42	20	3.6,	4.8	—	408
36 Ophiuchi	17	15.4	−26	33	5.1,	5.1	152	4.7
Tau Ophiuchi[d]	18	03.0	−08	11	5.3,	6.0	283	1.7
Eta Ophiuchi	18	10.4	−15	44	3.0,	3.5	244	0.6
Gamma Coronae Australis	19	06.4	−37	04	5.0,	5.1	55	1.3
Alpha-1 Capricorni	20	18.0	−12	33	4.2,	9.5	221	45.5
Alpha-2 Capricorni	20	18.0	−12	33	3.8,	11.2	180	6.6
Zeta Aquarii	22	28.8	−00	02	4.4,	4.6	191	2.1

[a]Xi Scorpii. A third star, of magnitude 7.3, is at PA 51°, 7.6″ (prediction for 2000.0).

[b]Nu Scorpii. Each star is a double: Nu[1] Scorpii is 4.3, 6.8, PA 3°, 0.9″; Nu[2] Scorpii is 6.4, 7.8, 51°, 2.3″ (prediction for 2000.0).

[c]Zeta[2] is the star with greater apparent brightness.

[d]Tau Ophiuchi. A third star of magnitude 9.3, is at PA 127°, 100″.

[e]Alpha Capricorni. Alpha[1] and Alpha[2] form a naked-eye double, separated by 6′.

to have variability until 1975. Stars E and F are both eleventh magnitude but people have claimed to see them with as small as a 3-inch. Several dimmer stars in the system are beyond most amateur telescopes.

Iota Orionis. Triple star, with bright components "white and grayish," according to Muirden. But Allen calls the colors of the three stars "white, pale blue, and grape red." Not far from Theta[1] and Theta[2] Orionis in the Sword of Orion, its field is covered with the nebulosity of NGC 1980. Iota A itself is a spectroscopic binary.

Sigma Orionis. Five visible components. A and E are 41″ apart, a double that can be seen through binoculars. A and B are only 0.25″ apart. At 11.2″ away is tenth-magnitude C and 12.9″ away is 7.5 magnitude D. The real span from A to E is at least ⅓ of a light-year!

Zeta Orionis. Triple. Close pair, much color controversy. NGC 2024 and IC 434 are nebulosities near this star, and the Horsehead Nebula appears as an indentation in the latter. Splitting Zeta easy in a little more than 3-inch.

Beta Monocerotis. See Activity 14 for this lovely triple star.

Alpha Canis Majoris. See Activity 2 (and elsewhere) for more on Sirius (and see Figure 12).

k Puppis. Bright, almost equal, and easy to split. Spectra B8 and B5.

Gamma Velorum. Resolvable in good binoculars. Relfix. Primary is most famous Wolf–Rayet star, hottest of all spectral types. Agnes Clerke thought its spectrum the most beautiful of all. Third star. Allen thought the three stars' colors were "white, greenish-white, and purple."

Upsilon Carinae. Spectra A9 and F0. Relfix.

Alpha Crucis. See Activity 3.

Gamma Centauri. Brilliant and equal, a magnificent though close (and closing) double. Duplicity first noted by John Herschel in 1835.

Gamma Virginis (see Figure 13). "Porrima"—named in honor of the goddess of prophecy. Magnitudes 3.65 and 3.65, spectra F0 and F0. White or yellow–white or pale white pair whose separation varies from 0.3″ to 6.0″ in 172-year orbit—least separated (and unresolvable even by John Herschel) in 1836, will be again least separated in

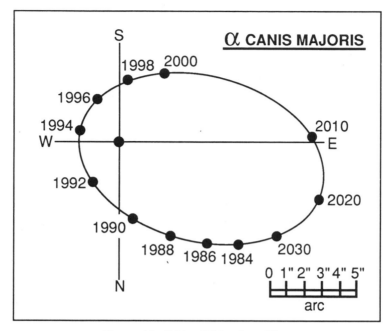

Figure 12 Orbit of Sirius A and B.

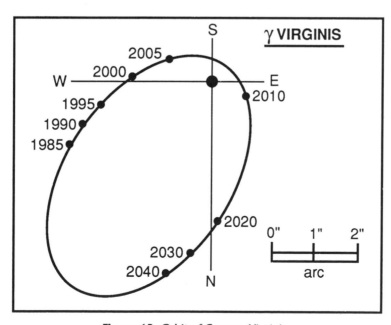

Figure 13 Orbit of Gamma Virginis.

about 2007. Duplicity discovered by Bradley and Pound in 1718. Only 32 light-years away. Burnham says they are like "twin head-lamps of some celestial auto, approaching from deep space."

Xi Scorpii. Tight pair, with rapidly changing PA: 48°0.67″ (1991), 61°,0.49″ (1993), 94°,0.27″ (1995)—but back out to 0.4″ by year 2000. The gold and gold pair are equally bright, and have the same spectral class, F5. A third star is a G7 orange dwarf. At least five stars in the system.

Alpha Centauri. See Activity 3 and Table 7.

Beta Scorpii. AB unresolvable in amateur telescopes, but AC makes a fine and easy pair. Famous for being near ecliptic and getting occulted by Moon—or even by Jupiter. Muirden thinks the colors are off-white and bluish.

Nu Scorpii. Quadruple star. Nu^1 needs about 5″ aperture telescope to split, but Nu^2 only about 2½″.

Alpha Scorpii. See Activity 4 and Table 7.

Zeta Scorpii. $Zeta^1$ and $Zeta^2$ are very widely separated, with $Zeta^2$ being the star of greater apparent brightness. This is an optical pair, with $Zeta^1$ possibly 40 times farther. If $Zeta^1$ is a member of the cluster NGC 6231, then its distance is about 5,700 light-years and it is one of the most luminous of all stars, perhaps bettering Deneb or Rigel with an absolute magnitude of -8.

36 Ophiuchi. Period about 550 years. PA decreasing. Main pair of equal magnitude and easy. Muirden calls them "yellow." Third star is about 732″ away in about PA 74, and shines at magnitude 7.5. Spectra of the three stars are K0, K2, and K5.

Tau Ophiuchi. Muirden says "yellowish and white," but spectra of both are F2V. Period about 280 years. Ninth-magnitude third star 100″ away.

Eta Ophiuchi. Bright but close pair, widening from 0.5″ in 1990 to 0.55″ in 1995. Only 70 light-years away, so separation is only about that of Sun and Uranus. Period only 88 years. Even on nights of excellent "seeing," a challenge for telescopes in the 8- to 12-inch range.

Gamma Coronae Australis. Almost edge-on system with period of about 120 years. Almost equally bright and spectra of both F8. PA changing rapidly—134° in 1985 to 55° in 2000.

Alpha Capricorni. Alpha[1] is a naked-eye double with Alpha[2]. Alpha[2] appears brighter at 3.6, Alpha[1] is 4.2. They are an optical pair, with Alpha[2] being a class Ib supergiant and Alpha[1] only a class III star. Alpha[2] is about 100 light-years away, Alpha[1] about 5 times farther. Their spectra are G9 (Alpha[2]) and G3 (Alpha[1]). Each star has a faint companion for telescopes (see Table 7). To see the dim companion of Alpha[2] requires at least a 6-inch, but usually more.

Zeta Aquarii. Central star of the Water Jar asterism in Aquarius. Muirden again calls this pair "cream-colored." Spectra are F2 and F2 or F2 and F1. This binary rather recently had its least separation in a roughly eight-century-long orbit. In 1990, the separation was 1.9″, PA 207°; in 1995, 2.0″ and 199°. After 2000, the split will become quite easy.

Questions

1. What magnifications and telescopes do you require to split the many south celestial hemisphere doubles listed above? What are your impressions of their colors?

2. What other doubles do you notice near, or even in the same field as, these stars?

18.

The Colors of Double Stars

Observe our selection of vividly colored double stars and make your own judgments as to what the hues are. Then, compare your estimates with those of Smyth, Webb, and other observers given here.

In the previous two activities, we encountered many lovely star colors. But most star colors are subtle. And in the case of double stars, contrasting colors of the two component stars can lead us to a perception of stronger hues than we would otherwise see. A further complicating factor is that color is more prominent in a brighter star, up to a point—a large telescope that gives brighter images may really begin to wash out the colors of bright stars. Still more complicating is the fact that color perception varies physiologically from person to person, and is probably even more greatly affected by the color vocabulary and other psychologically influenced factors in individuals.

Is there any hope for objectivity in estimating star colors? Despite all the potentially confusing elements, there is, of course, the potential for considerable agreement. This might be improved by having several observers looking at the stars through the same telescope at the same session, and by one observer using several different telescopes at the same session. Ultimately, a greater awareness of your use of color vocabulary grows. And, indeed, the sharpening of your observing skills is perhaps as great a benefit as any conclusions you manage to reach.

A great start in the direction of encouraging observers to study star colors was made in an article by Jacqueline Mitton and Alan MacRobert in the February 1989 issue of *Sky & Telescope*. Among other things, they presented a giant table of data and color descriptions of some double stars which the devoted nineteenth-century observer Admiral William Henry Smyth examined with his 5.9-inch refractor. The data are modern, but the descriptions were Smyth's. Our reproduction of this table (Table 8) shows that Smyth's color appraisals were indeed among the most picturesque ever made.

In our current activity, however, I would like to take this project one step further. Smyth's famous observer's handbook was the *Bedford Catalogue*, originally published in 1844. But the other great (and later) nineteenth-century observer's handbook was the Reverend T. W. Webb's *Celestial Objects for Common Telescopes*. Webb gives color estimates for a large number of stars, many of the estimates his own—often even several of his own for a particular double star which he observed in different years with different results (that is, with different star colors). Webb also gives many of the color appraisals of other nineteenth-century observers (very occasionally, he gives one of Smyth's).

The text below provides most of these descriptions from Webb's book of the stars on the Smyth list compiled by Mitton and MacRobert. I've also included some color appraisals by two of today's observers, James Muirden and John Sanford, plus a few general comments by Robert Burnham, Jr. (author of the great observer's handbook of the late twentieth century). In a few cases where they are not simply citations of Smyth's colors, I've taken the color estimates from R. H. Allen's wonderful 1899 work on star names (now retitled in its reissue by Dover Publications: *Star Names, Their Lore and Meanings*).

In the following discussion, any descriptions that are not otherwise identified are from Webb. Add your own to these! Try to use neither too large nor too small a telescope for the stars in question. Another trick which sometimes works to obtain a stronger perception of color is to defocus slightly the stars' images. And make certain you split the double enough. Above all else, remember that it is best for you not to go out to the telescope with these color appraisals fresh in your mind. Try to make your own unbiased observation at first, then come in to compare it to the descriptions presented here. If just reading these tints stimulates your sense of beauty, think what actually seeing these lovely hues glittering against a black backdrop will do!

55 Piscium. Very yellow, very blue.

Eta Cassiopeiae. Yellow, purple; yellow, pale garnet. John Herschel and South: red, green. Dembowski: Yellow and generally red. Espin: *comes* [companion] always pale red. Allen: orange and violet. Burnham: observers describe as "topaz and garnet," gold and purple. Muirden: A is cream-colored and B has a port-wine tint.

Lambda Arietis. Yellow, bluish. Dembowski: white, olive or azure.

Alpha Piscium. Greenish-blue, blue. Webb says companion "troublesome as to color, usually ruddy, or tawny, sometimes blue." Burnham says primary has been called everything from greenish-yellow to brown (but surely only the dimmer star would have been called brown?).

Gamma Andromedae. Gold, blue. Burnham: "golden-yellow or slightly orange . . . and the companion . . . a definite greenish-blue."

Iota Trianguli. Yellow, blue. Muirden: yellow, blue and delicate.

30 Arietis. Yellow, bluish-gray; yellow, pale lilac. Dembowski: "white, yellow or azure." Burnham: "Both stars are yellow [presumably he means should be yellow to judge from spectral class] but many observing lists refer to the smaller star as bluish or lilac."

Eta Persei. Very yellow, very blue. Burnham claims Webb called them greenish-white and ashy, but I can't find this in *Celestial Objects for Common Telescopes.*

32 Eridani. Yellow, blue; topaz, bright green.

Omega Aurigae. Greenish, bluish with white and ruddy.

Lambda Orionis. Yellowish, purple.

Table 8

Some Vivid Double Stars of William Henry Smyth

Star	RA h m	Dec. °	Magnitudes	Sep. "	Spectra	Smyth's Description
55 Psc	00 40	+21.4	5.4, 8.7	6.5	K0, F3	Orange, deep blue; good contrast, a rich specimen of opposed hues
η Cas	00 49	+57.8	3.4, 7.5	12.4	G0, M0	Pale white, purple
λ Ari	01 58	+23.6	4.9, 7.7	37.4	F0, G1	Yellowish-white, blue
α Psc	02 02	+02.8	4.2, 5.2	1.9	A2, A2	Pale green, blue; splendid object
γ And	02 04	+42.3	2.3, 4.8	9.8	K2, A0	Orange, emerald green; splendid
ι Tri	02 12	+30.3	5.3, 6.9	3.9	G5, F6	Topaz yellow, green; exquisite
30 Ari	02 37	+24.6	6.6, 7.4	38.6	F5, F5	Topaz yellow, pale gray
η Per	02 51	+55.9	3.8, 8.5	28.3	K3	Orange, smalt [deep] blue; the colors in clear contrast
32 Eri	03 54	−03.0	4.8, 6.1	6.8	G5, A2	Topaz yellow, pea green; brilliant contrast
ω Aur	04 59	+37.9	5.0, 8.0	5.4	A0	Pale red, light blue
λ Ori	05 35	+09.9	3.6, 5.5	4.4	O5, O5	Pale white, violet
8 Mon	06 24	+04.6	4.5, 6.5	13.4	A5, F4	Golden yellow, lilac
20 Gem	06 32	+17.8	6.3, 6.9	20.0	F8	Topaz yellow, cerulean blue
14 Lyn	06 53	+59.4	5.7, 6.9	0.4	G0, A2	Golden-yellow, purple; very delicate and pretty . . . with the colors distinct
38 Gem	06 55	+13.2	4.7, 7.7	7.0	F0, G4	Light yellow, purple; colors so marked that they cannot be entirely imputed to the illusory effect of contrast
ι Cnc	08 47	+28.8	4.2, 6.6	30.5	G5, A5	Pale orange, clear blue; colors finely contrasted
ω Leo	09 28	+09.1	5.9, 6.5	0.5	F9	Pale yellow, greenish; at times both stars looking yellow

	RA	Dec			Sep.	Spectra		Description
γ Leo	10 20	+19.8	2.2,	3.5,	4.4	K0,	G7	Bright orange, greenish-yellow; splendid
ι Leo	11 24	+10.5	4.0,	6.7,	1.5	F2,	F8	Pale yellow, light blue
β Leo	11 49	+14.6	2.1,	8.5,	264.0	A3,	F7	Bluish, dull red
2 CVn	12 16	+40.7	5.8,	8.1,	11.4	M1,		Golden yellow, smalt blue; very fine
24 Com	12 35	+18.4	5.2,	6.7,	20.3	K0,	A3	Orange, emerald tint; colors very brilliant
ε Boo	14 45	+27.1	2.5,	4.9,	2.8	K0,	A0	Pale orange, sea green; the colors distinct and strongly contrasted
ξ Boo	14 51	+19.1	4.7,	7.0,	7.0	G8,	K4	Orange, purple; the colors in fine contrast
ζ CrB	15 39	+36.6	5.1,	6.0,	6.3	B6,	B7	Bluish-white, smalt blue
ρ Oph	16 26	−23.4	5.3,	6.0,	3.1	B3,	B2	Pale topaz yellow, blue (color index + 0.24; interstellar reddening?)
λ Oph	16 31	+02.0	4.2,	5.2,	1.5	A1		Yellowish-white, smalt blue
α Her	17 15	+14.4	3.5v,	5.4,	4.6	M5,	G5	Orange, emerald or bluish-green
39 Oph	17 18	−24.3	5.4,	6.9,	10.3	K2,	F6	Pale orange, blue; very fine; a neat double star
ρ Her	17 24	+37.1	4.6,	5.6,	4.1	Ap,	B9	Bluish-white, pale emerald
95 Her	18 02	+21.6	5.0,	5.1,	6.3	A3,	G5	Light apple green, cherry red
70 Oph	18 05	+02.5	4.2,	6.0,	1.6	K0,	K6	Pale topaz, violet
59 Ser	18 27	+00.2	5.3,	7.6,	3.8	G0,	A6	Yellow, indigo blue
ζ Lyr	18 45	+37.6	4.3,	5.9,	43.7	Am,	F0	Topaz, greenish
15 Aql	19 05	−04.0	5.5,	7.2,	38.4	K0,	K0	White, lilac tint
β Cyg	19 31	+28.0	3.1,	5.1,	34.4	K3,	B8	Topaz yellow, sapphire blue; the colors in brilliant contrast
π Aql	19 49	+11.8	6.1,	6.9,	1.4	F2,	A2	Pale white, greenish
γ Del	20 47	+16.1	4.5,	5.5,	9.6	G5,	F8	Yellow, light emerald; beautiful
δ Cep	22 29	+58.4	4v,	7.5,	41.0	G,	A0	Orange, fine blue; in fine contrast
σ Cas	23 59	+55.8	5.0,	7.1,	3.0	B1,	B3	Flushed white, smalt blue; colors clear and distinct

8 Monocerotis. Yellowish, bluish.

20 Geminorum. Yellow, bluish; yellow, blue.

14 Lyncis. Gold, purple. (12 Lyncis has more interesting color controversy in Webb: greenish-white and bluish; yellow and ruddy.)

38 Geminorum. Yellowish, bluish; yellow, purple.

Iota Cancri. Yellow, blue. Muirden: yellow, blue. Sanford: gold, pale blue.

Omega Leonis. No comment on color from Webb.

Gamma Leonis. Gold, greenish-red; yellow, greenish-yellow; yellow, deeper yellow. Muirden: fine crocus-yellow and a greenish-yellow. Sanford: "Two orange–yellow stars."

Iota Leonis. Yellowish, bluish; bright orange, greenish-yellow; pale yellow and pale blue or greenish. Webb also says "tawny"—about primary or companion?

Beta Leonis. Webb cites only Smyth.

2 Canum Venaticorum. Very gold, blue; yellow, rosy. Dembowski: yellow, azure. Franks: orange, blue.

24 Comae Berenices. Yellow, very blue. (Much more controversy over colors of Alpha and 12 Comae.)

Epsilon Bootis. Very yellow, very blue; light yellow, greenish. Secchi: "most beautiful yellow, superb blue." Allen: pale orange, bluish-green (probably just adapted from Smyth). Muirden: golden, blue–green. Sanford: yellow–orange, bluish-green.

Xi Bootis. Clean yellow, purplish-red. Burnham says colors have been described usually as yellow and reddish-violet. Muirden: light yellow and tawny or warm gray. Sanford: yellow, deep orange.

Zeta Coronae Borealis. Flushed white, bluish-green.

Rho Ophiuchi. Pale yellow, tawny.

Lambda Ophiuchi. Yellow, bluish.

Alpha Herculis. Very yellow, intense blue; orange, bluish-green. Mary Proctor: orange, emerald-green (drawing upon Smyth, or completely independently?). Allen: orange–red, bluish-green. Muirden: gold, greenish-gray.

39 Ophiuchi. Pale orange, clear blue.

Rho Herculis. Greenish-white, greenish; white, bluish.

95 Herculis. Webb says he sees same colors as Smyth. Secchi: "red the larger, green the brighter"—whatever that means! Webb suggests the tints may vary, mentions Lewis saw both stars yellow.

70 Ophiuchi. Yellow, purple; yellow, orange. Burnham says observers see yellow and red or gold and violet.

59 Serpentis. Yellow, blue. Sir John Herschel: orange, green.

Zeta Lyrae. Yellow, greenish; pale yellow, pale lilac.

15 Aquilae. White or yellow–white and red lilac; yellow, ruddy purple.

Beta Cygni. Muirden notes that some people find the companion blue, others greenish. Burnham calls primary's color "topaz" or golden-yellow.

Pi Aquilae. Yellow, green; red–white, azure white. Secchi: yellow, blue. Dembowski: both white.

Gamma Delphini. Gold, bluish-green; yellow, pale green. William Herschel: white (presumably both white). Muirden: yellow, white. Burnham: called everything from white and yellowish (John Herschel and South) to reddish-yellow and grayish-lilac (Gore). Allen: gold, bluish-green. Franks: golden-yellow, greenish-blue.

Delta Cephei. Very yellow, blue. Allen: yellow, blue.

Sigma Cassiopeiae. Green, very blue; white, tawny.

Questions

1. What colors do you estimate for each of these double stars? What do you learn about your color vocabulary in your attempts to name the hues?

2. How do your color estimates compare with those of Smyth, Webb, and the others? Can you draw any conclusions about the physiology of your color vision or your color vocabulary by this comparison? What conclusions of this sort can you draw about the different observers? (For instance, does Sanford see or name orange in certain stars more readily than the other observers? than you?)

19.

Colors of Single Stars, Especially the Reddest

Rate interesting stars on a 0-to-10 scale of colors from blue to red. Compare your results with what would be expected from the spectral class and B–V color index of these stars. Observe especially the reputedly greenish star Beta Librae, and all of the extremely red stars listed or discussed here.

You may read astronomers who state categorically that no single star shows much color except the very reddest. Double stars can push our perception into the illusion of seeing intense versions of the complementary colors they seem to show even if their true tints are weak—or not even at all the colors we think we see.

There is a high degree of truth in what these people are saying. But sometimes the point is carried too far. We hear that Betelgeuse looks a little yellow, and that's all! Such exaggeration may result partly from the physiological fact that some individuals can see the red end of the spectrum significantly better than others, and significantly further (that is, to a much longer wavelength). Perhaps there really are people who see Betelgeuse as only a little yellow. But it is more likely, I think, that some people making statements based on theoretical considerations have simply never taken the time and energy to go outside and look carefully at star colors.

What is the best objective means for rating star colors? We can, of course, rely on the spectral class, which relates closely to the surface temperature, which relates closely to the star color. Perhaps even better is the *color index*. The brightness of a star is measured photoelectrically through two different filters which pass different wavelength bands, B and V. The B–V color index figure is the star's magnitude as recorded through the "blue" filter less its magnitude as recorded through the "visual" filter. A white star's two magnitudes are about equal, giving a color index of 0.0. A blue star will have a color index slightly lower than zero (say -0.2). Yellow, orange, and red (or "orange–red") stars range upward from 0.0, to about $+1.8$ for the average M5 star.

Of course, these measures do not tell us exactly what we will see— let alone what you will see as opposed to me or someone else.

A way to obtain other, more personal information about what you see is to rate the colors of stars on a 0-to-10 scale. Your figures may start out very imprecise. But before long you will get more of a feel for the numbers and more skill at evaluating subtleties of tint. Of course, you must be sure that the telescope–eyepiece combination you are using and the "seeing" you are observing in are not producing spurious colors (today's good telescopes and oculars generally shouldn't). Also, you may find that you get quite different ratings with different telescopes (only with different size telescopes, or at different magnifications?), not to mention under different sky conditions. In any case, here is a scale which I would suggest:

    0—Distinctly blue
    1—Blue
    2—Blue–white
    3—White
    4—Yellow–white
    5—Light yellow
    6—Deep yellow
    7—Light orange
    8—Deep orange
    9—Orange–red
  10—Red

Where do green stars fit on this scale? Is there enough room on the upper end to distinguish between Betelgeuse and one of the special very red stars of spectral type C?

I will address these questions (however short of adequately) in the course of now presenting some single stars whose color especially warrants our attention—and whose observation is the goal of this activity.

First, there is that matter of green stars. The only bright star reputed by some observers to look distinctly green is Beta Librae. No one can answer the question of what it looks like to you except yourself—observe it! But how might we account for some observers seeing green in this (and certain double star components) and other observers not? One answer may lie in the overlapping and confusion in what people call "blue" and "green." When we think of green grass and a deep blue sky, it might seem ridiculous that these colors could be confused. But consider what happens when you ask most people what color they think "turquoise" is: You should notice (if linguists' surveys are right) about half saying "blue" and half saying "green." The problem is not in the word but in the range of hue it covers. I might here mention that the artist and astronomer Guy Ottewell has said that he often sees with the naked eye a hint of green in Jupiter—a planet most people would consider to be yellow–white. All of us bring a very different experience with color to our perception and judgment of hues—in fact, the perception and judgment are perhaps usually almost inextricably intertwined.

Of course, vivid green is detected by everyone who looks at the excited, rarefied gases of the Great Orion Nebula (in a fair-sized telescope) or bright aurorae. But this wouldn't happen in a star. What other chemical causes that could produce green would happen? We must mention a physiological twist: with increasing age, the lenses of our eyes become yellowed, making our violet-end perception less good (also, some people are born with better violet perception than others—and, just like at the red end, the ability to see further along the spectrum . . . in this case, to a shorter wavelength). Thus, we have some people (usually older people?) calling the color of many planetary nebulae "green" and others (usually younger people?) calling the color "blue." But in such a case it would not be a matter of vocabulary, but very definitely a matter of physiology.

Whatever we think of various star colors, however strongly we agree or disagree with the view about only very red stars "really" showing color, those very red stars hold a special fascination.

Table 9 is based on a table that appeared in the same article mentioned in the previous activity (an article on star colors by Jacqueline Mitton and Alan MacRobert in the February 1989 issue of *Sky & Telescope*).

All of the stars in Table 9 that you can locate, you should observe. Even the fainter ones should not be too difficult to spot (if you have a large enough telescope) because of their striking colors. They are indeed very much ruddier than stars like Betelgeuse and Antares. Perhaps there is not enough room on the scale I have given above for all the levels of redness actually perceived?

To the list of some well-known stars, a few more should be added for us to observe. But before mentioning these, we should consider a few facts about the spectral types R, N, and C.

The types R and N were originally introduced for stars not necessarily cooler than the M-type stars, but rather showing some important different chemical compositions as evidenced by lines in their spectra. More recently, the type designation C has been introduced to subsume what used to be R and N. C stands for "carbon star," and the reason that these objects can be dramatically redder than M stars is the fact that their atmospheres actually block blue wavelengths from reaching us: An already predominantly red star does not get to display for us virtually any of its much shorter wavelengths.

Table 9
Some Well-Known Red Stars

Star	RA h m	Dec. ° '	B–V	Magnitude	Spectrum	Notes
α Ori	05 55.2	+07 24	1.85	0.4–1.3	M2	Betelgeuse
Y CVn	12 45.1	+45 26	2.54	5.5–6.0	N7.7	Named "La Superba" by Secchi
α Sco	16 29.4	–26 26	1.83	0.9–1.8	M1	Antares
μ Cep	21 43.5	+58 47	2.35	3.6–5.1	M2	William Herschel's "Garnet Star"
TX Psc	23 46.4	+03 29	2.60	5.3–5.8	C5	19 Piscium

Reddest Stars in *Sky Catalogue 2000.0*, Volume 1

Star	RA h m	Dec. ° '	B–V	Magnitude	Spectrum	Notes
R Scl	01 27.0	–32 33	3.86	6.5–8.1	N7.7	
U Cam	03 41.8	+62 39	4.29	8.1–8.6	N7.7	Argelander: "extraordinarily red"
W Ori	05 05.4	+01 11	3.45	6.2–7.0	C6	
SAO 172106	06 39.5	–30 02	3.4	7.8	K5	
X Cnc	08 55.4	+17 14	3.36	6.5–7.0	N7.7	
RY Dra	12 56.4	+66 00	3.26	6.8–7.3	N7.7	
HD 113842	13 07.5	–60 16	3.6	7.2	M0	
V Pav	17 43.3	–57 44	3.70	5.6–7.5	N7.7	
T Lyr	18 32.3	+37 00	3.67	8.3–8.9	C6.5	Secchi: "Intense"
V Aql	19 04.4	–05 41	4.19	7.4–8.0	N7.7	Schmidt and Vogel: "intense fire-red"
HD 189256	19 57.2	+44 16	3.43	7.85	N7.7	
RS Cyg	20 13.4	+38 44	3.31	6.5–9.3	N pe	

Other famous red stars now classified as type C, but not appearing in the Mitton–MacRobert table, include R Leporis, V Hydrae, and S Cephei. All of these vary greatly and rather irregularly in brightness. According to Robert Burnham, Jr., S Cephei has a color index of about 5½ magnitudes. If he means a UV color index of about +5.5, then S Cephei is easily redder than any of the reddest stars listed in *Sky Catalogue 2000.0*, Volume 1. This seems borne out by the C7 (and previously N8) spectral class of this star. Presumably its roughly eighth-to-eleventh-magnitude range makes it too faint for the *Sky Catalogue*. S Cephei also earns a subscript 4 ($C7_4$) for its amount of carbon—a higher number than that for TX Piscium. Other stars worthy of note include V Hydrae (magnitude 6–11, N6, $C6_3$) and certainly R Leporis—the famous Hind's Crimson Star. R Leporis can become as bright as magnitude 6, but is usually much dimmer. Its color has been described as "an intense smoky red." Its spectral class is N6 or $C7_4$.

The positions of these stars can be obtained from either *Norton's 2000.0 Star Atlas* or *Burnham's Celestial Handbook* or both, depending on the star.

Questions

1. Can you rate the color of many stars on the suggested 0-to-10 scale (or one of your own devising)? How much do your ratings differ with different telescopes and on different nights?

2. What do you think is the color of Beta Librae? How many of the very red stars, especially the carbon stars, can you observe? What is your impression of them? Which ones seem reddest?

20.

Variable Stars—General Observations

Learn the basics about variable stars and variable star observing, partly by studying the two most famous variables, Algol and Mira.

Follow Algol throughout as much of one of its 10-hour eclipses as you can, observing it not just with the naked eye but also through a telescope and paying close attention to any possible color changes. Attempt to make brightness estimates of Algol as practice. Be sure to look for color changes in Mira as it changes brightness over weeks and months each year—and try to make some serious brightness estimates of it, for unlike Algol there is no telling just how bright Mira will become or how quickly it will change.

Nothing seems more enduring or constant than the stars. Luckily for us, this really is the case to a surprisingly high degree when it comes to our Sun. The fossil record on Earth shows that our Sun has been decidedly constant for at least hundreds of millions and probably several billion years.

But this is not true of a great number of stars. Our explorations of the H–R diagram in Activities 8 through 11 revealed an area of the diagram in which a star's attempts to achieve a balance between radiation pressure pushing out and gravity pulling in resulted in pulsations in size and variations in brightness—and other behavior sometimes even more dramatic.

Variable stars are common in the universe. So common, in fact, that professional astronomers cannot possibly hope to follow the brightness changes of most of them. But here, of course, is where the amateur astronomers come in. There are thousands of variable stars that need observing—and potentially thousands of amateur observers with enough determination and skill to follow their brightenings and dimmings.

More than with any subject of amateur astronomy, when you mention variable stars you have to mention an organization. The organization is AAVSO—the American Association of Variable Star Observers (25 Birch Street, Cambridge, MA 02138). Founded in 1911, AAVSO has archived a staggering total of roughly 7 million variable star estimates. The estimates received now total more than a quarter million a year. There are many other variable star observer groups around the world, but most amateur observers send their information to AAVSO, acknowledging its role as the premier organization.

After you try a little variable star observing to see how you like it, you can—whether or not you join AAVSO—purchase at minimal cost some of its nearly invaluable variable star observing charts. There are over 1,000 such charts, each identifying a variable star (some stars warrant several charts, at different scales) and its surrounding star field. More importantly, these charts give the magnitudes of *comparison stars* in the vicinity of the variable star. If you judge that the variable star is about halfway in brightness between two comparison stars which are say magnitude 7.2 and 7.6, then your estimate for the variable at that time would be 7.4. Veteran observers have developed the ability to often tell brightness differences of as little as 0.1 magnitude.

What does AAVSO, or the devoted observer on his or her own, do with these brightness estimates? The goal is to plot a *light curve*. Your diagram has magnitude on the vertical axis and time on the horizontal axis. You plot the brightness estimates as a series of dots and then draw a line that connects these dots to form a curve.

The length of time between one peak or maximum and the next is the variable star's *period*. The magnitude change from its minimum to maximum brightness is the star's *amplitude*. Some variable stars have a period and amplitude that repeat identically every time. Others vary their brightness far more irregularly (the light curve is at least a little different each time). In addition, some variable stars vary only once in a great while, or even just once—explosively.

Our goal in this activity will be to become acquainted with examples of some of the major types of variable stars. But first we need a few words on the nomenclature.

Variables are lettered in order of discovery within their constellations, starting with the letter R and proceeding through Z, these letters preceding the genitive form of the constellation's name (thus, R Hydrae or S Cephei). After the Z star, we use RS through ZZ, then AA through QZ (omitting J). After this total of 334, a more straightforward method of designating them—V335, V336, and so on—is used.

The first major classification of variable stars is into *intrinsic variables* and *extrinsic variables*. The intrinsic variables are ones that change brightness due to some actual physical change in the star. The extrinsic variables change brightness because of an outside factor: the eclipse of one star by another.

In our previous activities on double stars, we have already heard of these *eclipsing binaries*. They are all double stars in which the component suns eclipse each other (or at least one eclipses the other).

The most famous class is Algol type variables. These are named for Beta Persei, the star better known as Algol. Algol-type variables feature the eclipses fairly far apart (a few days) with the light curve flat between the dips.

The classic example is, of course, Algol itself. The name means "the ghoul" in medieval Arabic and the ancient Greeks chose to have this star mark the severed head of the monstrous Medusa which constellation hero Perseus is carrying (one look from Medusa or her Gorgon sisters could literally petrify you—turn you into stone). We have to wonder whether these names are coincidental or derive from some of the early astronomers' realization that this star was undergoing eerie brightness changes. As far as we know, however, the first recorded recognition of the star's variability came from Geminiano Montanari around 1667, and the regularity of the period was first established by John Goodricke in 1782. This is surprising when you consider that Algol is a second-magnitude star, the brightest that shows very frequent dramatic variations.

Actually, though, you will find that it is not as easy as you might think to catch Algol's dimming act by pure chance. An easily available source of predictions for when it will suffer eclipse each month is *Sky & Telescope*. Once you learn when one eclipse occurs, it is fairly easy to keep track of when further eclipses will occur for awhile because Algol's variations are regular. The star normally shines at magnitude 2.1 but every 2 days, 20 hours, 48 minutes, and 56 seconds Algol reaches a minimum of brightness of 3.4 in the midst of a 10-hour-long eclipse. Since Algol never fades to dimmer than 3.4, it is always an easy naked-eye object. But a look at it in the telescope is interesting (can you detect any visual color change from maximum to minimum?)—and, of course, most of the eclipsing binaries are much fainter.

Figures 14 and 15 show the light curve and an illustration of what

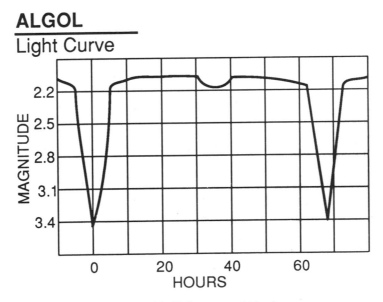

Figure 14 Light curve of Algol.

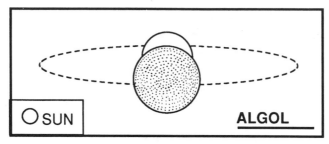

Figure 15 Diagram of the Algol system.

the Algol suns look like and how the eclipse occurs. As you can see, the eclipse occurs when the dimmer companion star passes in front of the brighter primary, obscuring up to about 79 percent of the latter at mid-eclipse (Algol's minimum). Notice that there is also an imperceptibly small secondary eclipse between the major ones—the illustration shows that this must occur when part of the dimmer star is obscured by the brighter, reducing the total light output of the system toward us very slightly.

The other large class of variable stars, intrinsic variables, can be divided into two major groups: the *pulsating variables* and the *eruptive variables*. Since the latter are usually harder to observe, we will save them (and many other variable stars) for the next activity. Right now, in fact, let us concentrate on just one type of pulsating variable, the long-period variable, and on its classic example—a variable star rivaled only by Algol in fame and ease of observation (though unlike Algol it usually requires a telescope to see).

Mira is the star Omicron Ceti, the brightest of the long-period variables and the possessor of one of the larger brightness ranges of all stars. In 1596, the Dutch astronomer David Fabricius became the first person we know of in Western civilization to record a bright star at this position in the neck of Cetus the Whale, but he apparently thought it was an exploding star of the kind that would not be seen again after it faded back to dimmer than naked-eye visibility. A number of years had to pass before the periodic nature of the star was recognized and it was the seventeenth-century German astronomer Hevelius who apparently was the first to suggest calling this star Mira—Latin for "the wonderful."

And a wonder it is. Omicron Ceti is too faint to see with the naked eye most of the time, and its average minimum is about magnitude 9. But then in a few months the brightness soars, eventually attaining an average maximum of about magnitude 3 before fading. The average period (between successive maxima) is about 330 days—thus, Mira tends to reach maximum about one month earlier each year, and is most conveniently observed in those years when the maximum falls during the autumn when Cetus is highest in the evening.

One of the exciting things about Mira, however, is that it does not behave quite the same way each cycle (compare Figures 16 and 17). Maybe once or twice a decade Mira soars to decidedly brighter than 3.0, and once—in 1779—this marvelous star was almost first magnitude, almost the equal of Aldebaran. Another dramatic factor is that Mira rises to maximum much more quickly than it falls: The average time from minimum to maximum is roughly 110 days.

Sky & Telescope also publishes monthly the predicted dates of maxima for long-period variables—including Mira.

MIRA
An Idealized Light Curve

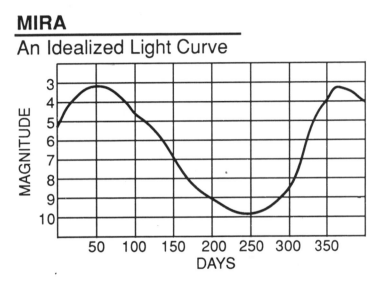

Figure 16 Idealized light curve of Mira.

MIRA
A Typical Four-year Light Curve

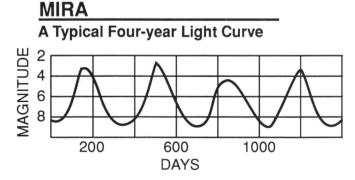

Figure 17 Sample of real light curve of Mira.

Mira is but one of many long-period variables, all red giants which are thought to be having pulsations which may result from the stars' going through the transition from hydrogen to helium "burning" in their cores. In the next activity, we will encounter other classes of pulsating variables which are more regular, and of far shorter period than the Mira-type stars.

Questions

1. Can you witness an entire eclipse of Algol? Do you notice any color change during its eclipse, or no color change (rate it on a scale like that in the previous activity)? Can you practice brightness estimates with Algol and come up with accurate results? (Be sure not to use Algol's neighbor, Rho, which is itself a variable.)

2. Can you make brightness estimates of Mira weekly, at least during the brightest portion of Mira's cycle? Can you follow the star through its entire period? How bright (or faint) does it become and how long is its period this time? Do you notice any color changes as it brightens or fades?

21.

Selected Variable Stars of Different Types

Try to view as many long-period variables as possible, and begin an ongoing surveillance of them. Take a look at some of the most prominent eclipsing binaries, including Beta Lyrae stars. Observe examples of the many different kinds of pulsating variables, including the very important classical Cepheids and RR Lyrae stars. Observe UV Ceti "flare" stars, check R Coronae Borealis to see if it is undergoing one of its immense fadings, and view a few dwarf novae like SS Cygni, making brightness estimates.

Long-period variables are often suggested as being easy projects for novices, their brightness changing slowly. They are certainly important to study. Table 10 presents a selection of them, all possessing an average maximum brightness of 7.0 or brighter.

But there are many different kinds of variable stars. And it is surely good for the observer to become acquainted with as many kinds as possible. Therefore, let us take a tour of variable star types, citing examples to observe when possible. Even those whose variations are too small for visual observers, and must be measured photoelectrically, are interesting to know about and to take a thoughtful look at.

Eclipsing binaries, which are extrinsic variables, come in several types.

The *Algol type* was described in the previous activity. Besides Algol itself, two good examples are U Cephei and U Sagittae. U Cephei shines at 6.8, fades for 4 hours until reaching 9.2, at which it stays for 2 hours. The period is very slowly increasing (apparently from gas streaming from one star to the other). It is about 2 days, 11 hours, and 50 minutes. U Sagittae is located only about 1.7°W of the Coathanger asterism (see Activity 25). This star falls from 6.4 to 9.2, but the fall is very rapid, the eclipse being total. The period between eclipses is 3 days, 9 hours, 8 minutes, and 5 seconds, and the star stays at minimum for about 1 hour and 40 minutes.

The *Lyrid type,* or *Beta Lyrae stars,* are such close pairs that they are stretched into ellipsoids and nearly touch. Beta Lyrae (see Figure 18) has two maxima of magnitude 3.4, but the minima are 3.8 and 4.1 (then 3.8 again, and so on). An excellent comparison star is Gamma Lyrae, the other star on the south end of the little pattern of Lyra (the famous Ring Nebula lies between these two stars). Gamma is magnitude 3.25. About every 13 days, Beta fades and is dramatically fainter than Gamma. About halfway between these deeper maxima occurs the less deep one, also noticeable in comparison to Gamma. Beta Lyrae is one of the most puzzling of all star systems, but there seems no doubt that a vast streamer of gas flows from the larger to the smaller sun (see Figure 19). Another Beta Lyrae star is 68 Herculis whose maxima are 4.7, with minima alternating between 5.0 and 5.4. The period from one deep minimum to the next is just over 2 days.

Dwarf eclipsing type, or *W Ursae Majoris stars,* are smaller, with shorter periods than Algol types. W Ursae Majoris fades from about magnitude 7.9 to 8.6. The full period is just over 8 hours—this is how long it takes for the component stars to complete one orbit of each other.

Ellipsoidal variables actually don't eclipse, but change in brightness due to our seeing different amounts of their surface—the long sides or

Table 10
Long-Period Variables with Maximum of 6.5 or Brighter

Star	RA h	m	Dec. °	"	Max. Mag.	Period days
S Scl	00	15.4	− 32	03	5.5	362.57
R And	00	24.0	+ 38	35	5.8	409.33
o Ceti	02	19.3	− 02	59	2.0	331.96
R Tri	02	37.0	+ 34	16	5.4	266.9
R Hor	02	53.9	− 49	53	4.7	407.6
R Ret	04	33.5	− 63	02	6.5	278.46
R Lep	04	59.6	− 14	48	5.5	427.07
S Pic	05	11.0	− 48	30	6.5	428.0
R Oct	05	26.1	− 86	23	6.3	405.39
U Ori	05	55.8	+ 20	10	4.8	368.3
V Mon	06	22.7	− 02	12	6.0	340.5
R Gem	07	07.4	+ 22	42	6.0	369.91
R Cnc	08	16.6	+ 11	44	6.1	361.60
R Car	09	32.2	− 62	47	3.9	308.71
Y Dra	09	42.4	+ 77	51	6.2	325.79
R LMi	09	45.6	+ 34	31	6.3	372.19
R Leo	09	47.6	+ 11	26	4.4	309.95
S Car	10	09.4	− 61	33	4.5	149.49
R UMa	10	44.6	+ 68	47	6.5	301.62
R Vir	12	38.5	+ 06	59	6.1	145.63
R Hya	13	29.7	− 23	17	3.5	388.87
S Vir	13	33.0	− 07	12	6.3	375.10
R CVn	13	49.0	+ 39	33	6.5	328.53
R Cen	14	16.6	− 59	55	5.3	546.2
R Boo	14	37.2	+ 26	44	6.2	223.40
S CrB	15	21.4	+ 31	22	5.8	360.26
R Nor	15	36.0	− 49	30	5	507.50
T Nor	15	44.1	− 54	59	6.2	240.7
R Ser	15	50.7	+ 15	08	5.2	356.41
VZ Aps	16	16.3	− 74	02	6	385
U Her	16	25.8	+ 18	54	6.4	406.1
S Her	16	51.9	+ 14	56	6.4	307.28
RS Sco	16	55.6	− 30	35	5.0	281.45
X Oph	18	38.3	+ 08	50	5.9	328.85
R Aql	19	06.4	+ 08	14	5.5	284.2

Table 10 (continued)

Star	RA h	m	Dec. °	"	Max. Mag.	Period days
R And	00	15.4	−32	03	5.5	362.57
R Cyg	19	36.8	+50	12	6.1	426.45
RT Cyg	19	43.6	+48	47	6.0	190.28
χ Cygni	19	50.6	+32	55	3.3	408.05
RR Sgr	19	55.9	−29	11	5.4	336.33
RU Sgr	19	58.7	−41	51	6.0	240.49
RT Sgr	20	17.7	−39	07	6.0	306.46
U Cyg	20	19.6	+47	54	5.9	463.24
T Cep	21	09.5	+68	29	5.2	388.14
S Gru	22	26.1	−48	26	6.0	401.51
R Aqr	23	43.8	−15	17	5.8	386.96
R Cas	23	58.4	+51	24	4.7	430.46

The designation uses official abbreviations of constellation names (see Appendix 2 for identifications); the RA and declination are in 2000.0 coordinates; the maximum magnitude is usually the brightest that the star will achieve at the best of a number of peaks, the typical maximum being dimmer; the period is the average and is not always the amount listed (certainly not the precise number of days, to the tenth or hundredth of a day, that is listed).

Check the current issue of *Sky & Telescope* (Calendar Notes of the Celestial Calendar section) for the days of the current month on which some of the above stars reach maximum. To follow these stars to their minima (which range from about ninth to fourteenth magnitude), you need excellent finder charts, such as those of AAVSO.

the short ends. Zeta Andromedae, magnitude 4.1, is an example, but its variation is too slight to notice.

Intrinsic variables can be divided into two major groups, the pulsating variables and the eruptive variables. Pulsating variables include irregular, semiregular, long-period or Mira type, RV Tauri type, classical Cepheids, W Virginis type (or type II Cepheids), RR Lyrae stars (cluster variables), Delta Scuti type (or dwarf Cepheids), and Beta Canis Majoris (or Beta Cephei) type.

Irregular variables are giant stars with no certain period. Betelgeuse and Mu Cephei are sometimes classed as irregulars, other times as semiregulars. Examples of *semiregular variables* include Alpha Herculis and Rho Persei. Alpha Herculis ranges from about 3.1 to 3.9, but usually less extremely during its main period of about 90 days (it and other semiregulars seem to possess several periods superimposed on one another). Rho Persei, neighbor of Algol, is another semiregular, with a main period of about 33 to 40 days, but with some much longer cycles. The leisurely variations take the star from about 3.3 (a bit brighter than Algol at its faintest) to 4.0.

BETA LYRAE
Light Curve

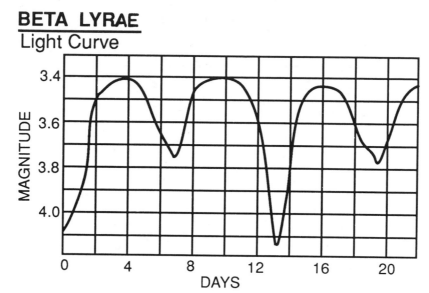

Figure 18 Light curve of Beta Lyrae.

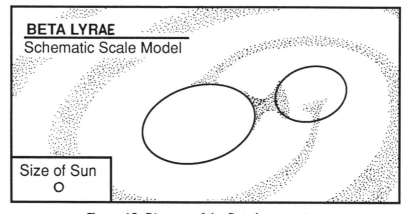

Figure 19 Diagram of the Beta Lyrae system.

A very remarkable star that is usually classified as a semiregular variable is L_2 Puppis. Though really too far south for a decent view to observers at 40°N, this star varies from about sixth to third magnitude, and sometimes a bit brighter. The average period is about 140 days.

Long-period variables include Mira (see the previous activity) and the stars in Table 10.

RV Tauri stars are rare, G- or K-type stars with variations up to several magnitudes and superimposed periods. RV Tauri itself has a semiregular period of 79 days, during which there are two maxima and two minima. The magnitude range is from about 9.5 to 13, so a good finder chart is certainly needed.

The *Cepheids,* or *classical Cepheids,* are among the most important of all variable stars. They have precision in their periods and follow the *period–luminosity* relation so that we can judge their luminosities by the length of their periods (the longer the period, the brighter the star)— and thereby determine their distances and use them as "measuring-sticks of the universe." The class is named for Delta Cephei, whose variations were discovered by John Goodricke in 1784. Delta varies from magnitude 3.6 to 4.3 and may be compared to the fixed-brightness stars Epsilon (4.2) and Zeta Persei (3.4). The star brightens for about 1½ days and fades for about 4 days, with a total period of 5 days, 8 hours, and 48 minutes (see Figure 20). The second most noted example of these very luminous stars is Eta Aquilae, whose period is 7.17644 days and which falls from 3.7 to 4.5. Another is RT Aurigae (48 Aurigae), not discovered until the twentieth century, yet varying from about 4.9 to 5.8, with a period of 3.728261 days.

RR Lyrae stars, or *cluster variables,* are as important as the classical Cepheids as "standard candles." They are much smaller Cepheids, with periods usually less than 1 day, and are in greater abundance in globular clusters and the *galactic halo.* RR Lyrae itself brightens in a few hours from 8.0 to 7.1, then declines to minimum far more slowly (see Figure 21). The period is just over half a day. The RR Lyrae stars are not luminous enough to have been detected with our past technology.

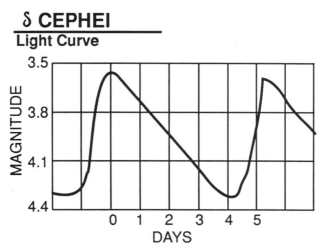

Figure 20 Light curve of Delta Cephei.

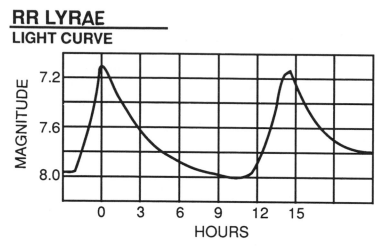

Figure 21 Light curve of RR Lyrae.

Delta Scuti type stars, or *dwarf Cepheids,* are even smaller and of shorter period than the RR Lyrae stars. The brightness variations are very slight. Examples other than Delta Scuti include Beta Cassiopeiae, Epsilon Cephei, Delta Delphini, and Upsilon Ursae Majoris. They may be a very common type of star.

Beta Canis Majoris, or *Beta Cephei type stars* (also called *quasi-Cepheids*), have very short periods and variations too small for amateurs to study visually. They are very luminous stars and include Gamma Pegasi, Delta Ceti, and a number of other stars of fairly great apparent brightness.

Eruptive variables include UV Ceti type "flare stars," R Coronae Borealis type stars, dwarf novae, recurrent novae, novae, novalike or P Cygni variables, and supernovae.

UV Ceti and similar stars have been discussed in Activity 12. The nearest star, Proxima Centauri, is another example.

R Coronae Borealis type stars are sometimes called *reverse novae—* instead of undergoing immense brightenings, they undergo immense fadings. R Coronae Borealis remains at about magnitude 6 for several years, then begins to dim. In just a few weeks, it will have faded to anywhere from about magnitude 7 to magnitude 15 (average about magnitude 12.5). Other examples of this rare class include RY Sagittarii and XX Camelopardalis. The explanation for the dimmings is believed to be clouds of carbon that condense around the star and block light periodically. Burnham says that R Coronae (and presumably the other stars of its type) may be little more than helium cores being converted into carbon with their outer hydrogen having been consumed or blown away.

Dwarf novae are also called *U Geminorum* and *SS Cygni type stars.* These are members of double star systems that keep undergoing brightness outbursts of up to 5 or 6 magnitudes at irregular intervals, usually intervals lasting for a number of months. SS Cygni is the brightest member of the class, usually shining at about magnitude 12, but at intervals of somewhere between 20 and 90 days rapidly brightening, flaring up to magnitude 8 in just a day or two. See *Burnham's Celestial Handbook* for finder charts for this and U Geminorum, two dim but exciting stars.

The other types of eruptive variables are even more dramatic stars. They are discussed separately in the next activity.

Questions

1. How many of the long-period variables on our list can you observe? How much do they deviate from the period suggested? How dim do they get? Do any of them exceed the maximum magnitude listed?

2. How many eclipsing binaries, and how many different kinds of eclipsing binary, can you observe? What irregular and semiregular variables can you study? What Cepheids, RR Lyrae, and other kinds of shorter-period pulsating stars can you view?

3. Can you observe any of the flares of the UV Ceti stars or the slower, but still dramatic increases of the dwarf novae? Is R Coronae Borealis or one of the other stars of its type undergoing one of their great dimmings—how dim do they get?

22.

Novae and Other Unusual Bright Variables

Keep a watch out for novae, perhaps even memorizing star fields down to a certain magnitude and scanning them for novae. Observe and estimate (on a regular basis) the current brightness of the most famous recurrent novae (especially T Coronae Borealis, "the Blaze Star") and

of both the permanent nova P Cygni and strange Eta Carinae.
Estimate on any suitable night the magnitude of the peculiar variable
Gamma Cassiopeiae. Check often the brightness of certain stars
reputed to have produced dramatic "flashes" (brightenings), especially
Beta Eridani and Epsilon Pegasi.

Stars that suddenly appeared where none had been before were known since ancient times as *novae*—"new stars." Only in modern times was it proven that these stars had existed before, but merely been so immensely fainter that they were not previously recognized. Novae brighten by 7 to 16 magnitudes, then fade back to something like their preexplosion brightness, sometimes emitting temporary shells of gas to glow.

Astronomers in recent decades have theorized that all novae may be members of double star systems in which the addition of material from one companion to another causes the second to become too massive and unstable and "novate." The resultant explosion only ejects a very small part of the star's matter.

Whatever novae are, we can only keep our eyes open for telescopic stars brightening—perhaps up to near the naked-eye limit, once in a great while to rival even the brighter stars (like Nova Cygni 1975 rivaled Deneb). But both the nova's rise and fall are rapid. Only a few days after maximum light, a nova may be a magnitude or two dimmer.

And if novae are mysterious, imagine how much more mysterious are certain classes of stars that simulate them in some respects.

The *recurrent novae* are stars that have brightness outbursts almost as great as those of novae—but outbursts which occur more than once over the decades. The classic example is the amazing Blaze Star, T Coronae Borealis.

T Coronae now lingers at around tenth magnitude, but on the night of May 12, 1866, this star was noticed when it was at the same brightness as Alpha Coronae Borealis—2.2—before brightening slightly more. Then, in 8 days, it had faded to below naked-eye visibility, and eventually became much fainter. Next, 80 years passed. Suddenly, on February 9, 1946, T Coronae was noticed at magnitude 3.2, but it was already fading, so that perhaps its maximum had again been something like 2.0.

No one knows the explanation for the Blaze Star's behavior, nor when it might flame again—nor whether several of its quick brightenings have been missed altogether. A good idea is to check its position in the Northern Crown every time the constellation is visible. One interesting suggestion is that "true novae" are themselves recurrent—just on a much longer time scale than T Coronae Borealis. There are two other stars that have behaved like dimmer versions of T Coronae Borealis: U Scorpii and RS Ophiuchi, both of which have been repeat performers.

P Cygni is sometimes a *permanent nova* or *novalike star*. This star was first noticed when it appeared as a third-magnitude object in 1600. After various fadings and brightenings, modern times have found it at about magnitude 4.9. But the remarkable fact is that this star may be so distant and shining through so much light-absorbing dust that it may be one of the few most luminous stars known—with an absolute magnitude of perhaps -9 even now.

A star something like P Cygni but maybe even more enigmatic is the far-southern star Eta Carinae, associated with one of the heavens' great wonders, the Eta Carinae Nebula. Eta was first noticed, by Edmund Halley, as a fourth-magnitude object in 1677. For the next century and a half, the star fluctuated irregularly between the second and fourth magnitudes. Then came the stunning brightening. Between 1820 and 1843, the star had several surges of brightness, each one stronger than the previous. These culminated in April 1843, when Eta Carinae reached a peak brightness of -0.8—brighter than Canopus and outshining every star in the sky except Sirius! The star then began a fairly steady but slow decline, not dimming to about 2.0 until 1859. By the late 1860s, however, Eta Carinae was sinking to dimmer than the naked-eye limit, where it has remained (with a few interesting variations) ever since.

When brightest in 1843, Eta Carinae may have had a peak absolute magnitude about midway between novae and supernovae—about -11. Will it someday become that most powerful of all exploding stars, a supernova? No one knows, but this far south ($-59°$ declination) star deserves close attention.

The thrilling subject of supernovae is touched upon in several places in this book (for instance, in Activities 11 and 31). A discussion of the potential majesty of a supernova occurring here in our own galaxy merits a whole chapter of my book *The Starry Room* (Wiley, 1988).

But I would like to close this current activity with an appeal for observers to make a regular habit of watching certain stars that have been claimed as having had dramatic increases in brightness.

The brightening of Gamma Cassiopeiae was not dramatic, but it was strange and well documented. Before 1910, the star always appeared to shine at 2.25. Then, it began an agonizingly slow brightening of about half a magnitude in 26 years. A slight further increase—to magnitude 1.6—was accomplished by April 1937, but then by the end of that year the brightness fell back to 2.25. A slow dimming proceeded for several years until Gamma became about 3.0 in 1940. Very slowly the brightness then increased, eventually returning to about magnitude 2.2—where the star has remained. Gamma is the middle star in the **W** or **M** of the main pattern of Cassiopeia. It can be compared to Alpha and Beta Cassiopeiae, which are both of that familiar magnitude 2.25 (actually Beta is one of the Delta Scuti variable stars, but the variations are too small to be noticed). It can also be compared to Delta (2.7—variable by 0.1 magnitude every 759 days, probably due to a partial eclispe!) and Eta (3.5) or Epsilon (3.4).

The other stars of unusual brightening I wish to mention are very much different than Gamma Cassiopeiae. Their brightenings have occurred as what might be called "flashes," and have not been well documented. In the August 1989 issue of *Sky & Telescope,* Brad Schaefer offers a list of otherwise seemingly normal stars for which there is evidence of brief brightenings of at least a magnitude. Stars with normal magnitudes brighter than 5.0 on his list are Epsilon Pegasi, Tau Coronae Borealis, Nu Ophiuchi, Beta Camelopardalis, Alpha Circini, Zeta Lyrae, Beta Eridani, and 66 Ophiuchi. Some of these could be explained away as various observers' mistakes or instrumental glitches, but probably not all of them (this appraisal comes from Schaefer, who debunked the "Aries flasher" and some other cases of flashes by proving they were satellite glints). Most spectacular of the flashes on the Schaefer list in *Sky & Telescope* are the brightening of magnitude 2.4 Epsilon Pegasi for more than 11 minutes and to a peak magnitude of about 0.7, and the brightening of magnitude 2.8 Beta Eridani to maybe brighter than magnitude 0 for over 2½ hours!

Questions

1. Can you scan for novae by examining regions in which you (at least temporarily) have memorized the stars down to a certain magnitude?

2. Can you check on the current brightness of the recurrent novae T Coronae Borealis, U Scorpii, and RS Ophiuchi? Can you check the current brightness of the permanent nova P Cygni or the perhaps even more luminous and more strange Eta Carinae?

3. What is the brightness of Gamma Cassiopeiae tonight? What do you find when you check the bright stars reputed to have had major visual "flashes," especially Epsilon Pegasi and Beta Eridani?

23.

Checking Limiting Magnitude and Light Pollution, Transparency, and "Seeing"

Observe the selected section of the star cluster M67 in Cancer and find out what the limiting magnitude is with your telescope, and with other telescopes, if possible. Test your limiting magnitude under different conditions of sky transparency—and with differing amounts of light pollution. At each important observing session, view the test double stars used to determine the image size for evaluation of "seeing" on the Tombaugh–Smith scale. Determine the best and worst nights of "seeing" (and how much detail on the planets and Moon is visible at different levels of "seeing" quality) and how "seeing" varies with weather situations, the seasons, and the site from which you observe.

Just as close double stars on a night of steady atmosphere—good "seeing"—offer a test of your telescope's resolving ability (ability to distinguish fine details), so too can faint stars on a night of clear air—good *transparency*—offer a test of your telescope's (and your own eyes') light-gathering ability. The brightness of the faintest star you can perceive is the *limiting magnitude* for the night with whatever instrument (naked eye, binoculars, small or large telescope) you are using.

Knowing your limiting magnitude on the best night you ever get is fascinating (what marvels beyond marvels will the sky give you—or the atmosphere permit it to give you—on a night like this?). Of considerable interest also, however, and much greater practical importance is how good your limiting magnitude is under many different conditions (more or less hazy skies, more or less strongly moonlit skies, and so on). What was it on the night you saw certain faint extensions of a particular nebula, or an unusually dim galaxy? The "seeing" also plays a role even in the visibility of "extended" (larger than point) objects—though a much greater role in the resolvability of double stars or details on the planets, Moon, and Sun.

For a given observing session, how can we best test the limiting magnitude (as a measure of transparancy once we know the standard limits of our eyes and telescope)? For a given observing session, how can we best test what we might call the *limiting resolution* (as a measure of the seeing once we know the standard limit of our eyes and telescopes)?

Articles appearing over 30 years apart in *Sky & Telescope* offer useful answers as to how we can proceed.

The fruitful discussion of limiting magnitude in telescopes appears in two 1989 articles by Bradley Schaefer.

The article in the March 1989 issue of *Sky & Telescope* proposes that the magazine's readers test their limiting magnitudes on stars in the star cluster M67 in Cancer. Schaefer provides photographs showing part of the cluster with labeled stars, stars whose magnitudes are listed in an accompanying table. Of course, to try this test, you must have M67 suitably high in your sky—higher than 30°, says Schaefer. He states that if it is lower in the sky the varying amount of *extinction* (light loss) caused by both the atmosphere and whatever haze or dust is in it is too difficult to predict accurately. Schaefer has other cautions and counsels which should be read in the article.

Schaefer's second article, in the November 1989 issue of *Sky & Telescope*, reports the results of his study of participating readers' efforts. Schaefer is able to generate several interesting graphs, the most important of which is adapted as our Figure 22. Schaefer stresses that the three ways in which you can make a major improvement in your limiting magnitude are to use somewhat higher magnification (this reduces the total amount of light coming to your eyes from the sky background), obtain a larger-aperture telescope, and observe in darker (less light-polluted) skies.

Indeed, fewer and fewer observers these days get a chance to come anywhere near to the ultimate limiting magnitudes of which their eyes and telescopes are capable due to the tremendous brightening of the sky by glow from artificial lights. For more on this problem and what we can and must do to reduce it, see the Telescopes, Observing Conditions, and Observing Techniques section.

Even if you must settle for usually observing in badly light-polluted skies, of course, you should seek your limiting magnitude. Your figures could even help the battle against light pollution by providing additional data on its effects. An interesting twist to the Schaefer project would be to check the limiting magnitude in M67 when it is in areas of your sky with varying degrees of light pollution. What happens to the limiting magnitude when M67 moves from the reasonably dark southeast part of your sky over into the southwest that is markedly afflicted with the skyglow from a city? You may want so send your results on this light pollution question to the International Dark-Sky Association (IDA), 3545 North Stewart, Tucson, AZ 85716.

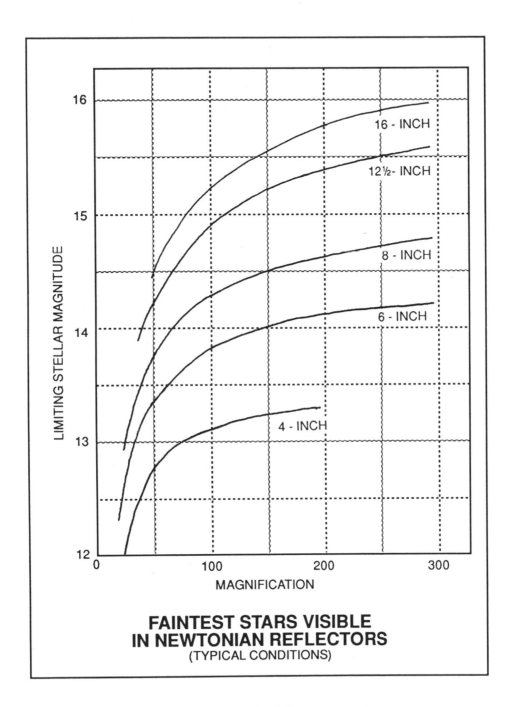

Figure 22 Limiting magnitude for different telescopic apertures.

What is a good empirical measure of "seeing" which can be related to the estimates of "seeing" you might make on a 0-to-10 scale? That is the question answered admirably well in an article by Clyde W. Tombaugh and Bradford A. Smith. The article appeared in the July 1958 issue of *Sky & Telescope* and very much deserves to be resurrected.

Tombaugh compared the numerical estimates of "seeing" he made with the image diameter of stars. He found that for every three numerical steps of improvement in "seeing" on his scale there was a fourfold decrease in the diameter of the image disk or blur, a 16-fold decrease in its area. The worst "seeing" he ever had was when gusts of gale wind made the image of Delta Geminorum in a 7.3-inch telescope at 171× swell to 3 or 4 times the apparent diameter of Jupiter and disappear! On the other hand, in 25 years of (evaluated) observing up to the time of this article, Tombaugh had recorded a "9" on his "seeing" scale less than a dozen times—but a 9 on his scale, he found, corresponded to a star image blur only ⅛ of an arc-second across!

But how can we judge the size of star images accurately? The solution is to observe double stars. Ideally, the test stars should be: rather near the north celestial pole (for north temperate observers) so always visible; fairly bright; and consisting of stars not greatly different in brightness. Bradford A. Smith compiled a list of such stars, but I have had to update this due to the changing separations (not to mention position angles). My list (see Table 11) is somewhat shorter and uses a few different stars, but I think it is adequate. You can, of course, supplement it with a few seasonal double stars you know well that are suitable. (Depending on your interest and your possession of certain star atlases and catalogs, you may want to make a list of your own—indeed you must if you live in the Southern Hemisphere.)

Observe the stars on my list (making certain that none is too low in the sky, where "seeing" is markedly worse) and note how large their image size looks in comparison to their known separation. Then, choose the numerical rating that corresponds to the image size you have determined from the following table of Tombaugh's:

"Seeing" Quality	Image Diameter
−4	50″
−3	32
−2	20
−1	12.6
0	7.9
+1	5.0

+2	3.2
+3	2.0
+4	1.3
+5	0.79
+6	0.50
+7	0.32
+8	0.20
+9	0.13

You may already have realized that this scale works independently of your telescope size in this sense: The "seeing" quality could be +7 and yet an observer with a 6-inch would not see the star images any smaller than about 0.79″ (Dawes' limit for a 6-inch) or a "seeing" quality of +5, due to the limitations of his or her telescope. (It would take at least a 16-inch to take full advantage of such conditions.) An observer with a 6-inch might decide that when he or she could resolve down to 0.79″, the "seeing" on his or her scale should be the highest possible, a 9. But this is surely not as good a method as using the Tombaugh scale which allows the results of all observers to be easily compared.

In the 1958 article, by the way, Tombaugh stresses that his experience with different "seeing" conditions had been gathered from observing at a great variety of places—Flagstaff, Arizona, being the place where

Table 11
Double Stars for the Tombaugh "Seeing" Scale

Star	Magnitudes	PA °	Dist. ″	RA h m	Dec. ° ′
Psi² Draconis	4.9, 6.1	15	30.3	17 42	+72 09
40/41 Draconis	5.7, 6.1	232	19.3	18 00	+80 00
Xi Cephei	4.4, 6.5	274	8.2	22 04	+64 38
20 Draconis	7.1, 7.3	68	1.3	16 56	+65 02
48 Cassiopeiae	4.7, 6.4	263	0.9	2 02	+70 54
OΣ235 Ursae Majoris	5.8, 7.1	341	0.6	11 32	+61 05

The position angle and distance (separation) between components are predictions for the year 2000.0; the RA and declination are in year 2000.0 coordinates. Of these stars, only the last two have rapidly changing PA and distance:

	PA °	Dist. ″	Period years	Year	Notes
48 Cassiopeiae	220	1.0	60	1926	Widest about 1935
	47	0.3	—	1962	PA increasing
OΣ235 Ursae Majoris	360	0.7	73	1930	Widest, 1.0″, in 1950
	95	0.8	—	1968	PA increasing

he witnessed both the best and the worst "seeing." Nevertheless, some locales do have consistently better "seeing" than others (a friend of mine complained about the poor "seeing" in the Colorado Rockies where he lives and once only half-joked that the naked-eye stars on a night here in South Jersey looked so nontwinkling compared to what he was used to it was like looking at "a sky full of planets.") Study the "seeing" conditions at your home observing sight and other locations (remember to be careful to try minimizing very local sources of turbulence, like the turbulence caused by your body heat on certain nights).

Questions

1. What is the limiting magnitude of your telescope as judged from observing test stars in the area of M67 mentioned above (refer to Schaefer's article in the March 1989 issue of *Sky & Telescope*)? With other telescopes? Under different weather conditions and transparency? With different amounts of light pollution?

2. What is your rating of the "seeing" quality on different nights (or at different times during an observing session) using the Tombaugh–Smith method of test double stars and quality scale? Can you document consistently better or worse "seeing" at different locales or in different parts of the country—or in different seasons and different weather conditions at one place?

STAR CLUSTERS
AND NEBULAE

24.

Open Star Clusters—1

View the open clusters on our list, studying and sketching their structures. Look for star colors and double stars among their members. Make comparisons of them, especially when they are near one another as in the cases of M46 and M47, and the Auriga clusters. Look for other objects near the clusters (like the cluster behind M35's fringes and the nebula probably in front of M46).

Stars may form by the dozens or hundreds in groups that maintain their identity at least through the early ages of their stars' lives, perhaps much longer. The result we see is *galactic star clusters,* more commonly known as *open star clusters,* because their density of stars is less and their tenacity for staying together is weaker than the other major kind of star cluster (the globular cluster).

Our goal in this and the next activity is to sample a fairly large selection of open star clusters. But, as usual, some explanation is required first if our tour of visual splendors is to take on greater meaning and be even more beautiful and interesting.

First, a few words on designations.

Most of the clusters, nebulae and galaxies in this and the following activities are *M objects* or *NGC objects.* M objects are Messier objects from the eighteenth-century French astronomer Charles Messier's catalog of over 100 clusters, nebulae, and galaxies. Observers with larger telescopes and star atlases today try to see as many as possible of the 7,000+ NGC objects (objects in John L. E. Dreyer's *New General Catalogue of Nebulae and Clusters*). Objects with an IC in their designation are from the two Index Catalogues which supplemented the NGC in the few decades after its 1888 publication. Still later, a few catalogs of special objects—for instance, very large sparsely starred clusters which the NGC had missed—were published by people like Collinder (Cr) and Melotte (Mel).

Second, a few words on an important characteristic of open clusters.

The NGC numbers its objects in order of right ascension, a sensible system. William Herschel and his son John had tried categorizing clusters into eight classes of objects, which was not very successful. However, their ideas of categorizing clusters as to whether these were "very compressed," "compressed," or "scattered" was one which was of some use in giving the prospective observer an idea of what he could expect to see. In our own tables of open clusters (Tables 12 and 13), I have used a rating system based on an improved version of this kind of cluster classification: Harlow Shapley's classification in which c is "very loose and irregular," d is "loose and poor," e is "intermediate rich," f is "fairly rich," and g is "considerably rich and concentrated." To make these easier to compare, I have turned these letter designations into a 1-to-5 scale where 1 is c, 2 is d, 3 is e, 4 is f, and 5 is g. Thus, a 1 is the most scattered, a 5 is the most densely concentrated.

Much information is provided in Table 12. But here are additional notes about the clusters of autumn and winter, and some special sights to look for in them.

NGC 752. A big, bright, well-placed, underrated low-power cluster. It is also interesting for being one of the few star clusters of intermediate age (NGC 2158—see below under "M35"—and NGC 7789 in Cassiopeia are others).

The Double Cluster (NGC 869 and NGC 884). Known since ancient times (but apparently missed by Messier), these twin, side-by-side clusters are easily seen with the naked eye in decent skies and offer one of the heavens' finest and easiest telescopic views. A field of a degree or more is needed to fit both clusters. Red stars add to the beauty. The brightest stars here are supergiants that would rival Betelgeuse and Rigel if the Double Cluster was not so immensely far—between about 7,000 and 8,000 light-years away. In fact, the Double Cluster is located in another spiral arm of our galaxy—the Perseus Arm, the one beyond our own on the way out from the center of the Milky Way galaxy. These clusters are among the very youngest known, with an age of perhaps only a few million years (the oldest open cluster may be NGC 188 in Cepheus, over 10 billion years old).

M34. Superb sight—but only with low power (too sparse otherwise).

Alpha Persei Cluster. Still not included on all lists because formerly considered not to be a true cluster. To the naked eye (and binoculars), the stars huddle rather near second-magnitude Alpha Persei (Mirfak), the one star in the cluster to have already left the main sequence and become a giant. But of telescopes, only an RFT (rich-field telescope) can include the entire cluster in one view.

The Pleiades (M45). The most conspicuous of all clusters to the naked eye, the Pleiades or Seven Sisters have charmed cultures throughout history (see Figure 23). The Pleiades have links to the Bible, Hallow-

Table 12
Open Clusters—1

Cluster	RA h	RA m	Dec. °	Dec. '	Constellation	Mag.	Size '	Con.
NGC 752	1	58	+37	41	Andromeda	5.7	50	2
NGC 869 (h Persei)[a]	2	19	+57	09	Perseus	4.3	30	4
NGC 884 (Chi Persei)	2	22	+57	07	Perseus	4.4	30	3
M34 (NGC 1039)	2	42	+42	47	Perseus	5.5	35	2
Alpha Persei cluster	3	22	+49		Perseus	1.2	185	—
The Pleiades (M45)	3	47	+24	07	Taurus	1.2	110	1
NGC 1502	4	08	+62	20	Camelopardalis	5.7	8	3
The Hyades	4	27	+16		Taurus	0.5	330	1
Collinder 464	5	22	+73		Camelopardalis	4.2	120	—
M38 (NGC 1912)	5	29	+35	50	Auriga	6.4	21	3
M36 (NGC 1960)	5	36	+34	08	Auriga	6.0	12	4
M37 (NGC 2099)	5	52	+32	33	Auriga	5.6	24	4
M35 (NGC 2168)	6	09	+24	20	Gemini	5.3	28	3
NGC 2232	6	27	−04	45	Monoceros	3.9	30	—
NGC 2244	6	32	+04	52	Monoceros	4.8	24	1
NGC 2264	6	41	+09	53	Monoceros	3.9	20	1
M41 (NGC 2287)	6	47	−20	44	Canis Major	4.6	38	3
M50 (NGC 2323)	7	03	−08	20	Monoceros	5.9	16	3
M47 (NGC 2422)	7	37	−14	30	Puppis	4.5	30	2
M46 (NGC 2437)	7	42	−14	49	Puppis	6.1	27	4
M93 (NGC 2447)	7	45	−23	52	Puppis	6.2	22	5
NGC 2451	7	45	−37	58	Puppis	2.8	45	—
NGC 2477	7	52	−38	33	Puppis	5.7	27	5
NGC 2516	7	58	−60	52	Carina	3.8	30	5
NGC 2547	8	11	−49	16	Vela	4.7	20	2

[a]h Persei and Chi Persei together are known as the Double Cluster.

—The RA and declination are in 2000.0 coordinates; the magnitude is visual but approximate (sometimes made deceptively bright by the presence of one bright star); the size is usually photographic and thus for visual purposes quite approximate; "Con." is the concentration in numerical rating based on the Shapley classification system (see text for explanation).

Figure 23 The Pleiades.

een, Devils Tower in Wyoming, and Tennyson. The nine brightest Pleiads (magnitude 5.6 or brighter) form a tiny dipper shape in the sky and are concentrated into an area a little more than a degree wide, which at the cluster's distance is only about 7 light-years wide in space. This cluster is the fourth closest, perhaps a little over 400 light-years away. Even very small telescopes show several wide, bright double stars here and that the brightest Pleiad, magnitude 2.9 Alcyone, has an eye-catching little triangle of ninth-magnitude stars near it. The Pleiades cluster is young, its hot, luminous, rapidly spinning blue–white suns still bearing traces of their swaddling clothes—the elusive nebulosity which is most prominent near the Pleiad star Merope (see Activity 28). The star Pleione is known to be occasionally variable, and may have some relation to the tale of the Lost Pleiad.

NGC 1502. Makes a naked-eye glow in a dim constellation.

The Hyades. This cluster forms the V-shaped outline of Taurus the Bull's face, though the most brilliant star of the V, first-magnitude Aldebaran, is not a member of the cluster (shining about half the distance of the cluster from us). The Hyades are the second-closest cluster (after the Ursa Major Cluster), centered only about 130 light-years away. Though brighter than even the Pleiades, the Hyades stars are scattered over too wide an area to draw the eye as quickly or give as rich an appearance. Binoculars or richest-field telescopes are needed to take all or most of the main part of the cluster into one field of view. A telescope shows well the cluster's double stars and also the varied colors of the Hyads (of the five brightest Hyads, three are K-type and one is a G-type giant, all far more luminous than the Sun). Fifteen cluster members are brighter than 5.0. Whereas all the brightest Pleiads are B-type giants, there are no B-type stars among the several hundred members of the Hyades. A far more extensive *Taurus Stream* includes stars that seem to have a proper motion similar to the Hyades and thus may be related—examples include Capella and Cor Caroli (Alpha Canum Venaticorum).

Collinder 464. Little known—very big and sparse, far north.

M38, M36, and M37. Three beautiful and rather rich clusters in Auriga. M38 and M36 are only about 2.3° apart. M36 is somewhat like a mildly less luminous version of the Pleiades (lots of B-type stars) that is 10 times more distant. M38 lies at about the same distance as M36, is bigger and richer, and possesses some stars other than B-type, including the yellow giant which is M38's brightest member (magnitude 7.9). Note the cross or pi (π) shape of stars in M38. M37 is the brightest, largest, and richest of the Auriga clusters. It is probably a little farther than M38 and M36, and certainly older. Look for the ruddiness of a magnitude 9.5 red giant near M37's center, and the curving lines of stars as in M35 and M41.

M35 (and NGC 2158). M35 is a large naked-eye cluster conveniently located at the northern feet of Gemini. Low power is called for. Note the comparative scarcity of stars near the center, also the glorious curving lines of stars throughout. With a medium-sized telescope, also look through the southwest fringes of M35 for the little glow of eleventh-magnitude NGC 2158. NGC 2158 is about 6 times farther than M35 (which itself is about 2,800 light-years away), so is actually a mighty cluster in its own right. The sixteenth-magnitude stars of NGC 2158 will not be resolved in less than about a 16-inch telescope. NGC 2158 seems to be intermediate in type between open clusters and the globular clusters, and is one of the rare clusters of intermediate age (perhaps about 800 million years old).

NGC 2232, 2244, and 2264. Both NGC 2232 and 2264 feature a fifth-magnitude star with a cluster of fainter stars. NGC 2244 is enwreathed by the much larger Rosette Nebula (see Activity 28) and NGC 2264 is associated with nebulosity and the difficult but wondrous dark cloud called the Cone Nebula.

M41. M41 is a big, glorious low-power cluster conveniently located about 4° S of Sirius. A naked-eye spot of glow, it was apparently mentioned by Aristotle in 325 B.C. Look for curving lines of stars, and a reddish star near the center (brightest in the cluster, at magnitude 6.9). The cluster's distance is about 2,350 light-years.

M50. M50 is a bit more than a third of the way along the long line drawn from Sirius to Procyon. Burnham says the curving arcs of stars at its edge give the whole a heart-shaped outline. M50 is somewhat farther than M41. It includes a red giant somewhat south of the cluster center.

M47 and M46. M47 and M46 are nicely contrasting clusters hardly more than 1½° apart. M47 is brighter but much sparser than M46. Smyth called M47 "lozenge-shaped," and Walter Scott Houston pointed out that to see the "dim sheen" of the cluster's fainter stars requires about a 10-inch telescope. M46 is a big, round cluster of mostly magnitude 10 to 13 stars which is several times farther from

117

us than M47. Look for the 65″ wide planetary nebula NGC 2338 just 7′ N of M46's center. This object is not related with the cluster and is probably closer to us.

M93. M93 is smaller than M46. The center is concentrated, and from it run branches of stars. Smyth thought it looked like a starfish; K. G. Jones thought it looked like a butterfly with open wings.

NGC 2451 and 2477. These are only 1° from each other. NGC 2451 is bright because it includes the fourth-magnitude star c Puppis. NGC 2477 is very near the star b Puppis and Burnham calls it the finest of the Puppis clusters (but it is quite southerly). None of NGC 2477's stars are brighter than about magnitude 10, but a medium-sized telescope begins to show this incredibly rich (transitional between open and globular?) cluster well.

NGC 2516. A spectacularly rich, bright cluster of the far south.

NGC 2547. Composed of magnitude 7 to 15 stars and is about 2°S of the brilliant Wolf–Rayet star Gamma Velorum.

Questions

1. What are the structures of the various clusters as you sketch them from your telescopic views? Do you see certain lines or curves of stars become more apparent or less with increasing magnification or with a larger-aperture telescope?

2. What star colors do you notice in the clusters? Can you locate NGC 2158 behind the fringes of M35, or NGC 2348 probably in front of the stars of M46? How do the three great Auriga clusters compare to each other? What other clusters do you happen upon in Auriga (or in any of your observations of the other clusters on our list)?

3. Do you agree with the Shapley classifications (sparseness or richness of stars)? What might they be for the clusters for which Table 12 doesn't give the data?

25.

Open Star Clusters—2

View the open clusters on our list, studying and sketching their structures. Look for star colors and double stars among their members. Make comparisons of them, especially when they are near one another. Look for other objects and clusters near the clusters on our list.

We continue the survey of open clusters started in the previous activity.

M48. No cluster exists in the spot Messier gave but his description is almost certainly that of a large cluster 4° S of his position, so that cluster has been universally accepted as M48. It is an impressive object but lies in a rather desolate area of western Hydra, and does not seem to be much observed. (See Table 13.)

M44. M44 is the famous Beehive cluster, known as Praesepe (the "manger" for the stars Asellus Borealis and Asellus Australis in Cancer) since ancient times. At a distance of a little over 500 light-years, M44 is an easy naked-eye object but usually just beyond the ability of the naked eye to distinguish as separate stars. Galileo was the first to see the component stars properly. Any small telescope gives a good view, and the roughly 1½° width of the cluster calls for low power. There is a variety of spectral types and colors, and the stars of similar brightness seem to pair and bunch (much indeed like bees in a hive). Like M35, the Pleiades, and the Hyades, M44 is close enough to the ecliptic to often be a target for the Moon and the planets. Remarkably, M44 is moving parallel to and at nearly the same velocity as the Hyades—spurring speculation that they had a common origin. The two clusters are of similar age, but are very far apart in space.

M67. This rich cluster of magnitude 10 to 16 stars is less than 2°W of Alpha Cancri. M67 is very unusual for an open cluster in that it lies 1,500 light-years above the equatorial plane of the galaxy. This is no doubt the reason its stars have not scattered (not often does it have neighbors to gravitationally pull them) even though it is about 10 billion years old, one of the very oldest of open clusters.

Table 13
Open Clusters—2

Cluster	RA h m	Dec. ° '	Constellation	Mag.	Size '	Con.
M48 (NGC 2548)	08 14	−05 48	Hydra	5.8	55	4
The Beehive (M44) (NGC 2632)	08 40	+20 00	Cancer	3.1	95	2
M67 (NGC 2682)	08 50	+11 49	Cancer	6.9	30	4
NGC 3114	10 03	−60 07	Carina	4.2	35	3
NGC 3532	11 06	−58 40	Carina	3.0	55	4
NGC 3766	11 36	−61 37	Centaurus	5.3	12	5
Coma Star Cluster	12 25	+26	Coma Berenices	1.8	275	1
Kappa Crucis Cluster*a*	12 54	−60 20	Crux	4.2	10	5
NGC 6025	16 04	−60 30	Triangulum Australe	5.1	12	2
NGC 6193	16 41	−48 46	Ara	5.2	15	3
NGC 6231	16 54	−41 48	Scorpius	2.6	15	3
M6 (NGC 6405)	17 40	−32 13	Scorpius	4.2	15	3
IC 4665	17 46	+05 43	Ophiuchus	4.2	41	1
M7 (NGC 6475)	17 54	−34 49	Scorpius	3.3	80	3
M23 (NGC 6494)	17 57	−19 01	Sagittarius	5.5	27	3
M21 (NGC 6531)	18 05	−22 30	Sagittarius	5.9	13	2
NGC 6530	18 05	−24 20	Sagittarius	4.6	15	3
M24*b*	18 17	−18 29	Sagittarius	4.5	90	—
M16*c* (NGC 6611)	18 19	−13 47	Serpens	6.0	35	1
NGC 6633	18 28	+06 34	Ophiuchus	4.6	27	2
M25 (Ic 4725)	18 32	−19 15	Sagittarius	4.6	32	2
M11 (NGC 6705)	18 51	−06 16	Scutum	5.8	14	5
The Coathanger*d*	19 25	+20 11	Vulpecula	3.6	60	—
M39 (NGC 7092)	21 32	+48 26	Cygnus	4.6	32	3
M52 (NGC 7654)	23 24	+61 35	Cassiopeia	6.9	13	3

*a*The Kappa Crucis cluster is NGC 4755, and is also commonly known as the Jewel Box.

*b*M24 is the Small Sagittarius Star Cloud.

*c*M16 is here a star cluster but is better known as the nebula (the Star-Queen Nebula or Eagle Nebula) associated with these stars.

*d*Also known as Brocchi's cluster and Collinder 399.

The RA and declination are in 2000.0 coordinates; the magnitude is visual but approximate (sometimes made deceptively bright by the presence of one bright star); the size is usually photographic and thus for visual purposes quite approximate; "Con." is the concentration in numerical rating based on the Shapley classification system (see Activity 24 for explanation).

STAR CLUSTERS AND NEBULAE

NGC 3532 and 3766. NGC 3532 and 3766 in Carina are big, bright, and rich clusters for southern viewers.

NGC 3766. NGC 3766 is a small but extremely rich cluster in Centaurus.

The Coma Star Cluster. Originally the tuft on Leo the Lion's tail, this star cluster (and later its whole constellation) was named for the shorn locks of hair of Queen Berenice II of Egypt, which she offered in thanks to the gods upon the safe return of her husband from war. This cluster does look like beautifully disheveled hair, stretching across 5° with fifth- and sixth-magnitude (and fainter) stars. Only the richest-field telescopes can show the whole cluster at once. The Coma cluster is the third closest, at about 250 light-years, and though filling about the same volume as the Pleiades has only about one-quarter as many stars. It may be disintegrating more rapidly than most clusters. It is older than the Pleiades and offers a variety of spectral types.

The Kappa Crucis Star Cluster. Also known as "the Jewel Box," NGC 4755 is small but richly packed with bright stars, and is one of the heavens' finest telescopic sights. At a distance of about 7,700 light-years, this cluster is comparable to the Double Cluster in several respects (including its extreme youth), but lies in almost the opposite direction. Near the brilliance of the Jewel Box is the blackness of the Coal Sack—the most famous of the dark nebulae (see Activity 31).

NGC 6025 and 6193. NGC 6025 and 6193 are small but rather bright clusters of the south, located in Triangulum Australe and Ara, respectively.

NGC 6231. NGC 6231 is a spectacular cluster half a degree north of the wide double Zeta Scorpii. It is located 5,700 light-years away and Burnham says that its central region is similar in size to the Pleiades—but if it were as close as the Pleiades, it would feature stars shining as brightly as Sirius! The cluster is part of the I Scorpii Association of stars which spreads over several degrees and marks part of the spiral arm next inward toward the galactic center from our own spiral arm. The whole region is fabulous, but a bit far south for 40°N viewers to see well except on excellent nights.

M6 and M7. These are farther-north wonders of Scorpius than NGC 6231, lying just Sagittarius-ward of the Scorpion's upraised sting.

M6 is only 3½° from M7 and the two were known as fuzzy patches of light to the naked eye even in ancient times. Both are comparatively near clusters and truly magnificent. M6 has been called the Butterfly Cluster by Burnham, who points out that the brightest cluster member is a golden K-type 6.2 magnitude star on the northeast "wing-tip." M7 is even brighter and larger, an easy naked-eye object which looks like a real cluster even in binoculars. Low magnification must be used on a telescope to get all of this splendid giant in the field of view.

IC 4665. This is a huge but very sparse cluster visible to the naked eye near Beta Ophiuchi.

M23. M23 would be a major attraction in most regions of the heavens, but, being located in Sagittarius, it is often overlooked. Sanford notes the curving lines of stars in it.

M21. M21 is a cluster near (but not related to) the famous M20, the Trifid nebula (see Activity 29). It is small and not very rich but is bright and adds to the splendor of its spectacular locale.

NGC 6530. NGC 6530 is the cluster in M8, the huge Lagoon Nebula (see Activity 29). This cluster is very bright and spectacular in its own right—study it while you are tracing the areas of nebulosity.

M24. M24 was once considered to be a much smaller, less impressive cluster. Now the title is assigned (correctly) to the entire Small Sagittarius Star Cloud, the 2° by 1° patch which looks like the brightest knot of the Milky Way to the naked eye and provides one of the most star-crowded fields of view possible in the telescope.

M16. M16 is the title that astronomers usually associate with the Eagle nebula, but until the nebula filters and larger telescopes of recent years came into use, the sight often consisted of just this large, sparse but bright enough cluster of stars.

NGC 6633. This is a bright, not very famous cluster in Ophiuchus.

M25. M25 is more famous, but still grossly underobserved because of the objects of premier wonder all about it. This bright, large cluster seemed especially beautiful to me when Comet Austin was near it at the beginning of June 1990. It was left out from the Herschels' catalog by mistake and so was also missed by the NGC (it was finally captured by one of the Index Catalogues, the supplements to the NGC). M25 is almost unique among open clusters in possessing a bright classical Cepheid variable star, U Sagittarii, which varies from 6.3 to 7.1 in a period of a bit over 6.7 days. The star becomes somewhat yellower as it fades to minimum. It is one of two bright stars near the cluster center.

M11. M11 gets my vote as favorite open cluster for telescopic viewing and I could argue the case for its being the most splendid of all. Most observers agree it is one of the few best. Admiral Smyth described the central formation of its stars as resembling "a flight of wild ducks," leading to its being called the Wild Duck Cluster. In a medium-sized telescope, I see M11 as an avalanche of tenth- to twelfth-magnitude stars falling from a single eighth-magnitude gem, and throwing up a dust of fainter stars. As Walter Scott Houston says, a good 10-inch telescope can show hundreds of stars in this cluster—all aglow in the midst of the intense Scutum star cloud, and set off with several dark nebulae not far from the cluster.

The Coathanger (Brocchi's Cluster). This curious cluster features a perfect line of six stars and a hook of four (along with fainter other stars) which together look exactly like a coathanger. It is bright enough to see as a spot with the naked eye, and little magnification is needed to see the strange figure.

M39. This is a large bright cluster a full 9°NNE of Deneb. Perhaps its out-of-the-way location has contributed to its being underrated. In a good low magnification view, it looks surprisingly like a smaller version of the Pleiades. If the cluster were not twice as far as the Pleiades, it would appear only mildly inferior. Aristotle may have mentioned M39's visibility as a naked-eye patch of glow.

M52. M52 is a small but rich and fairly bright cluster. Smyth noted an eighth-magnitude orange star and a shape somewhat like a flying bird. M52 is one of the many and varied clusters in Cassiopeia—try hunting around and identifying the objects after you come upon them and marvel.

Questions

1. What is the structure of the different clusters as you sketch them? How much do the lines and curves and vacancies of stars seem to

become more or less prominent with your changes of magnification and aperture?

2. What star colors and double stars can you find in these clusters? What interesting nearby clusters and other objects do you happen upon as you look for the clusters on our list? How do the various clusters compare, especially ones that are near each other?

3. Do you agree with the Shapley classifications (sparseness or richness of stars)? What might they be for the clusters for which Table 13 doesn't give the data?

26.

Globular Clusters

Learn about globular clusters and study and sketch a selection of the most interesting. Note each globular's overall shape, degree of concentration, and how many of its individual stars are resolved at different magnifications with different size apertures. Look for structural oddities like the dark lanes in M13 and the very concentrated center of M15. Compare the different globulars, especially ones rather near each other in the sky and those reputed to have similarities. Try to observe a few of the most distant globular clusters of our galaxy, and one which may not be part of the Milky Way, "the Intergalactic Wanderer."

Globular clusters are dramatically different from open clusters (see Figure 24). Whereas open clusters may contain hundreds of stars, globulars feature thousands and in a few cases several million stars. There are something like 18,000 open clusters in our entire galaxy, but maybe no more than 200 globular clusters. Open clusters are almost entirely confined to near the equatorial plane of our galaxy, whereas the globulars form a spherical halo about the center of the galaxy, often at great distances from the center and far above or below the equatorial plane. Open clusters feature *Population I* stars (younger, later-generation stars— like our Sun), while globular clusters contain the older *Population II* stars. Open clusters may be immersed in nebulosity or at least still associated

Figure 24 A globular cluster.

with wisps of it; globular clusters and their Population II stars have long since used up gas and dust and have no nebulosity connected with them.

The central hub of the galaxy and the spherical halo about it contain only Population II stars (the gas and dust from which Population I stars are still being born is confined to the spiral arms). There are a small number of Population II stars orbiting on their own in the halo, amazing escapees from the globular clusters. But when we look out over distances of as much as tens of thousands of light-years from us around our galaxy, what we see are the mighty spherical star aggregations called globular clusters.

Let us take a tour of some of the finest globular clusters in the heavens. Because the globulars form a spherical halo with the center of the galaxy in its middle, we should expect to see more when we look in the direction of the center of our galaxy. This is true, because in that direction we see ones above and below the galactic center, plus even some on the opposite side of the center from us. Of course, globulars near the galactic center or directly on the other side of it must remain hidden from us as the center itself is, due to the many light-years of dust and gas in the spiral arms which we must stare into when we look toward the center. The center is located in western Sagittarius, a summer constellation for the Northern Hemisphere—and so the vast majority of globular clusters are in that summer half of the heavens.

One more point before we begin our tour: As with open clusters, there is a system used to classify how compressed (how densely populated with stars) the various globulars are. The system uses 12 classes which range from the most highly condensed globulars (class I) to the most loosely condensed (class XII). The ease with which an amateur telescope can resolve individually even some of the outer stars of a globular depends on how condensed the cluster is (also partly on how bright the individual stars are compared to the telescope's limiting magnitude). In Table 14, I have for greater accessibility converted the Roman numerals of the concentration class numbers to Arabic numerals.

Table 14
Selected Globular Star Clusters

Cluster	RA h m	Dec. ° '	Constellation	Mag.	Size '	Con.
47 Tucanae	00 24	− 72 05	Tucana	4.5	31	3
NGC 362	01 03	− 70 51	Tucana	6.6	13	3
M79 (NGC 1904)	05 25	− 24 33	Lepus	8.4	3	5
NGC 2808	09 12	− 64 52	Carina	6.3	14	1
NGC 5139 (Omega Centauri)	13 27	− 47 29	Centaurus	3.7	36	8
M3 (NGC 5272)	13 42	+ 28 23	Canes Venatici	6.4	16	6
M5 (NGC 5904)	15 19	+ 02 05	Serpens	5.8	17	5
M80 (NGC 6093)	16 17	− 22 59	Scorpius	7.2	9	2
M4 (NGC 6121)	16 24	− 26 32	Scorpius	6.0	26	9
M13 (NGC 6205)	16 42	+ 36 28	Hercules	5.9	16	5
M92 (NGC 6341)	17 17	+ 43 08	Hercules	6.5	11	4
NGC 6397	17 41	− 53 40	Ara	5.6	26	9
M22 (NGC 6656)	18 36	− 23 54	Sagittarius	5.1	24	7
NGC 6752	19 11	− 59 59	Pavo	5.4	20	6
M55 (NGC 6809)	19 40	− 30 58	Sagittarius	7.0	19	11
M15 (NGC 7078)	21 30	+ 12 10	Pegasus	6.4	12	4
M2 (NGC 7089)	21 34	− 00 49	Aquarius	6.5	13	2

The RA and declination are in 2000.0 coordinates; the magnitude is visual but approximate; the size is usually photographic and thus for visual purposes quite approximate; "Con." is the concentration in numerical rating based on I (most concentrated) to XII (least concentrated), here converted from Roman numerals to Arabic numerals.

47 Tucanae. This is generally considered to be the second most spectacular of the globular clusters. It is far too southerly for observers at mid-northern latitudes, shining magnificently just 2½°W of one of the Milky Way's companion galaxies, the Small Magellanic Cloud (SMC). At between 15,000 and 20,000 light-years away from us, 47 Tucanae is only about one-tenth the distance to the SMC. The cluster is one of the closest of the globulars, but also one of the intrinsically greatest. Its brightest stars are about magnitude 11½, so 4-inch telescopes can begin to resolve some of them.

NGC 362. NGC 362 lies only a few degrees north of the Small Magellanic Cloud in Tucana and though a respectably bright globular it is quite outclassed by the great 47 Tucanae.

M79. M79 in Lepus is the only even moderately bright globular among the traditional winter constellations. This is its chief claim of interest.

NGC 2808. NGC 2808 is a fairly impressive but highly condensed globular for far-south viewers.

Omega Centauri. Omega Centauri is even greater than 47 Tucanae, and thus the greatest object of its class. It is far enough south to be only just visible from the southern three-quarters of the United States. In the tropics and Southern Hemisphere, it is high enough to be easily visible to the naked eye, and was indeed mentioned as a spot of glow in ancient times by Ptolemy. Edmund Halley was the first to identify it as a star cluster. Omega Centauri contains over a million stars and spans more than 300 light-years (the central, visually prominent mass is about 100 light-years in diameter).

M3. M3 is isolated, with few good stars nearby to guide us to it. It lies a little more than halfway along the long line in the sky you can draw from Cor Caroli (Alpha Canes Venaticorum) to Arcturus. M3 is one of the few finest globulars of the north celestial hemisphere. It contains more variable stars than perhaps any other globular cluster known. A few stars in the edges are resolved with a 4-inch, hundreds with a 6-inch, and stars down to near the center with a 12-inch. The cluster is about 35,000 to 40,000 light-years distant.

M5. M5 is, along with M13 and M3, one of the three brightest globulars north of the celestial equator. It is a little farther than M13, and its true brightness and numbers of stars must be similar. M5 lies only 20′ from the double star 5 Serpentis, making for a gorgeous sight at low power. The age of M5 is thought to be about 13 billion years, perhaps old even for a globular cluster. This cluster is decidedly elliptical.

M80 and M4. These are two greatly contrasting clusters near Antares. The large M4 is located only 1.3°W of Antares and is extremely loose for a globular. It may be tied with NGC 6397 in Ara for the title of closest globular at a distance of about 6,900 light-years. The first structure to be noticed in a 4-inch or larger telescope as it begins to resolve the cluster is a strange bar of eleventh-magnitude stars through the cluster's center. M80 is about 4°NNW of Antares and appears much smaller than M4, being about 4 to 5 times farther. It is highly condensed and moderate-sized telescopes can only begin to resolve a few of its faint stars.

M13. M13 is the most famous of all globular clusters, the best in the north celestial hemisphere and better seen from 40°N than rivals like M22 because it passes so much higher in the sky—indeed, almost overhead. M13 contains about a million or more stars, and is located roughly 20,000 to 25,000 light-years away. Although perceivable to the naked eye on one side of the Keystone asterism of Hercules, M13 was apparently first reported by Edmund Halley. A 4- to 6-inch telescope begins to show the glittering pinpoints of individual stars in the cluster. In a 10-inch telescope M13 is grand almost beyond belief, like a benevolent monster with mighty arms or tentacles of stars. One peculiarity of M13 is dark lanes which when well-glimpsed seem to form a Y shape, meeting at a spot to the southeast of the core. The faint galaxy NGC 6207 is found quite close to M13 in the sky—through a 13-inch I am surprised how prominent this galaxy can be. In regard to M13's popularity as a wonder of summer nights, I think of Walter Scott Houston's question at Stellafane when he was told people were looking at M13—"Have they worn it out yet?"

M92. M92 is a second fine globular cluster in Hercules. It can just be glimpsed with the naked eye on superb nights. It is smaller and less bright than M13 and also harder to resolve. A large telescope shows a central area of this cluster as especially impressive. M92 is about 35,000 light-years distant.

NGC 6397. This is possibly the closest known globular cluster, rivaled by M4. One of the least concentrated of globulars, it is also one of the finest, looking perhaps as large as M4 but a little brighter.

M22. M22 has its advocates as the superior of M13 for mid-northern latitude observers. The problem for most of us is, of course, M22's relatively low altitude. M22 does seem to be brighter and bigger, though the blending of its fringes with the foreground stars of the Milky Way equatorial plane makes it difficult for an observer to tell where it does end. M22 appears less condensed than M13 or 47 Tucanae, though not quite so loose as Omega Centauri. Taking into account its dimming by dust here near the galaxy's equatorial plane, astronomers think that M22 may be a little less than 10,000 light-years away, one of the very closest globulars. This cluster is also very conveniently located, glowing about 2.3°NE of Lambda Sagittarii, the star marking the top of the Teapot asterism of Sagittarius. Which is a grander sight, M13 or M22? Both have their distinctive appearance, and both are grand enough to keep most of us happy for a lifetime of viewing.

NGC 6752. NGC 6752 in Pavo may be the most neglected of all the truly great globular clusters. It is almost as large and bright as M22. A double star with components of magnitude 7.7 and 9.3, separated by 3″, can be found in this cluster's fringes.

M55. M55 is in a rather desolate area just off from the incredibly rich attractions around the Sagittarius Arm of the Milky Way, and is significantly farther south than M22. But it deserves more attention. Its most interesting characteristic is its extreme looseness. Amateur telescopes seem to show space between stars even in its central regions. Robert Burnham explains that is deceptive, however, because when the magnitude limit goes down to seventeenth magnitude many faint stars spring up in those gaps. M55 is probably a little less than 20,000 light-years away.

M15 and M2. These superb globulars lie at almost exactly the same right ascension, M2 almost right on the celestial equator and M15 a little over 12°N of the equator. These must be great clusters, considering how bright they are at distances of about 35,000 (M15) and 50,000 (M2) light-years away. Both appear highly concentrated, and M15 has an especially condensed center. The fact that M15 is a source of X-ray energy has suggested that there might be a *black hole* at its center, but recent satellite imagery has cast doubt on this idea. M15 does seem to have some dark areas like the lanes in M13. It also has a very faint planetary nebula which is actually part of the cluster, a real novelty. M15 is only about 4°NW of Epsilon Pegasi, the second-magnitude star at the tip of the nose of Pegasus.

The ambitious observer may want to try seeing two other globular clusters, noted not for their apparent brightness but rather for their distance. NGC 2419, a globular in Lynx about 7°N of Castor, is only a few arc-minutes wide visually and only about eleventh magnitude. But this is either the Milky Way's most remote globular cluster or what its nickname suggests, "the Intergalactic Wanderer." NGC 2419 is 210,000 light-years from the Milky Way's center and really does seem to be in independent motion. The only other known globular which is not within 65,000 light-years of the Milky Way's center is NGC 7006 in Delphinus, 150,000 light-years out and at 185,000 light-years from the Sun even a little more distant from us than NGC 2419.

Questions

1. What differences in structure (including overall shape—some globulars seem more elliptical than others, presumably due to faster rotation) do you find between the different globular clusters? How large a telescope aperture is needed to achieve various degrees of resolution of each cluster?

2. Can you detect the dark lanes in M13? If so, at what magnification and aperture size do they seem most prominent? Can you find the galaxy fairly near M13 in an 8-inch or larger telescope? How about the planetary nebula in M15 with a very large telescope? How do M15 and M2 compare? M13 and M92? M13 and M22? Omega Centauri and 47 Tucanae?

3. Can you find "the Intergalactic Wanderer" and the distant NGC 7006 in Delphinus?

27.

Stellar Associations, Moving Groups, and Streams

With a telescope view the individual members of the Ursa Major Cluster and Stream, considering their significance. Study the stars and nebula of the young and rapidly expanding Zeta Persei Association. Observe many of the stars of the vast Scorpius–Centaurus Association. Look at the entire seemingly small (less than 4° wide) I Scorpii Association in a rich-field telescope, then study its component superluminous stars and clusters in detail contemplating the great distance and marvelous location of this association. While performing all these observations, pause to note whichever section of Gould's Belt is currently visible and meditate upon the major structures of our galaxy which these patterns and associations indicate.

In the previous activities, we have examined the open clusters and the far more condensed objects known as globular clusters. But there are groupings of stars that are far less condensed than even the sparsest open clusters yet sharing similar direction and velocity of motion through space, suggesting a common origin. There are two kinds of loose confederations of stars like this, radically different in age and perhaps also in nature.

Associations are confederations of young stars that have just formed (or, in the case of the T Tauri stars in T associations, are in the process of forming). These outbreaks of rampant star birth occur in the clouds of gas and dust of spiral arms like our own, perhaps set off by *density waves* as the galaxy rotates. O–B associations contain brilliant young stars of spectral types O and B.

Moving groups seem to be confederations of older stars that have drifted farther and farther away from their fellow members, a stage in the disintegration of what were once stars close enough together to have warranted being called a cluster. If a cluster still exists in the midst of such an arrangement, then the escaped, far-outlying stars could be called a *stream*.

Let's discuss and observe moving groups and streams first.

How widely spread out must stars moving through space together be before they are called a moving group and not a cluster? A debatable case is that of the Ursa Major Cluster—or Ursa Major Moving Group! I have hedged on the question. The recent tendency in popular astronomy books seems to be to consider these stars a cluster, and in the previous activities I called the Hyades the second-closest open cluster in deference to the idea that the Ursa Major Cluster is indeed a cluster. Nevertheless, I have thought it more advisable to discuss this confederation of stars in our activity on moving groups. I wonder if the transition from calling it a moving group to calling it a cluster has not arisen largely from Burnham's use of a synonym of moving group—*moving cluster*—and his subsequent shortening of it to just cluster.

131

Every stargazer in the northern half of the world has seen the core of the Ursa Major Cluster, though few have realized its identity as such. The core is none other than the five central stars of the Big Dipper—all of the seven except for Alpha Ursae Majoris at the bowl end and Eta Ursae Majoris at the handle's end. Not counting Alcor and the Big Dipper, about 11 other stars have been considered likely members, of which the ones brighter than magnitude 5.5 are: 21 Leo Minoris, 78 Ursae Majoris, 37 Ursae Majoris, and Alpha Coronae Borealis. The membership of the last of these, the pretty star called Gemma or Alphecca, is apparently not certain.

So how close is the Ursa Major Cluster? It is centered about 75 light-years from Earth and measures about 18 by 30 light-years. That translates to a diameter of about 23° in our sky! Only the naked eye can take in the whole assemblage, interspersed with many other unrelated stars, in one field of view. But aren't each one of the members of this nearest fellowship of stars worthy of telescopic examination and pondering?

An even more exciting point is that there seems to exist an Ursa Major Stream surrounding the Ursa Major Cluster. Similar motions through space have been identified for Beta Eridani, Beta Aurigae, Delta Leonis—and for Sirius itself! The stars of this stream are thus distributed across almost a hemisphere of the heavens. It is possible that our solar system is passing right through the outer edges of the Stream. This is a most beguiling thought. But let us remember: This interpretation of the data is by no means proven.

For speculation about the also fascinating Taurus Stream, see the entry on the Hyades in Activity 24.

How widely spread out must bright young stars moving through space together be before they are called an association and not a cluster? A borderline case here appears to be the Alpha Persei Cluster—also sometimes called the Alpha Persei Association. The nearby II Persei Association, sometimes called the Zeta Persei Association, seems clearly to deserve the title. As Figure 25 shows, the stars (over 20 in number, actually) of this small association appear to be diverging from a common point of origin which they must have left little more than a million years ago (less time than there have been humans capable of looking at the stars and wondering). We seem to be seeing how massive young stars forming in a loose enough group will soon easily escape from their siblings' mutual attraction.

Besides Zeta and Xi Persei, this O–B association includes 40, 42, and Omicron Persei. Zeta and the latter three can be observed together in a wide telescopic field of view, but only the widest could also capture Xi. Just north of Xi, however, is an elusive but wonderful object which is

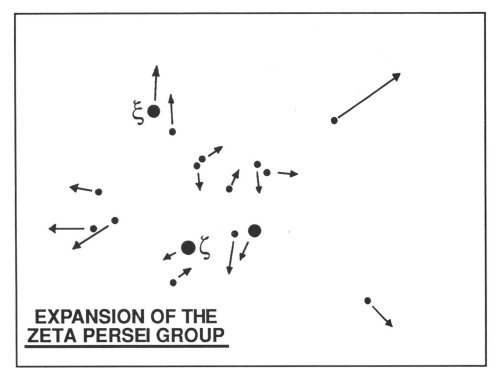

**EXPANSION OF THE
ZETA PERSEI GROUP**

Figure 25 Expansion of the Zeta Persei association or group.

further indication of this association's youth—the California Nebula (see the next activity for details on it). The Zeta Persei Association is about 1,000 light-years away and about 100 light-years across.

What other kinds of O–B associations are there? There is another one in Perseus, surrounding the great Double Cluster. This then, is an association about 7,000 to 8,000 light-years away in the next spiral arm outward from our own. An association may have several clusters within it: There is an Auriga association about 4,000 light-years away which apparently includes the three most famous Auriga clusters. An association may have clusters, runaway stars, and vast areas of nebulosity surrounding a mighty central nebula—which is a description of the Orion Association. Most of the bright blue stars, the clusters, and the nebulae of Orion are part of this complex centered roughly 1,500 light-years from us but extending across an area at least many hundreds of light-years wide and deep. We are looking here into the center of our own spiral arm, where a density wave or some other event not many millions of years ago must have set off this awesome display in the clouds of gas and dust.

133

Facing the other way, we can see more signs of this "recent" great upheaval of star birth. The Scorpius–Centaurus Association is the closest to us—it is centered about 550 light-years away, with some member stars as close as 450 light-years from us. Its brightest star is Antares, but the association is thought to be only about 20 million years old, so the other stars are still B-type. Some of the major members include Theta Ophiuchi, Beta and Nu and Delta and Sigma Scorpii, Alpha and Gamma and Lambda Lupi, Epsilon and Delta and Mu and Eta Centauri, and Beta Crucis. All in all, over 100 members are known, extending across about 90° of sky!

Another amazing O–B association is located in Scorpius, but is about a dozen times farther than the Scorpius–Centaurus Association. Whereas the Scorpius–Centaurus Association marks the inward side of our spiral arm, this other association is located in the next spiral arm inward toward the center of the galaxy. It includes the marvelous open cluster NGC 6231 and its neighbor, the superluminous star Zeta^1 Scorpii—both objects previously discussed in this book. But there are other clusters nearby, including (about a degree north and a little east of NGC 6231) a rich area of stars marked on some old star atlases as "H12." The region from Zeta and extending about 3°N of it is so curious and spectacular it has been given a special name, "the Table of Scorpius," and is actually composed largely of the I Scorpii Association. Photographs have revealed that this distant association is surrounded by a loop of nebulosity about 4° wide, which in linear measure at that distance is about 300 light-years.

Although the stars of even the most widely spread associations can be observed individually in a telescope, the still larger structures which they decorate or spottily outline are the province of the naked eye—and the mind's eye. We have seen how there are stellar associations in the center of our Orion Arm (sometimes called the Cygnus–Carina Arm) and toward the inner edge of it. We have learned that there is an association around the Double Cluster marking our outer neighbor arm, the Perseus Arm, and our inner neighbor arm, the Sagittarius Arm. But anyone who studies the bright stars of winter with the naked eye may notice that they are arranged slightly—at an angle of about 15° to 20°—aslant of the Milky Way band, or rather of the equatorial plane of our galaxy. This strip of bright stars actually extends from Perseus, Taurus, Orion, and down through Carina around to Centaurus and Scorpius. It includes both the Orion and Scorpius–Centaurus associations and is known as Gould's Belt (of Bright Stars) in the sky or, sometimes, the Local System in space. It is just a spur—albeit a glorious spur—on the

Orion (or Cygnus–Carina) Arm. Yet it is apparently possible that even the so-called Orion Arm is really just a vast spur on the Perseus Arm.

And where is our Sun and its family headed in all this? Apparently we are heading toward a spot in the vicinity of Cygnus for now. But, if we step out and look at our situation from an outside and longer-term view, some astronomers have speculated (and speculation it clearly is) that our solar system may be eventually cutting across the Orion Arm and across the gap (no doubt far from empty, but rather replete with dark clouds) into the Perseus Arm.

Questions

1. Can you observe all of the bright stars of the Ursa Major Cluster, both in one view with the naked eye and individually with the telescope? How about the members of the Ursa Major Stream?

2. Can you fit much of the Zeta Persei Association into one field of view and picture the past and future of these breakaway stars? Can you observe Xi Persei and the California Nebula (see the next activity for advice on the latter)?

3. Can you view many of the stars of the Scorpius–Centaurus Association? Can you observe the entire I Scorpii Association in the Table of Scorpius in one rich-field telescope view, then study its glorious and intricate components (mentally excluding known foreground objects like Zeta² Scorpii) with higher power?

4. While observing parts of the Orion Association and Scorpius–Centaurus Association, can you stop to note Gould's Belt and ponder the arrangement of associations and spiral arms and where we fit in to the hints of this patterning we see in our sky?

28.

Diffuse Nebulae—1

Observe the nebulae on our list, making careful sketches of what you see. Try to detect the greatest extent and structure of the Merope Nebula and other Pleiades nebulosity that you can. Try to glimpse the California Nebula, with or without a nebula filter. Spend lots of time sketching the incredibly intricate streamers, wisps, stars, mottlings, and various levels of brightness in the incomparable Great Orion Nebula, also noting where you see green, red, or purple in it. Also observe and sketch M43 and NGC 1977. If you are far enough south to observe it, sketch the awesomely distant Tarantula Nebula. Observe and sketch the two nebulae near Zeta Orionis and the neglected but surprisingly prominent M78.

Nebula means "cloud" in Latin. In astronomy, a nebula is a cloud of gas and dust in space. The first major classification is into *diffuse nebulae* and *planetary nebulae*. The former are the clouds from which stars are born, the latter are the clouds that dying stars eject (*supernova remnants* or SNR are the clouds from the more violent deaths of the most massive stars).

In the present activity and the next, we will discuss the diffuse nebulae.

Diffuse nebulae can themselves be divided into two major types: *emission nebulae* and *reflection nebulae*. In an emission nebula, the gas itself glows, fluorescing due to the ultraviolet radiation of hot (hotter than 20,000 K) stars shining in it or near it. In a reflection nebula, the cloud is merely a passive reflector of the stars shining in or near it. The Great Orion Nebula is an example of an emission nebula, its gas fluorescing from the radiation of the O-type stars of Theta[1] Orionis, the Trapezium. The Merope Nebula and other nebulosity associated with the Pleiades is a reflection nebula, because the B-type stars of the Pleiades are not quite hot enough to fluoresce the gas.

Another term you will hear in relation to diffuse nebulae is *HII regions*. These are merely the areas of diffuse nebulae that are near enough to hot stars to fluoresce. The regions of the nebulae too far from the hot stars to glow are the *HI regions*. (By the way, if a nebula is far from any stars but happens to lie between us and a much more distant bright nebula, we may see the first as an inky silhouette—a *dark nebula*, which we will consider in Activity 31.)

The "H" in these terms is the symbol for the chemical element hydrogen, the most common element in the universe and in these nebulae. In the Great Orion Nebula, there is about 10 times more hydrogen than helium, and about 100,000 times more helium than anything else. Next, in order of decreasing amount, are carbon, oxygen, nitrogen, sulfur, neon, chlorine, argon, and fluorine. Interestingly, it is the oxygen that is most important to the color of the Great Orion Nebula which the eye most easily perceives.

That color is green and it comes from two wavelengths of doubly ionized oxygen. The other colors which one should be able to glimpse in bright diffuse nebulae—usually quite subtle colors unless the nebula is very bright and the telescope quite large—are the red from hydrogen in the HII regions and the blue of reflected starlight in reflection nebulae. In an earlier book I speculated that, as in some aurorae, the violet that some of us glimpse in parts of the Great Orion Nebula could be due to the emission of ionized molecular nitrogen at the extreme violet end of visible light. But it occurs to me that a more likely explanation might be that it is really the purple of the combination of hydrogen red and reflection blue (in the cooler edges of the nebula) that we are really seeing (or even a combination of green and red?).

The goal of this activity is to survey some of the more important and observable diffuse nebulae in the heavens (see Table 15).

Merope Nebula. It takes about a B0 or hotter (O-type) star to make an emission nebula and the Pleiades are not quite hot enough. But long-exposure photographs show them immersed in the blue fog of a reflection nebula. The naked eye can actually glimpse hints of this nebulosity, but a good medium-sized telescope, rich-field or other, is needed to see the details—not the colorful strands of photographs but at least some elongated patches and wisps of pale nebulosity. The most prominent section of the Pleiades nebula extends about 20' S from Merope (the star located at the southeastern corner of the bowl in the tiny dipper shape of the cluster's brightest members). How do you know you are really seeing the Merope Nebula? Walter Scott Houston advises checking the Hyades stars to determine if what you are seeing is caused by condensation (from dew or your body heat). If none of the Hyades stars show the effect, and the Pleaides stars other than Merope show it in much less measure than Merope, and you are essentially seeing the glow extending only south (not in other directions) from Merope, your observation is positive.

California Nebula. At Stellafane (the annual meeting of amateur astronomers in Vermont) in 1977, I heard someone suggest we look for

Table 15
Selected Diffuse Nebulae—1

Nebula	RA h m	Dec. ° '	Constellation	Mag.	Size '
NGC 1435 (Merope Nebula)	03 46	+23 47	Taurus	—	30 × 30
NGC 1499 (California Nebula)	4 01	+36 37	Perseus	—	145 × 40
M1 (NGC 1952) (Crab Nebula)[a]	5 34	+22 01	Taurus	8.2	6 × 4
M42 (NGC 1976) (Great Orion Nebula)	5 35	−05 35	Orion	2.9	66 × 60
NGC 1977	5 35	−04 52	Orion	4.6	20 × 10
M43 (NGC 1982)	5 36	−05 16	Orion	6.9	20 × 15
NGC 2070 (Tarantula Nebula)	5 39	−69 06	Dorado	—	40
NGC 2024	5 41	−02 27	Orion	8	30 × 30
IC 434	5 41	−05 16	Orion	—	60 × 10
M78 (NGC 2068)	5 47	+00 03	Orion	8	8 × 6
NGC 2237 (Rosette Nebula)	6 32	+05 03	Monoceros	—	80 × 60
NGC 2261 (Hubble's Variable Neb.)	6 39	+08 44	Monoceros	10	2
NGC 3372 (Eta Carinae Nebula)	10 44	−59 52	Carina	5.0	120

[a]Supernova remnant.

The RA and declination are in 2000.0 coordinates; the magnitude is approximate; the size is usually photographic and thus for visual purposes quite approximate.

the California Nebula with Dennis diCicco's lightweight 16-inch. Clouds foiled our plans but I was intrigued because I had hardly heard of the California Nebula before and didn't know it was a visual object. Later, I discovered for myself that this large nebula could be faintly glimpsed in a clean dark sky with a 3-inch rich-field telescope. In recent years the use of nebula filters has made the California Nebula (so named for its shape) a more well-known object, with a few intrepid observers even using the filters to glimpse this nebula with the naked eye. It stretches for about maybe 3° or more, just north of Xi Persei, and marks the north edge of the Zeta Persei Association, whose expansion from a common point of origin it seems to share.

Crab Nebula. See Activity 30 for details on this supernova remnant.

The Great Orion Nebula (M42), M43, and NGC 1977. The Great Nebula in Orion is easily the brightest of the diffuse nebulae. In fact, it is easily the most spectacular of all objects beyond our solar system to see

138

in a telescope. There is simply more here to see than in any other deep-sky object. The nebula would be more easily visible to the naked eye if it were not so close to—in fact surrounding—Theta Orionis. But even binoculars begin to show its glowing fanlike wreath well, and the smallest telescopes reveal considerable structure. As we move from about a 4- to a 6-inch telescope, the predominant green color of the nebula becomes increasingly obvious. Contrary to what is often said, red and purple or violet do also become visible to the eye in this nebula, and even with 10-inch or 8-inch telescopes to the trained eye.

How to begin to describe the structure of M42? There is intricacy here that literally can absorb the observer for an hour or more at a time. The brightest part of the nebula is the Huygenian region (named for Christiaan Huygens), surrounding the striking multiple star Theta[1], whose four brightest members form the pattern known as the Trapezium. Photographs usually must overexpose this region in order to show the furthest reaches of the nebula, but the eye can see detail in both this brightest part and some of the faintest wisps or streamers. Indenting part of the Huygenian edge of the nebula is the dark cloud region which Admiral Smyth nicknamed "the Fish's Mouth." Across a gulf of darkness on that side of M42 shines the bright and sizable M43, a section of the Great Orion Nebula which if somewhere else in the sky would be thought one of the heavens' best sights—but which here is often overlooked!

At low power try to trace a full loop of nebulosity (more than a degree in diameter) in M42 and trace from either side the longest extent possible of streamers. At higher power look for stars within the nebulosity (including the fainter members of the Theta[1] system) and in some areas look for prominent mottling.

Our fascination with M42 itself can easily lead us to overlook the rest of the glorious sword of Orion, with its several double and multiple stars and several nebulosities—including the reflection nebula NEC 1977.

Tarantula Nebula. No nebula compares with M42 in apparent grandeur, but the largest and brightest nebula known in the universe is so much larger in true size that it is an admirable sight even though it is 100 times farther away than the Great Orion Nebula. This amazing Tarantula Nebula is visible in the far-south sky in one of the Milky Way's little companion galaxies, the Large Magellanic Cloud (LMC). The nebula is the LMC's most prominent feature, easily visible to the naked eye and in the telescope stretching tendrils far out from the central region and its fine star cluster and brightest star. In 1987, a supernova exploded rather near the Tarantula Nebula and for awhile rivaled it as a naked-eye object.

NGC 2024, IC 434, and M78. The first two of these nebulae are located near Zeta Orionis, the eastern star of Orion's Belt. At least 6 inches of aperture may be needed to see them fairly well, whereas with a 13-inch the former begins to appear as prominent as it does in photographs. Observations of them, or at least of IC 434, are hampered by having Zeta in the field of view. A dark nebula in front of the long strand of IC 434 is the famous Horsehead Nebula, a difficult target (see Activity 31). M78 is a bright reflection nebula, located virtually right on the celestial equator. This often overlooked object actually consists of a main mass and two fainter patches nearby. You can easily see that the nebula is surrounded by areas of dark nebula.

Questions

1. Can you observe the Merope Nebula? How long an extent of it do you see? Do you detect any structure? How much (if any) nebulosity can you be sure of around some of the other Pleiades stars?

2. Can you detect the California Nebula? What optical instrument do you use? What is the view like in other instruments? How much of the nebula's extent do you make out? If you use a nebula filter, what difference does it make in your view?

3. How far out can you trace streamers from the Great Orion Nebula? What colors other than green—if any—do you detect? What do your detailed sketches of the nebula show, and how do they compare with professional photographs of the nebula? Can you find the fainter stars of the Theta[1] system and other dim stars in the nebula? Do you notice any mottling in certain places? What different features or colors of M42 become visible with different magnifications and apertures? Can you also sketch M43 and NGC 1977?

4. How much intricate structure of the Tarantula Nebula and its star cluster can you trace if you are far enough south to observe it? Can you find NGC 2024 and IC 434 near Zeta Orionis? What structure do they show (for instance, the Horsehead Nebula as a seeming indentation in IC 434!)? What shape do you sketch for the main mass of M78 and its auxiliary patches?

29.

Diffuse Nebulae—2

Observe and sketch the diffuse nebulae on our list. Try to discern as much of the Rosette Nebula as you can, with and without a nebula filter. Check the current brightness and structure of Hubble's Variable Nebula, and look for color. If you are far enough south, view the Eta Carinae Nebula, looking for the Keyhole, the clusters, Eta Carinae and its small cloud, and the color and overall structure of this massive object. Observe the Trifid Nebula, sketching its dark channels, observing its multiple star, and looking for color in both its emission area and its dimmer reflection area. Observe the Lagoon Nebula, identifying the bright Hourglass section and 9 Sagittarii and the fine cluster in the Lagoon, and sketching how much or little extent and detail is visible in this nebula with instruments ranging from the naked eye and binoculars up to large telescopes. See how much nebulosity a small telescope can show you with the fine star cluster in M16. Then, use a larger telescope and/or a nebula filter to identify the dark Star-Queen and other detail. Check out the Omega or Swan (M17) nebula so near M16, determining how small a telescope is needed to show its color and how large a telescope is needed to show the glow around the main part. Look for the large North American Nebula with the naked eye, binoculars, and a rich-field telescope. Then, determine how large a telescope is needed to again detect parts of this object and sketch details of its structure.

We continue with our tour of diffuse nebulae from the previous activity. Data are provided in Table 16.

Rosette Nebula. This nebulosity forms a giant delicate wreath in which the cluster NGC 2244 shines. In a rich-field telescope the main stars of the cluster form an odd parallelogram and the elusive nebula may be glimpsed. The Rosette becomes much plainer—no longer the challenging object it was once considered—with the use of a nebula filter. See how much of its full extent you can detect and sketch, then compare this with photographs.

Hubble's Variable Nebula. This nebula looks like a small intense comet with the star R Monocerotis as the comet's nucleus. The nebula

Table 16
Selected Diffuse Nebulae—2

Nebula	RA h m	Dec. ° '	Constellation	Mag.	Size '
NGC 2237 (Rosette Nebula)	6 32	+5 03	Monoceros	—	80 × 60
NGC 2261 (Hubble's Variable (Nebula)	6 39	+8 44	Monoceros	10.0	2
NGC 3372 (Eta Carinae Nebula)	10 44	−60 01	Carina	5.0	120
M20 (NGC 6514) (Trifid Nebula)	18 03	−23 02	Sagittarius	8.5	29 × 27
M8 (NGC 6523) (Lagoon Nebula)	18 04	−24 23	Sagittarius	5	90 × 40
M16 (NGC 6611) (Star-Queen Nebula (Eagle))	18 19	−13 47	Serpens	6.0[a]	35
M17 (NGC 6618) (Omega Nebula)	18 21	−16 11	Sagittarius	7	46 × 37
Veil Nebula[b]					
NGC 6960	20 46	+30 43	Cygnus	—	70 × 6
NGC 6992	20 56	+31 43	Cygnus	—	60 × 8
NGC 7000 (North American Nebula)	20 59	+44 20	Cygnus	—	120 × 100

[a]Magnitude of the associated cluster.   [b]Supernova remnant.

The RA and declination are in 2000.0 coordinates; the magnitude is approximate; the size is usually photographic and thus for visual purposes quite approximate.

and star are usually about tenth magnitude and quite prominent, since the nebula (or its brightest portion) is only about 1′ long. But both the star and nebula are variable, and can fade by several magnitudes. Large telescopes reveal bluish color and details, and make seeing the star easier within its bright background.

Eta Carinae Nebula (or Keyhole Nebula). I have read the opinion that in extremely large telescopes this nebula may be more fascinating than even the Great Orion Nebula. Though much dimmer than M42, this far-southern wonder spreads across a full 2° and contains six star clusters. In *Touring the Universe through Binoculars,* Phil Harrington says that this "monstrous glowing cloud seemingly blossoms forth like a huge ghostly orchid." Indeed, the nebula seems to have a number of separate lobes or petals, separated by dark lanes. The brightest lobe contains a large dark cloud which has been called "the Keyhole," providing the whole nebula with a nickname. The whole bright Keyhole Nebula is better known as the Eta Carinae Nebula because it contains the mysterious novalike star or *slow nova*, Eta Carinae. Though at sixth magnitude or so in recent decades, there is no telling when this star might flare up spectacularly again (see Activity 22 for more details on the star). A cloud less than half an arc-minute wide is concentrated around Eta Carinae and expanding, apparently from the nineteenth-century outburst which brightened the star so greatly. The distance to Eta Carinae still seems to be quite uncertain (is it less than 4,000 or as much as 9,000 light-years away?), so the true brightness of the star and size of the nebula are not precisely known.

Trifid Nebula (M20). This beautiful nebula owes its name to its being split into three sections by dark lanes (see Figure 26). Actually this is just the emission nebula part, a smaller reflection nebula part lying adjacent to the north. Photographs show magnificently the details of the nebula, including the rest of the emission part and the blue of the reflection part. A medium-sized telescope begins to reveal these features clearly and the colors slightly. The Trifid contains a multiple star which suffers only by comparison to Theta^1 Orionis in M42. The Trifid may be associated with the Lagoon Nebula in space if their distances are both a little less than 5,000 light-years, but the Trifid may be 1,500 light-years farther from us. The star cluster M21 is near the Trifid, and the Lagoon Nebula lies only about 1½° to the south-southeast.

Lagoon Nebula (M8). Although the Lagoon Nebula is obvious to the naked eye and binoculars in good skies, it is actually less prominent in regular small telescopes than the Trifid Nebula (presumably because M8 is spread out over a large area). The greater light-gathering power of larger telescopes brings the Lagoon Nebula back into glory. Of course, even a fairly small telescope can show the bisected nebula and the dark "lagoon" (really a channel) which separates the halves, the magnitude 6.0 illuminating star 9 Sagittarii (an O5 spectral class star), and the loose cluster NGC 6530. Near 9 Sagittarii is the brightest part of the nebula which, due to its shape, is often called "the Hourglass." It measures about 30″. A very large amateur telescope (with perhaps a nebula filter) can show the round little dark areas known as Bok globules (clouds about ⅛ of a light-year across which are thought to be stars in their initial stages of formation). Some color begins to become visible in the Lagoon in medium-sized telescopes. The entire Moon-sized nebula and its environs offer hours of study and beauty.

Star-Queen Nebula or Eagle Nebula (M16). None of the early deep-sky observers except perhaps Messier detected anything but the star

Figure 26 The Trifid nebula.

cluster here. Today's better telescopes and our knowledge of where and what to look for mean that an 8-inch or 10-inch can reveal at least faintly some of the details in this nebula which photographs bring out so magnificently. And the use of a nebula filter may work wonders on this object. The names of the nebula are derived from the shape of an area of a dark cloud silhouetted against the bright parts of the nebula. Robert Burnham, Jr., invented the title of "the Star-Queen" for this silhouette and even if his imagining weren't appropriate (I personally think it very much so, and the figure of the queen quite convincing) perhaps we owe it to him to use this title for what seems to be his favorite nebula (that's

144

the kind of repayment for his classic *Celestial Handbook* which I think he would appreciate). M16 is located in Serpens near the intersection with Sagittarius and Scutum, just 3°N of the superb M17. The Star-Queen Nebula is believed to be about 8,000 light-years away, thus in the Sagittarius Arm, the next spiral arm inward from our own.

The Omega (or Swan, Horseshoe, or Checkmark) Nebula (M17). This nebula is only a few degrees south of M16, and only a few degrees north-northeast of M24 (the Small Sagittarius Star Cloud). "Omega Nebula" seems to be the most common name for this object, even though its shape in at least small telescopes is more like a swan or checkmark than a horseshoe or the capital Greek letter omega. M17 is extremely prominent in even rather small telescopes. Interestingly, there seems to be no star cluster or single superluminous star responsible for causing this emission cluster to glow—perhaps the star or stars are hidden in the nebulosity. In a large amateur telescope with a nebula filter, a dim glow becomes visible around the bright part, though apparently not within the curve of the Swan's neck where a dark cloud must reside.

North American Nebula. Max Wolf should probably have named this the North America (not North American) Nebula, but whatever its title the fact remains that it has the rough shape of North America. This nebula lies about 3°E of Deneb, which is no longer thought to be the illuminating star. The nebula is well known from long-exposure photographs, but there may still be popular confusion about its visibility to the naked eye and telescopes. The naked eye has little trouble seeing the nebula as a brightening of the Milky Way in a clear, dark sky. But a little magnification is needed before you can fairly say that you are making out any details of the shape. A small rich-field telescope can provide a fine view, but regular telescopes spread the light of the big nebula too much, reducing its contrast with the dark sky. Of course, with the light-gathering power of much larger telescopes (10-inch and more), and especially with the help of a nebula filter, parts of the nebula can again be glimpsed and perhaps even studied in detail. The Pelican Nebula, a huge "island" off the "Atlantic Coast" of the North American Nebula, is much dimmer, but Phil Harrington says that under excellent conditions giant binoculars can reveal the contrast between the edges of the Pelican and the dark clouds around it, making its outline discernible.

Veil Nebula. See Activity 30 for details on this supernova remnant. There are scores of other patches of diffuse nebula now within the range

145

of large amateur telescopes and nebula filters. When you have put lots of time and attention into observing skillfully the nebulae of this and our previous activity, you may be ready to hunt for these others.

Questions

1. Can you detect any of the Rosette Nebula around the cluster NGC 2244 in a rich-field telescope or regular telescope (if the latter, preferably of at least 6 inches and at low power)? How much of the structure can you sketch (compare it to photographs)? How much does a nebula filter help with this object?

2. How bright is Hubble's Variable Nebula tonight? Can you detect any color in it or any details, and if so with how large a telescope? What changes in its form (if any) do you notice over days, weeks, or months?

3. Can you observe the far-south wonder of the Eta Carinae Nebula? Can you locate the Keyhole dark nebula in it? Can you observe all six of its clusters? How much color do you see in it using a telescope with a certain aperture? Can you observe the small, expanding cloud around Eta Carinae itself?

4. How small a telescope shows the dark channels that divide the Trifid Nebula's emission section into three parts? Can you identify the multiple star that illuminates the Trifid? Can you see red color in the emission part of the Trifid? Can you detect the reflection part of the nebula well enough to glimpse a hint of blue in it (partly in contrast to the emission area's red)?

5. What kind of views of the giant but perhaps too widely spread out Lagoon Nebula can you obtain with rich-field and regular telescopes of various sizes (not to mention the naked eye and binoculars)? Can you sketch the details of the channel that bisects the nebula and the fine star cluster in the nebula? Can you observe 9 Sagittarii and the bright Hourglass nearby? With a large telescope and nebula filter, can you detect any of the nebula's Bok globules? With a rich-field telescope, can you include M8, M20, and the cluster M21 and make a low-power study of them and their environs?

6. How much nebulosity can you make out in M16, the Star-Queen Nebula, with telescopes of various sizes? How much more is revealed with the use of a nebula filter? How much detail can you trace in the dark Star-Queen figure? What details are visible in the prominent Omega or Swan Nebula with telescopes of different sizes? Can you see

a dimmer glow around the main part of the nebula in a large telescope? With a rich-field telescope, can you survey M16 and M17 and their spectacular neighborhood (including M24)?

7. Can you detect the presence of the North American Nebula with the naked eye, its shape with binoculars and a rich-field telescope, and any trace of even its edge with a small regular telescope? How large a telescope is needed to start detecting parts of the nebula? What do your sketches show compared with the famous photographs of the nebula?

30.

Planetary Nebulae

Observe and sketch the planetary nebulae on our list. Look for the structure of the Little Dumbbell, and structure in the Eskimo Nebula and Ghost of Jupiter. Determine how large a telescope you need to detect the eyes of the Owl Nebula, the "ansae" of the Saturn Nebula, the unevenness of the illumination along the band of the Ring Nebula. Note the predominant color of all the planetaries and see if you detect several colors in the Ring Nebula and the Dumbbell Nebula with a fairly large telescope. See if you can blink the Blinking Planetary, and how many central stars you can identify (though it is not always easy to determine which is the correct star). Find out what optical instruments bring you your best views of the giant Helix Nebula. Study and sketch in great detail the magnificent forms of the Ring Nebula and the Dumbbell Nebula.

Planetary nebulae (see Table 17) have nothing in particular to do with planets. The name arose because the appearance of many of these clouds of gas resembles the blue–green little disks of the planets Uranus and Neptune in the telescope.

At the start of Activity 28, I wrote that these *planetaries* are the clouds of gas expelled by dying stars. But exactly how close to dying the stars are, and how peacefully the nebula is produced, and why it is produced, and how long planetary nebulae last are all questions that

Table 17
Selected Planetary Nebulae

Nebula	RA h m	Dec. ° '	Constellation	Mag. C. Star	Mag. Neb.	Size
NGC 246	00 47	− 11 53	Cetus	12	8.5	240 × 210
M76 (NGC 650-1) (Little Dumbbell Nebula)	01 42	+ 51 34	Perseus	16–17	12?	120 × 60
NGC 2392 (Eskimo Nebula)	07 29	+ 20 55	Gemini	10	8.3	40
NGC 3132 (Eight-Burst Nebula)	10 08	− 40 26	Vela (−Antlia border)	9–10	8.2	84 × 53
NGC 3242 (The Ghost of Jupiter)	10 25	− 18 38	Hydra	11.5	8	40
M97 (NGC 3587) (Owl Nebula)	11 15	+ 55 01	Ursa Major	14	11	150
NGC 3918 (the Blue Planetary)	11 50	− 57 11	Centaurus	?	8	12
NGC 6210	16 45	+ 23 49	Hercules	12.5	9	14
NGC 6543	17 59	+ 66 38	Draco	10	8.6	22 × 16
M57 (NGC 6720) (Ring Nebula)	18 54	+ 33 02	Lyra	14–17 (var.?)	9	70 × 150
NGC 6826 (the Blinking Planetary)	19 45	+ 50 31	Cygnus	11	9	25
M27 (NGC 6853) (Dumbbell Nebula)	20 00	+ 22 43	Vulpecula	13.5	8.1	480 × 240
NGC 7009 (Saturn Nebula)	21 04	− 11 22	Aquarius	12	8.4	26
NGC 7293 (Helix Nebula)	22 30	− 20 48	Aquarius	13	6.5	900 × 720
NGC 7662	23 26	+ 42 33	Andromeda	13	8.5	30

The RA and declination are in 2000.0 coordinates; the magnitudes may be approximate; the size (given in arc-seconds) is usually photographic and thus for visual purposes quite approximate.

remain controversial. We now believe that the planetaries are probably not produced by novae, the lesser star explosions that flare up fairly commonly in our galaxy. But how does a planetary nebula form?

The best we can do is review some of the facts about planetary nebulae and the stars that have made them—for the latter are generally still quite detectable, each planetary having its own *central star*.

The central stars are the hottest suns known, with surface temperatures of many reaching 100,000 K and higher, and therefore emitting powerful ultraviolet radiation which causes the gas of the planetaries to fluoresce green or blue with sometimes very great intensity. Other wavelengths of light are produced but are not seen visually because they are overwhelmed by the blue–green except in a few prominent nebulae. The true size of the nebula is usually about 1 light-year or less and although the typical shape is basically spherical, there is great diversity of structures within that basic form and some planetaries that at least seem to depart radically from sphericity—at any rate, as seen from our viewing angle and in the bright parts that we can behold.

Some of the lesser planetaries have such small apparent size that you cannot successfully scan for them with low power—without more magnification, they are indistinguishable from stars. A solution used to be to use a diffraction grating to detect the difference between stars and planetary nebula, but now the same purpose can be served more easily by an appropriate nebula filter. In any case, the planetary nebulae in our present survey are all sufficiently bright or large to make identification of them easy enough.

NGC 246. NGC 246 is a large, ghostly, and little-known planetary in Cetus. Its surface brightness dictates low magnification. Better save this one for after you have observed a dozen or so other planetary nebulae!

The Little Dumbbell Nebula. The name is derived from the shape, which slightly resembles that of the brighter, larger, more famous Dumbbell Nebula, M27 (see below). This smaller object, M76, is reputed to be the faintest object in the Messier Catalogue at about magnitude 12—but most observers find it considerably brighter. The Little Dumbbell is nevertheless not an easy object for small telescopes unless the sky is dark—as it was for my 4¼-inch when I picked this object up (with considerable satisfaction) as a teenager making the Messier rounds. In a 8-inch or larger telescope, the structure of this object is fascinating.

Eskimo Nebula. This is a fairly small but quite bright and therefore very high-surface-brightness object. Planetaries like this can take very high magnifications and still show more structure. Photographs portray an Eskimo face surrounded by a fur-lined hood. In a 16-inch the many strange details in this nebula were so bright and intense and blue that it looked like a special effect from a science-fiction movie!

Eight-Burst Nebula. This object lies right on the border of Vela and Antlia, but is usually listed with the former. It is really too far south for a good view for people who live around 40°N, but it is so intriguing that northerners should try anyway. Fairly large and certainly bright, this nebula has structure to divulge to large telescopes, but perhaps even more interesting is the unusual brightness—about magnitude 9—of its central star.

The Ghost of Jupiter. This object is not very southerly and is conveniently placed less than 2°S of Mu Hydrae—why hasn't it been observed more often? The nebula and its central star are rather bright, but it is the odd structure in this nebula which makes it most fascinating, though requiring a fairly large telescope (say, 10-inch) to see well. The dimensions given in Table 17 are only those of the remarkable eye-shaped brighter part of the nebula. Surrounding this is a fainter spherical shell which is about 40″ in diameter—indeed, about the average size of Jupiter.

Owl Nebula. The Owl Nebula is dim, but an interesting object for several reasons. First of all, its location is very near the bowl of the Big Dipper, and the fairly faint galaxy M108 is right on the way from Beta Ursae Majoris to the Owl. Second, the Owl is large, and telescopes smaller than a 10-inch can provide glimpses of the dark spots which look like eyes and give the nebula its name. In large amateur telescopes other structures, incuding one or two other spots (closer to the nebula's edge), become visible. The Owl is dim but can be found and enjoyed even in 4-inch telescopes.

The Blue Planetary. This far-south object is unusually bright for its being so small (compared to the size of the other bright planetaries).

NGC 6210 and NGC 6543. These two objects for a Northern Hemisphere summer night are a little larger and a little dimmer than the Blue Planetary, but still have high surface brightness. The latter lies almost right at the north ecliptic pole and has an unusually bright central star.

Ring Nebula (see Figure 27). This is the most famous of all planetary nebulae. Its brightness and especially its size are good, but it is the splendid eerie smoke-ring shape and favorable location which have made this object so popular. The location is favorable not only in the sense of being easy to find but also in presenting the nebula high in the sky for much of the world's population. The Ring Nebula is slightly less than half the distance from Beta to Gamma Lyrae. Even scanning at fairly low magnification you come upon it, a glowing little disk suspended well within a triangle of faint stars. A 4-inch telescope and more magnification show the hole in the middle of the disk and begin to reveal the blue–green color. An 8- or 10-inch telescope can use surprisingly high magnification and start showing that the ring is by no means evenly illuminated all around and that the hole is not entirely dark.

Artist Doug Myers and I discovered a few years ago that a 13-inch— later, and more marginally, even a 10-inch—could in moments of good "seeing" show subtle hints of three colors in the nebula: blue–green on the inside edge, yellow in the middle of the ring, and red on the outer edge. Another challenge for Ring Nebula observers is the famous central

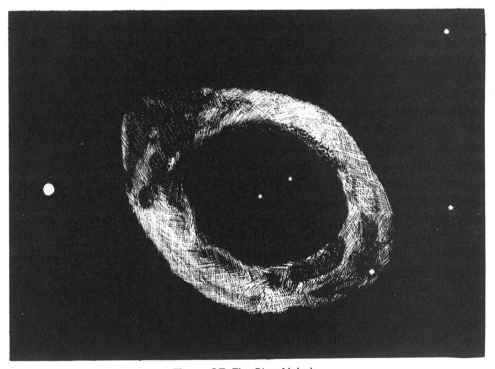

Figure 27 The Ring Nebula.

star. Walter Scott Houston was able to see this with less than a giant telescope even before the replacement of one of his eye lenses enabled him through that eye to see the star much more easily—because the new lens didn't block out as much ultraviolet. There has been controversy over whether this central star is variable in brightness. Certainly, different transparency and "seeing" conditions vary the visibility of any faint star in the neighborhood of a rather bright nebula. But perhaps some of the discrepancies result from differences in people's abilities to see well in the violet end of the spectrum. Many older people report planetaries green that younger observers report blue—surely due to the fact that the yellowing of the eyes' lenses as we age begins to block out more and more of the violet-end light.

The Ring Nebula is believed to lie somewhat more than 1,000 light-years away, which means that the true size of the visible structure is about half a light-year. Planetaries are tremendously more short-lived than most celestial objects. Evidence indicates that the Ring Nebula may be roughly 20,000 years old, perhaps the average age of these objects.

The Blinking Planetary. Another strange optical effect involves planetaries whose central star is nearly as bright as they are. If the observer gazes right at the central star, the nebula may appear to vanish, but then when averted vision (see the Telescopes, Observing Conditions, and Observing Techniques section) is used, the whole nebula springs back into view. The fairly bright, fairly small planetary nebula NGC 6826 in Cygnus is the classic test case for this technique. By the observer rapidly switching from direct to averted vision repeatedly, the nebula can appear to blink on and off.

Dumbbell Nebula. This is the most prominent of all planetaries, an object in which great size and great brightness are combined in proper measure to produce a spectacular sight. The nebula has more the shape of an apple core, especially in small telescopes. It is fascinating to study the object's structure and as larger telescopes are used to behold ever more light in what John Herschel called "the lateral concavities" (the eaten part of the apple). In the largest amateur telescopes, the initial shape is merely one superimposed with great brightness upon a full ellipse of light. Even with small telescopes, there is much to sketch in this object, not least of all the locations of stars around and in it. The 13.5 magnitude central star requires a rather large amateur telescope to glimpse, however. Doug Myers and I have observed several colors in the Dumbbell with a 13-inch in moments of good "seeing." Burnham says that the very slight measured expansion of the Dumbbell Nebula suggests that it may be older than most planetaries, perhaps 48,000 years old (but I've also seen sources which attributed extreme youth to this nebula). The Dumbbell is probably a little less than 1,000 light-years away, with a true size of about 2½ light-years—very large for a planetary.

Saturn Nebula. This bright planetary is on the small side and thus has very high surface brightness. Identifying it at low power is not a cinch for novices, but fortunately it is located only about 1°W of Nu Aquarii, so if you can find the right star you will find the right nebula. The name of the nebula derives from its possessing projections to either side which cover a span very similar to that of Saturn's rings. Some books maintain that these *ansae* (ring projections) are not seen in telescopes, but that is nonsense. Burnham says that the ansae may be glimpsed in a good 10-inch telescope. Steve Albers and I have glimpsed them under excellent conditions in his superb 6-inch Newtonian. This nebula may be a good test of violet-end sensitivity—do you see it as blue or green?

Helix Nebula. The largest and almost certainly the closest of the planetary nebulae, this object appears about half the apparent size of the Moon—but has such a low surface brightness that it may not appear at all in a regular amateur telescope. The Helix is best seen in dark skies with good binoculars or a rich-field telescope. The ring shape (really two rings offset to suggest the imagined helix) is certainly hard to discern visually. This is another object for which nebula filters should do wonders. The total magnitude of the Helix Nebula is about 6.5, suggesting that it might be spotted with the naked eye under excellent conditions.

NGC 7662. NGC 7662 is bright and fairly small. One large-telescope observer notes that with an aperture of over 16 inches the central area of this nebula appears pinkish.

Questions

1. How large a telescope is needed to see the dumbbell structure of M76? How much structure can you detect within the intense Eskimo Nebula? Can you see both the bright eye and the outer shell of the Ghost of Jupiter? Can you detect the dark eyes of the Owl Nebula?

2. At what magnification and aperture size does the hole in the Ring Nebula become apparent? The unevenness of illumination around its

band? The illumination inside the hole? Colors other than the standard blue–green?

3. How large a telescope is needed to see the "lateral concavities" of the Dumbbell Nebula begin to fill in with light? What colors can you see in the Dumbbell with various size telescopes? How detailed a sketch can you make of this nebula and the stars around and in it?

4. Can you blink the Blinking Planetary? What other central stars can you identify? How large a telescope is needed to see the "ansae" of the Saturn Nebula? With what kinds of optical instruments do you see the Helix Nebula best (and with what kinds don't you see it at all!)? How much do nebula filters help the visibility of the Helix? How much do they help the visibility of other planetaries?

31.

Supernova Remnants and Dark Nebulae

View the supernova remnants known as the Crab Nebula and the Veil Nebula. Determine how large a telescope is required to show an uneven edge to the Crab or details of its overall shape. Try to detect any of the filaments of the Crab. Look for the two most observable parts of the Veil Nebula with various optical instruments, noting its degree of visibility. Try to glimpse and sketch some of the filaments in the Veil. In far-south skies, study details of the edge and interior of the Coal Sack. Try to detect the Horsehead Nebula (and, of course, sketch what you see) with various telescopes. Study the Pipe Nebula, the Snake Nebula, the Northern Coal Sack, and the dark nebulae near M11.

For our final activity devoted entirely to nebulae, I will lump together two nebular loose ends: the supernova remnants and the dark nebulae.

Supernovae are the greatest explosions in the universe after the Big Bang itself—and unlike the Big Bang, there is no doubt that supernovae have occurred. One star may outshine a hundred million, even a billion average stars, perhaps the entire galaxy it is in. In Activity 11, we saw the causes that led massive stars to go suprenova. I might here add that the supernovae transmutation of simpler elements into heavier ones may have made the composition of our Sun and Earth—and life itself—possible.

Unfortunately, we cannot be assured of a supernova in our own galaxy for us to observe anytime soon—neither this year nor even in a lifetime (the last supernova in our galaxy visible to us occurred in 1604!). Our alternative is to look at the two most prominent examples of supernova remnants (SNR) in our heavens.

The Crab Nebula is the first object on Charles Messier's list. This is the cloud that has been produced by a supernova which was seen to flare up in Taurus in the year 1054. Its brightness exceeded that of Venus for a while when it was observed in broad daylight for 23 days in China. The Crab Nebula remains one of the few most important objects of professional astronomical study, as does the pulsar that the Crab supernova formed.

But the Crab is also a fascinating sight in amateur telescopes. Novice observers used to seeing the long-exposure photographs and to hearing about the importance of the Crab Nebula may at first be disappointed that the glow of the object seems rather amorphous and featureless in small telescopes. But a telescope of 8 or 10 inches can begin to change all that. In a good 10-inch, the edge of the Crab takes on a marvelously scalloped appearance and the observer catches glimpses of the famous filaments that run through the nebula. The observer begins to see why Lord Rosse in the nineteenth century compared the filaments to the legs of a crab, giving rise to the name.

M1 is conveniently located just over 1°NW of Zeta Tauri, the more southerly and dimmer horn tip of Taurus the Bull. It is thought to be about 6,300 light-years away.

The Veil Nebula is the name which I believe is now often given to not just NGC 6960 but to all of the Cygnus Loop of nebulosity. The name was originally the Bridal Veil nebula, and in Europe apparently it is still often called the Cirrus nebula. The loop has two sections that are commonly tried for by amateur observers, NGC 6960 (another name for this section besides Veil: Network Nebula) and NGC 6992 (sometimes called the Filamentary Nebula). There are actually other strands in the roughly 3° wide "bubble" that we trace on photos as a loop, but let's concentrate on those most prominent two. NGC 6960 (see Figure 28) is easiest to find because it runs right past the fourth-magnitude star 52 Cygni. It is about a degree long. Roughly 2½° to the east-northeast is NGC 6962, the easier of the two sections to see (if you locate the correct field of view). It is perhaps more than a degree long. Both of these

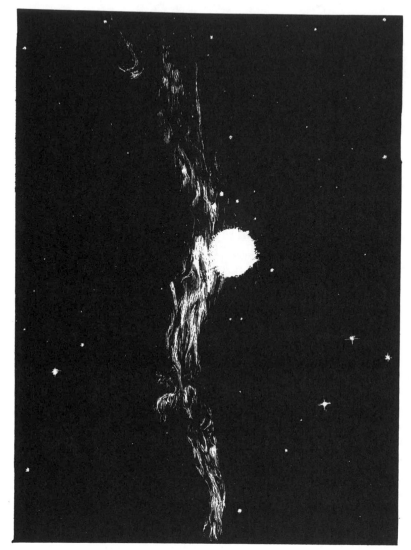

Figure 28 Part of the Veil nebula.

curved clouds can be detected with 7 × 50 binoculars or a similar
finderscope under excellent conditions. The further goal, however, is to
see them at greater magnification in a telescope where the beautiful thin
filaments that structure these clouds might be glimpsed. You might need
an 8-inch to suspect the filaments, and a larger telescope to start seeing
them well. With amateur telescopes of 20 inches or more, the view may
begin to approach that of the best photographs, though the red, white,
and blue of the filaments presumably remain subtle at best.

156

What is the Veil Nebula? There is little doubt that it is the remnant of a supernova explosion that must have occurred very roughly 30,000 to 40,000 years ago. But there are tremendous unanswered questions. Where is the star that exploded? Why are the delicate filaments visible in this nebula—for that matter, what are they, thin sheets of gas seen edge-on? The entire matter of why some supernovae leave spectacular remnants and others leave little if any capable of being detected by us is troublesome. But if the Veil Nebula vexes us, its beauty also stirs us.

From the glowing remnants of star explosions unimaginably bright, we now turn to the *dark nebulae*. We should look for "all that's best of dark and light" in the heavens, but extremely prominent dark nebulae are not very common. Until recent years, most amateur astronomers had heard of just a few examples, but more have been publicized and even suggested for observation with binoculars by Phil Harrington in his excellent and important book *Touring the Universe through Binoculars* (see the Sources of Information).

The most famous dark nebulae, other than the great naked-eye Rift splitting the Milky Way from Cygnus to Scorpius, are the Coal Sack and the Horsehead Nebula.

The Coal Sack is a huge naked-eye cloud, measuring 7° by 5°. It is the nearest of the dark nebulae, and if it is only 500 light-years distant, its true diameter must be about 60 light-years. The Southern Cross stands just beside it, and just north of it lies the splendid Kappa Crucis cluster. But within its large expanse only two dim stars brighter than the typical naked-eye limit may be glimpsed—and these near its edges. Low-magnification study on excellent nights reveals a beautiful structure of faint star patternings, however.

The Horsehead Nebula is a tiny and strictly telescopic object. Lying perhaps 1,200 light-years away, it is one of the most familiar photographic subjects in astronomy books and magazines, but its visual identification is difficult. Walter Scott Houston, Clyde Tombaugh, and Steve Albers have succeeded with 5- and 6-inch telescopes, but for most of us considerably larger telescopes will be needed. Figure 29 shows how to find the nebula. Note that you must be able to see the nebula IC 434 first if you are to see the form of the Horsehead silhouetted against it. Note also that the size of the Horsehead is surprisingly small—the distance from Zeta Orionis, eastern star of the Belt to it is only half a degree. Zeta must, of course, be kept out of the field of view.

What other prominent dark nebulae can be sought? There are the dark nebulae nearly surrounding and quite near to M11 (see Activity 25). There is the large Northern Coal Sack, just south of Deneb. Then there is the Pipe Nebula, which has a 5° long stem and 2° wide bowl,

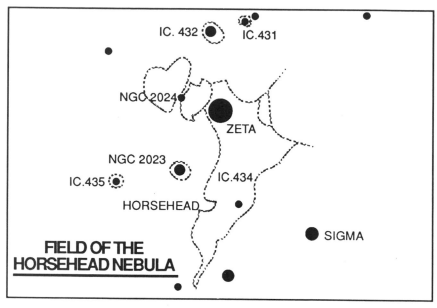

Figure 29 Map for locating the Horsehead Nebula.

located in Ophiuchus. The bowl is found at 17h33^m and $-26°$. The stem extends west from this. The Pipe Nebula can be glimpsed with the naked eye on good nights, but also rewards detailed telescopic observation. A much smaller dark nebula is the 30′ long Snake Nebula found at 17^{h}23^m and $-23°28′$.

Questions

1. Does your telescope show you an uneven edge to the Crab Nebula, or uneven light intensity across its extent? Can you detect any of the filaments, or any color?

2. With what optical instruments can you detect the two important parts of the Veil Nebula? How large a telescope do you need to detect the Veil's filaments? How do your sketches of the Veil with a fairly large or very large telescope compare to photographs of the nebula?

3. If you are far south, can you study details of faint patterns of stars in the Coal Sack, or details of its edges? Can you spot the Horsehead Nebula, and if so with what kind of telescope under what conditions? Can you observe the details of the Pipe Nebula and the Snake Nebula, the Northern Coal Sack, and the dark nebulae near M11?

GALAXIES AND QUASARS

32.

Galaxies—General Observations and Types

Learn the types of galaxies and observe examples of each type using our list. Sketch each galaxy carefully, determining if possible what limitations in your ability to see features are caused by the size of your telescope and what limitations are a result of the tilt of the galaxy itself. Observe M58 to see if you can detect a slight bar in it which is like the one that our Milky Way may have.

In the first section of this book, we studied the differnt kinds of stars, including those specialties (very common specialties) known as double stars and variable stars. In the second section, we examined the clusters, associations, and other groupings in which stars may be organized—and the various kinds of nebulae from which they are born and to which they give rise when they die.

Now we move on to a larger level of organization in the universe, objects tremendously more vast and more distant. Before, we dealt with objects dozens or hundreds or thousands of light-years away. Now the objects will be millions or even billions of light-years distant—yet still, I hasten to add, often within the range of backyard telescopes! Before, virtually everything we talked about was part of the Milky Way—as we ourselves are. But now we are leaving the Milky Way to explore vast systems of stars and nebulae that are the kin of our Milky Way: the galaxies.

The galaxies come in three most basic types: spiral, elliptical, and irregular.

The *ellipticals* (symbolized by the letter E) resemble the central bulges of spiral galaxies in consisting only of Population II stars (and little interstellar gas or dust), the ancient stars that we also find in globular clusters here in the Milky Way. Indeed, elliptical galaxies remind us of superglobular clusters. Many elliptical galaxies are small compared to the larger spiral galaxies, but a few are truly awesome giants.

The *irregulars* (I or Irr) resemble the collections of star clouds and nebulae (both bright and dark) that we find in the arms of spiral galaxies. Most of the irregulars are rather formless, but some may begin to show hints of spiral structure.

160

The *spirals* (S) have a central bulge filled with Population II stars, but also spiral arms filled with Population I stars (including blue giants) and lots of gas and dust. There are spirals in which the arms do not curve outward from a central point as in the "normal spirals." These fairly common *barred spirals* (SB) seem to have the arms radiating out from the ends of a long central bar-shaped formation of stars.

There is a special class of unusual *lenticular* galaxies which seem to be intermediate in type between spiral and elliptical galaxies, and receive the designation SO.

There is further classification of galaxies according to their structure (see Figure 30).

Ellipticals are classed from E0, E1 . . . E7 in order of increasing flattening (in other words, E0 galaxies are the most spherical, E7 the most highly elliptical). An E7 galaxy has a length-to-width ratio of 1.7 to 1. Spirals are classed as Sa, Sb, and Sc, depending on how tightly coiled the spiral arms are—Sa is the most tight, Sc is the least tight. This factor is also used with barred spirals, which receive designations SBa, SBb, or SBc. Irregulars generally don't have enough structure to permit any more detailed structural classification (they sometimes have I or II added

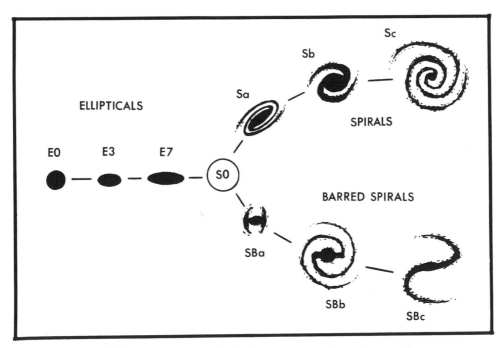

Figure 30 Diagram of types of galaxies (no suggestion of an evolutionary scheme is intended).

161

to their "Irr" to indicate whether they contain predominantly Population I or II stars—the latter presumably being usually the case).

In a number of cases, pluses and minuses and various other letters are actually added as suffixes or prefixes to these galaxy class designations. A class Sd—galaxies with a very concentrated center and weak spiral arms—is sometimes used. In addition, there may be considerable controversy as to which class a particular galaxy belongs. After all, in the case of spirals, if we see them from a nearly edge-on position it is difficult to determine how tightly the arms are coiled. Also, some galaxies have strange shapes that seem to be the result of some kind of explosion or the result of the collision of two galaxies (an event in which one galaxy generally slides right through the other—but not without distortions in the two galaxies' structures which can produce strange and lasting results). Certain galaxies are simply given the designation P to denote that they are peculiar.

But the unusual cases are not as important to us in our context as understanding and recognizing the major standard types. And questions about the odd galaxies are likely to arise only after another question which quickly comes to mind when you hear about spirals, ellipticals, and irregulars: Do these galaxy types represent different stages in the life of any galaxy? The answer seems to be No. We do not think that ellipticals become spirals, or vice versa. There is speculation, however, about whether spirals may tighten as they age.

To understand galaxies better, we should go out and look at them. The next two activities will be a tour of some of the brightest and most interesting galaxies. But our present activity is devoted to observing examples of each of the galaxy types. Many of the representative galaxies are ones we will encounter on our tour. But for those which are not, Table 18 provides the positional and other data.

I have attempted to select the brightest and largest galaxies possible, and in each case to provide examples for northerners and southerners, and even for different times of the year. But there are surprisingly few bright examples of some of these classes. Another fly in the ointment is the angle at which we see these galaxies. It would be wonderful if there were more galaxies we could view face-on. In reality, of course, we see them at all angles. Some of the galaxies I have selected will certainly not give you a picture-perfect illustration of their class. And even though selected for brightness and size many of these galaxies will require at least a medium-sized (say 8-inch) telescope to show their details well (indeed, if you have a small telescope, you may want to try only—or at least start with only—the brightest galaxies discussed in our next two activities).

Table 18
Galaxy Types and Examples

Galaxy Type	RA h	m	Dec. °	'	Constellation	Mag.	Size '
Elliptical galaxies							
E0—NGC 5846	15	06	+01	36	Virgo	11.4	3 × 3
E1—M87[a] (sometimes classified E0), M105[a]							
E2—M32[a]							
E3—M86	12	26	+12	57	Virgo	9.2	7 × 5
E4—M49[a]							
E5—NGC 4125[b]	12	08	+65	11	Draco	9.8	5 × 3
NGC 5253	13	40	−31	39	Centaurus	10.5	4 × 2
E6—M110[a]							
E7—NGC 4350	12	24	+16	42	Coma Berenices	11.1	3 × 1
S0 galaxies (intermediate between elliptical and spiral)							
S0—NGC 4429	12	27	+11	07	Virgo	10.2	5.5 × 2.6
Centaurus A[a]							
Spiral galaxies (normal spirals)							
Sa—NGC 4699	12	49	−08	40	Virgo	9.6	3.5 × 2.7
NGC 7213	22	09	−47	10	Grus	10.4	1.9 × 1.8
Sb—M31,[a] M81,[a] M104[a]							
Sc—M33,[a] M51,[a] M83,[a] M101[a]							
Spiral galaxies (barred spirals)							
SBa—NGC 2655	08	56	+78	13	Camelopardalis	10.1	5 × 4
NGC 4314	12	23	+29	53	Coma Berenices	10.5	8 × 4
SBb—NGC 1097	02	46	−30	17	Fornax	9.3	9 × 6
NGC 1300	03	20	−19	25	Eridanus	10.4	6.5 × 4.3
M95[a]							
NGC 4725	12	50	+25	30	Coma Berenices	9.2	11 × 8
SBc—NGC 925[c]	02	27	+33	35	Triangulum	10.0	10 × 6
NGC 1187	03	03	−22	32	Eridanus	10.9	5 × 4
NGC 4945	13	05	−49	28	Centaurus	9	20 × 4
Irregular galaxies							
Irr—Small Magellanic Cloud[a, d]							
Large Magellanic Cloud[a, d]							
NGC 4449	12	28	+44	06	Canes Venatici	9.4	5 × 4

[a]See Table 19 or 20 for statistics and Activity 33 or 34 for text discussion.

[b]Sometimes designated E5p (peculiar).

[c]Sometimes designated Sb/c.

[d]May show incipient spiral structure.

The RA and declination are in 2000.0 coordinates; the magnitude is visual but approximate; the size is usually photographic and thus for visual purposes quite approximate.

Despite these qualifications, I feel this tour of the galaxy types is a very valuable one. If nothing else, observing these galaxies in the context of noting their types will get you in the habit of inquiring about the physical nature underlying the appearances you see—and also help acquaint you closely with a number of very different galaxies.

One final question needs to be asked: What exact type of spiral galaxy is our own Milky Way galaxy? That is a difficult question, located as we are in one of the spiral arms with our view of the galaxy's center (and much else of it) hidden in visual wavelengths behind thousands of light-years of gas and dust. But studies of our galaxy's structure at radio, infrared, and other wavelengths offer some tantalizing clues. A pair of articles in the May 1990 issue of *Sky & Telescope* discusses two possibilities. One team of researchers thinks that our galaxy has a more compact and brighter central bulge than previously believed, more so than M31 (the Great Galaxy in Andromeda) does, for instance. They judge that the Milky Way should be classed as a normal spiral of type Sb or tending toward Sc ("Sbc"). Galaxy NGC 4565 in Coma Berenices might be what our galaxy would look like if seen from an edge-on view. However, another team of researchers finds evidence that the Milky Way may be a barred spiral—which, if true, would have several interesting repercussions in our thinking about our galaxy and our Sun's orbit in it. This second team of researchers suggests that the Milky Way's bar is a weak one. A galaxy of similar type would be M58 in Virgo.

Questions

1. How many of the different types of galaxies can you observe? How detailed can you make your sketches of them? In which galaxies is faintness a problem for making-out features with a telescope of the size you are using? In which galaxies is the tilt of the object the problem?

2. In instances where several galaxies are suggested per type, what similarities and what differences do you find between the individual galaxies?

3. Can you observe M58 (at 12^{h}38^m, +11° 49′, and magnitude 9.8) and note any gentle bar in it like our Milky Way may have (M58 has previously been classified as an Sb not an SBb galaxy)?

33.

Selected Galaxies—1

Observe the galaxies on our list, sketching each one. View the two brightest Sculptor galaxies, taking into account how clear and dark your sky is, if you are a northern observer. Study the fuller extent of the Great Andromeda Galaxy with the naked eye, binoculars, and a rich-field telescope, then use a regular telescope for closer views of its dust lanes, starlike nucleus, companions M32 and M110, its star clouds, and even its globular clusters (depending on the size of your telescope). If you are observing from a southerly position, study all the incredible telescopic riches of the Magellanic Clouds. Test the visibility of M33 with different optical instruments, and with medium-to-large telescopes study its component NGC 604 and other structure of its spiral arms. View the Seyfert galaxy M77, paying special attention to its central region. Observe and contrast the spectacular galaxy pair M81 and M82, looking for the strange mottling in M82 especially if you have a fairly large telescope.

The text of the previous activity is sufficient preparatory reading for a tour of selected bright or interesting galaxies. Let us begin our journies across millions of light-years of space—to catch glimpses of these vast systems as they were when the light set out from them millions of years ago. Data are given in Table 19.

NGC 55. One of the two bright Sculptor galaxies, this object is unfortunately quite low in the sky for observers around 40°N. It is seen nearly edge-on and extends about 25′ as seen in the telescope. NGC 55 may be either a loose barred-spiral or an irregular galaxy. It lies not far beyond our Local Group of galaxies, at a distance of about 8 million light-years. Burnham says that a good 10-inch can begin to show mottling in this galaxy—but northerners will, of course, have to pick a very clear, steady night.

M31 (Great Galaxy in Andromeda), M32, and M110. M31 (see Figure 31) is the largest member of our Local Group, the brightest galaxy visible to most Northern Hemisphere viewers, and one of the finest of all sights in amateur telescopes. The naked eye sees it as an elongated smudge of light. I agree with Walter Scott Houston that the

Table 19
Selected Galaxies—1

Galaxy	RA h m	Dec. ° ′	Constellation	Mag.	Size ′	Type
NGC 55	00 15	−39 11	Sculptor	8	32 × 6	SBm
M110 (NGC 205)	00 40	+41 41	Andromeda	8.0	17	E6
M32 (NGC 221)	00 43	+40 52	Andromeda	8.2	8 × 6	E2
M31 (NGC 224) (Andromeda Galaxy)	00 43	+41 16	Andromeda	3.5	160 × 40[a]	Sb
NGC 253	00 48	−25 17	Sculptor	7.1	22 × 6	Scp
Small Magellanic Cloud	00 53	−72 50	Tucana	2.3	280 × 160	Irr[b]
M33 (NGC 598) (Pinwheel galaxy)	01 34	+30 39	Triangulum	6.3	60 × 35	Sc
M77 (NGC 1068)	02 43	−00 01	Cetus	8.9	6 × 5	Sbp
Large Magellanic Cloud	05 24	−69 45	Dorado	0.1	650 × 550	Irr[b]
M81 (NGC 3031)	09 56	+69 04	Ursa Major	7.0	26 × 14	Sb
M82 (NGC 3034)	09 56	+69 41	Ursa Major	8.4	11 × 5	P

[a]Visual size of M31 can be much greater (see text).

[b]Both of the Magellanic Clouds seem to show signs of incipient spiral structure.

The RA and declination are in 2000.0 coordinates; the magnitude is visual but approximate; the size is usually photographic and thus for visual purposes quite approximate.

naked eye can perceive the greatest extent of M31, sometimes tracing it out for up to 5°. Good binoculars or a rich-field telescope give superb views of several degrees of the galaxy, but regular telescopes will see only the brighter, more central region—in blazing brightness and sometimes remarkable detail. A 6-inch or 8-inch telescope can begin to show the dust lanes in this gently tilted spiral and may reveal the starlike nucleus. Larger telescopes bring out these features in terrific splendor and can be used to spot not just star clouds but even globular clusters in this, a galaxy over 2 million light-years away. Pulling back a bit to low magnification—and smaller aperture if you wish (or have no choice)—you can study the grand sight of M31 with its two closest companion galaxies, M32 and M110 (the latter still sometimes known as NGC 205 to those who do not accept it as being a Messier object). M32 is smaller, but therefore appears brighter, than M110. It is a rounder elliptical galaxy, and appears much closer to M31. Several other companions much farther from M31 in the sky can be observed in amateur telescopes (for details on them, see *Burnham's Celestial Handbook*).

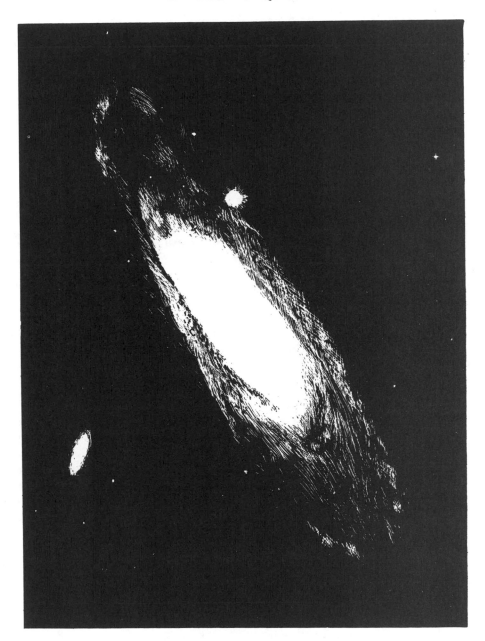

Figure 31 M31, the Great Galaxy in Andromeda.

NGC 253. NGC 253 in Sculptor is generally regarded as a kind of southern celestial hemisphere M31, and it is indeed a large and bright spiral. Lying much farther north than NGC 55, this galaxy is an impressive sight even to northerners. Mottling becomes easily visible in 8-inch and 10-inch telescopes. The galaxy lies a 7½° scramble south from bright Beta Ceti. Like NGC 55, this is one of the closest galaxies beyond our Local Group.

The Small Magellanic Cloud (SMC). This is one of the two prominent naked-eye companion galaxies of our own Milky Way which adorn the far-south skies. Though much the inferior of the LMC (see below), and given competition by the huge Milky Way globular cluster 47 Tucanae near it in the sky, the SMC (or Nubecula Minor) appears as a beautiful cloud about 4° by 3° across. A telescope reveals a number of star clouds and clusters in this apparently irregular galaxy less than 200,000 light-years away.

M33. The famous line about this galaxy is that it is sometimes easier to see in binoculars than in a 10-inch. In reality, I think no skilled observer in dark skies will be unable to find or see it with a medium-sized telescope. The naked-eye visibility of M33 is a mark of very good sky conditions, but its sixth-magnitude glow is admittedly spread across most of a degree and that suggests low surface brightness. M33 is probably a little farther than M31, but it is the closest example of an Sc galaxy and its sloppy arms are clumpy with star clouds. The easiest such component of the arms to see is NGC 604, about 10′ to the northeast of the galaxy's bright and condensed but far-from-stellar center. In true dimensions, NGC 604 is vastly larger than our galaxy's Orion Nebula, and it is even about half the size of the Tarantula Nebula. In medium-sized telescopes, NGC 604 will seem to be an object distinct from the visible main mass of the galaxy. With an 8-inch or larger telescope, much time can be spent sketching the various bright patches in the galaxy—for later comparison with photographs.

M77. M77 is the brightest of the Seyfert galaxies—galaxies with abnormally bright centers. There is speculation that the famous *quasars* may be more extreme versions of Seyfert galaxies. Perhaps a black hole in the center is causing the outpouring of tremendous energy. M77 is only 1°SE of Delta Ceti and is seen nearly face-on. Burnham says that telescopes as small as a 4-inch can sometimes just reveal the clumpiness which is an outstanding feature of this galaxy's spiral arms.

168

The Large Magellanic Cloud (LMC). This spectacular companion of the Milky Way galaxy appears as a bright patch roughly 10° across and about 22° from the SMC in our far-south sky. How lucky we are to have such a bright and varied companion just 170,000 light-years away. The brightest stars known are the supergiants of the LMC. The greatest nebula known in all the universe is the Tarantula Nebula which glows as an easy naked-eye object on the edge of the LMC. The LMC (also known as Nubecula Major) offers telescopic observers stars, clusters, associations, and star clouds galore, too numerous to detail here! In February 1987, a blue giant in the LMC went supernova, becoming a moderately bright naked-eye object near the Tarantula Nebula. It remains to be seen what kind of remnant nebula develops from Supernova 1987A in the coming years. Amateur astronomers with medium-sized and large telescopes have the means to scan numerous galaxies on the lookout for supernovae in these distant systems. The Australian minister Rev. Robert O. Evans has discovered well over a dozen supernovae in galaxies with 10-inch and 16-inch telescopes. Other amateurs have also succeeded.

M81 and M82. This is the most spectacular of all pairs of galaxies, the two bright objects lying just 38′ apart and offering a striking contrast. M81 is a large, bright, grand spiral of nearly symmetrical form. M82 is a long, cigar-shaped object with no trace of spiral structure but perhaps even greater surface brightness than M81. The two form an engaging sight in even very small telescopes. With 10-inch and larger instruments, intricate wonders are revealed. My view of M82 in a 16-inch on a good night revealed nearly as much detail of the dark clouds mottling it as one can see on professional long-exposure images of the galaxy. M82 offers more puzzles to professional astronomers than perhaps any galaxy but our own. One theory is that M82 was the site of a massive explosion about 1½ million years ago. As usual, a black hole has been suggested as the culprit. These two galaxies are the central members of a galaxy group that lies just beyond our own Local Group. They are probably between 6 and 10 million light-years away.

Questions

1. How do the two brightest Sculptor galaxies compare with each other? If you live at mid-northern latitudes, how much more does haziness on some nights spoil the view of the lower NGC 55? How large a telescope is needed to see mottling or other internal structure in either of these galaxies?

2. How large an extent of M31 can you see with various optical instruments (including your naked eye) on different nights? How well can you sketch the dust lanes and star clouds of M31? With what size telescope can you detect the starlike nucleus? How well can you see the shapes of M32 and M110?

3. If you observe at a southerly enough location, how much detail of star clouds, clusters, and nebulae can you study and sketch in the vast expanses of the Large and Small Magellanic Clouds?

4. What kind of view of M33 do you obtain with different optical instruments (from naked eye to large telescope)? How much structure can you trace in the loose spiral arms of this huge galaxy? Can you identify the largest component in the arms, NGC 604?

5. How much structure can you detect in the Seyfert galaxy M77 with various size telescopes? What is the highest magnification you can use on your telescope and still fit in and directly compare both the marvelous galaxies M81 and M82? How large a telescope is needed to see structure in them, particularly the complex mottling of M82 with dark dust clouds?

34.

Selected Galaxies—2

Observe and sketch the plentiful galaxies of spring on our list. Compare the component galaxies of the two attractive major groups in Leo. Contrast the needle-like edgewise spiral NGC 4565 with the nearly round spiral M94, looking for the special structures of both (like M94's intense center). Compare the dust features in the Sombrero

Galaxy, Black-Eye Galaxy, and Centaurus A, and study the unique structure of each of these galaxies, noting how large a telescope is needed to discern certain aspects of each of them. Observe M106, and observe M87 and M49, pondering the incredible true size and luminosity of the latter two and their position in the midst of the awesome Virgo Galaxy Cluster. See how small a telescope can reveal hints of the spiral arms in exquisite M51, and with larger telescopes study the structure of M51 and the strange galaxy that appears to be appended to it. Compare M51 with M83 and M101 (other nearly face-on, Sc galaxies). Try to see if you can note considerable blueness in M101, and compare your impressions of its color with that of all your other galaxies in medium-sized and large telescopes. For special challenges, look with low magnification for the low-surface-brightness form of Barnard's Galaxy and track down both sets of "Siamese Twins." For a large-telescope challenge, try to glimpse the dim galaxies of Stephan's Quintet.

The presence of the Milky Way band—marking the Milky Way galaxy's equatorial plane in which we ourselves live—makes a great deal of difference to our ability to see other, external galaxies. Only when we look up or down out of this plane do we see mostly unobstructedly to the other galaxies. On (Northern Hemisphere) autumn evenings, we look down (south) out of our galaxy and see the Sculptor galaxy group and the largest members of our own Local Group. On (Northern Hemisphere) spring evenings, we look up (north) out at more distant galaxy groups with significantly more members.

Why are there so many more galaxies in spring than autumn? It is mostly because in spring we are treated to a view of the 2,500-member Virgo Galaxy Cluster! This cluster extends across parts of Corvus, Virgo, Coma Berenices (it has sometimes been called the Coma–Virgo Galaxy Cluster), and Canes Venatici, making the whole region of the sky rich with (mostly faint) galaxies. The central part of the galaxy cluster, the richest of all, is in western Virgo, and was originally dubbed "the Realm of the Nebulae"—before it was realized that these fuzzy glows of light were not clouds of gas in our own Milky Way, but instead vast systems of billions of stars (and, often, nebulae, clusters, and so on) like our Milky Way. The name for this region of our sky has therefore become "the Realm of the Galaxies."

Data for the following galaxies appears in Table 20.

M95, M96, and M105. Here a regular spiral, a barred spiral, and a very round elliptical are close to each other—M95 and M96 are 42′

171

Table 20
Selected Galaxies—2

Galaxy	RA h m	Dec. ° '	Constellation	Mag.	Size '	Type
M95 (NGC 3351)	10 44	+11 42	Leo	9.7	7 × 5	SBb
M96 (NGC 3368)	10 47	+11 49	Leo	9.2	7 × 5	Sbp
M105 (NGC 3379)	10 48	+12 35	Leo	9.3	5 × 4	E1
M65 (NGC 3623)	11 19	+13 05	Leo	9.3	10 × 3	Sb
M66 (NGC 3627)	11 20	+12 59	Leo	9.0	9 × 4	Sb+
NGC 3628	11 20	+13 36	Leo	9.5	15 × 4	Sb
NGC 4038/9 (Ring-Tail Galaxy)	12 02	−18 52	Corvus	10.7	3 × 2	Scp
M106 (NGC 4258)	12 19	+47 18	Canes Venatici	8.3	18 × 8	Sb+p
M49 (NGC 4472)	12 30	+08 00	Virgo	8.4	9 × 7	E4
M87 (NGC 4486)	12 31	+12 24	Virgo	8.6	7	E1
NGC 4565	12 36	+25 59	Coma Berenices	9.6	16 × 3	Sb
M104 (NGC 4594) (Sombrero Galaxy)	12 40	−11 49	Virgo	8.3	9 × 4	Sb
M94 (NGC 4736)	12 51	+41 07	Canes Venatici	8.2	11 × 9	Sb−p
M64 (NGC 4826) (Black-Eye Galaxy)	12 57	+21 41	Coma Berenices	8.5	9 × 5	Sb−
NGC 5128 (Centaurus A)	13 26	−43 01	Centaurus	7	18 × 14	SOp
M51 (NGC 5194) (Whirlpool Galaxy)	13 30	+47 12	Canes Venatici	8.4	11 × 8	Sc[a]
M83 (NGC 5236)	13 37	−29 52	Hydra	7.6	11 × 10	Sc
M101 (NGC 5457)	14 03	+54 21	Ursa Major	7.7	27 × 26	Sc
NGC 6822 (Barnard's Galaxy)	19 45	−14 48	Sagittarius	9.2	10	Irr+

[a]M51's seemingly attached companion is NGC 5195, which shines at magnitude 9.6, measures 5' × 4', and is classified as P, for peculiar.

The RA and declination are in 2000.0 coordinates; the magnitude is visual but approximate; the size is usually photographic and thus for visual purposes quite approximate.

172

apart, with M105 about 48′ from M96. In addition, M105 forms its own tighter little trio with NGC 3384 and 3389, the former of which is sometimes considered to be one of the unusual S0 galaxies. All five of these galaxies are thought to be part of a rather close group in space.

M65, M66, and NGC 3628. The finest Leo trio of galaxies, M65 and M66 are just 21′ apart, with NGC 3628 just 35′ from M66. The first two galaxies are both Sb spirals but look quite different; NGC 3628 is an edge-on object with a fine dust lane and though fainter than the other two is larger (as much as 15′ long).

NGC 4038 (with one section called 4039). The Ring-Tail Galaxy may be two galaxies in collision with each other. The two extended filaments of this strange object have sometimes been called "the Antennae." A fairly large telescope is required to get a good view of the features in this rather small and roughly eleventh-magnitude object.

M106. M106 is a spiral, the largest and almost the brightest galaxy in Canes Venatici.

M49 and M87. M49 and M87 are major members of the Virgo cluster of galaxies, and two of the most luminous and massive elliptical galaxies known. M87 is the most massive object, located near the center of the galaxy cluster and possessing perhaps hundreds of times as much matter as the Milky Way. Its overbright central region and strong radio emission have been hypothesized to be effects of a massive black hole in the galaxy.

NGC 4565. This is the apparently largest edgewise spiral galaxy. Burnham says that with a 10-inch and excellent skies "it is a perfect little needle of light which can be traced out to nearly its full photographic diameter of 15′."

The Sombrero Galaxy (M104). The apparently brightest edgewise— or nearly edgewise—galaxy. Photographs of this amazing object may stir great expectations in the observer, but a medium-sized telescope can actually provide a view that will satisfy those expectations. The prominent dust lane splitting the Sombrero can be glimpsed in rather small telescopes. Although it is down near the border of Virgo and Corvus, the Sombrero is usually considered an outlying member of the Virgo cluster of galaxies. At a distance of roughly 40 million light-years, it is one of the more luminous and massive galaxies known.

M94. M94 has an intense 30″ wide central region. This very bright, compact, and circular spiral is thought to be about 20 million light-years away.

M64. M64, the Black-Eye Galaxy, is only about 1°ENE of the star 35 Comae. A telescope of about 6- to 8-inch aperture can reveal the large dust cloud just offset from the central area of this bright, open spiral. M64 is thought to be closer than the Virgo Cluster and not a member, although that cluster is centered only about 9° away.

Centaurus A (NGC 5128). A bright and large galaxy of unique appearance, once suspected to be galaxies in collision. Later thinking has theorized that some sort of explosion is responsible for its appearance. The name of the object is really its title as a powerful radio source. In the familiar photographs of this galaxy, it is seen as a ball of glow with a huge dust lane splitting it—as if an elliptical and spiral galaxy had merged. The usual classification is an S0—with a "P" for peculiar, to be sure. A medium-sized telescope may provide glimpses of the dust band, but larger telescopes are needed for a good view. Centaurus A is unfortunately a bit too far south to be seen well by observers around 40°N.

M51. M51, sometimes called the Whirlpool Galaxy, offers the easiest chance for observers with a small telescope to see beautiful spiral arms. Although a 10-inch or larger telescope might be needed to see the major features of the galaxy really well, even a 6-inch can show definite hints of the spiral structure. Most peculiar about M51 is the appearance of a very large patch of glow at the end of one of its spiral arms. This glow is indeed a companion galaxy (NGC 5195), but not really in the same plane as M51 or directly attached to its spiral arm. In smaller telescopes the spiral arm extension which seems to run to the companion is unlikely to be seen. M51 is located roughly 20 million light-years away.

M83. M83 is another large, bright, and nearly face-on spiral. It is located down near the Hydra–Centaurus border, but not far enough south for northerners to despair. In photographs M83 gives the appearance of perhaps being a barred spiral, but it is not usually classified as such; instead, it is regarded as an Sc with an unusual "three-branch" spiral structure. A fairly large telescope (10- or 12-inch) might be needed to see much of this structure. M83 has hosted an unusual number of supernovae in recent decades. It lies about as far away as M51.

M101. M101 appears as a larger face-on spiral than M83 or M51, but has its brightness spread over perhaps too large an area. This galaxy is one of the bluest, due to the large proportion of Population I stars in its arms. The distance is about 15 million light-years. M101 is located just above the handle end of the Big Dipper.

Barnard's Galaxy (NGC 6822). This object is difficult because of its low surface brightness. Large binoculars or a rich-field telescope are called for. An observer knowing properly where to look with a large telescope will locate some of the star clouds or HII areas. This feeble member of our Local Group of galaxies lies about 1.7 million light-years away.

Several other challenging extragalactic sights should be mentioned. One sight is the Siamese Twins—or are there two sets of these twins? Burnham gives this name to NGC 4567 and 4568, whereas John Sanford gives this name to NGC 4435 and 4438. Both sets of twins appear to be strange interacting pairs of about eleventh-magnitude galaxies. The former pair's position is listed in Burnham, the latter pair is at about 12^{h}28′ and +13°.

A famous challenge for observers with large telescopes is the group of galaxies known as Stephan's Quintet. First, find the ninth-magnitude large spiral NGC 7331 at 22^{h}37^m and +34°25′. Then, look about ½° to the southwest and search for the five thirteenth- and fourteenth-magnitude galaxies of Stephan's Quintet.

Questions

1. Can you observe all the members of the two best-known groupings of galaxies in Leo? How do they compare with each other, and at what magnifications can you fit all members of a group (or some of the close pairs) together?

2. Can you contrast the appearance of needle-thin edgewise spiral NGC 4565 and mildly tilted, nearly round spiral M94? Can you discern structure in them, and detect M94's intense central region? What are your impressions of the spiral M106 and the giant (in true size, mass, and luminosity) ellipticals M87 and M49?

3. What are the differences in the appearance of the dark dust clouds of the Sombrero Galaxy, Black-Eye Galaxy, and Centaurus A? How large a telescope do you need to start detecting those dust features? What other structure do you see in these distinctive galaxies?

4. How do the three apparently large, loose-armed, nearly face-on spirals M51, M83, and M101 compare? How small a telescope suffices to show spiral structure in M51? In the others? How large a telescope do you need to trace the spiral arm which seems to connect M51 with NGC 5195? What structure can a large telescope show you in this seemingly appended galaxy? Can you see anything like a slight central bar in M83? Do you notice that M101 is especially blue, and if so how does it compare with whatever color you see in the other galaxies on our list? How much aperture is needed to reveal any color in our various galaxies?

5. Can you succeed in seeing Barnard's Galaxy? What are your views of this low-surface-brightness object like in rich-field telescopes and in regular telescopes of various size? Can you observe and sketch both sets of Siamese Twins? Can you succeed in glimpsing some or all of the galaxies of Stephan's Quintet?

35.

Galaxy Clusters and Quasars

Observe as many galaxies as possible in the central region of the Virgo Galaxy Cluster. Attempt to see the brightest member of the far more distant Coma Berenices Galaxy Cluster. Try to view the brightest quasar, 3C 273, in an attempt to observe light that set out on its journey to you several billions years ago.

As our final adventure of this book, we throw all caution to the wind and dare—with backyard telescopes—to seek the ends of the universe and the beginnings of time.

Our first stage is to observe more of the giant Virgo Galaxy Cluster we discussed in the previous activity. Figure 32 presents a chart to assist in finding just a few dozen of the galaxies—those of thirteenth magnitude or brighter—in just the central region of the giant galaxy cluster. The chart covers little more than two fields of view of an average pair of binoculars. But you should use at least an 8-inch telescope, and probably larger, if you want to be sure of finding all these galaxies. In addition, a

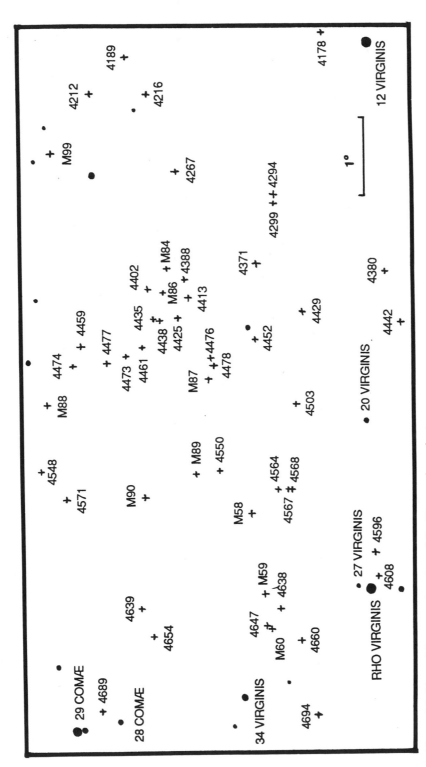

Figure 32 Map of the central region of the Virgo galaxy cluster.

177

star atlas showing all the background stars down to a much fainter magnitude would be highly advisable.

The Virgo Galaxy Cluster is thought to be centered a little over 40 million light-years from us. Its angular size of about 12° by 10° would thus work out to a diameter of more than 5 million light-years. But it has been discovered that the Virgo cluster is only the core of a much vaster *supergalaxy* composed of a number of galaxy groups—a total of 10,000 or 12,000 galaxies, one-quarter of them part of the Virgo cluster—and stretching at least 40 million light-years across. In fact, it is quite possible that our own Local Group of galaxies—the few dozen dominated by M31, M33, the Milky Way, and a few others—is on the outskirts of this supergalaxy and actually a part of it. The Supergalaxy (as we may want to call it if it is our own) bears a highly flattened shape, and it is possible that this is from rotation. Our Milky Way would thus be traveling with the Local Group (the Milky Way's three or more companions may be revolving around our galaxy and two of them, the Magellanic Clouds, like moths around the Milky Way's flame, are perhaps also moth-circling each other). But the whole Local Group might also be traveling around the Supergalaxy, taking at least hundreds of millions of years to complete one period.

The next question that presents itself is whether there are other galaxy clusters beyond the Supergalaxy, perhaps themselves banding together to form other supergalaxies?

There certainly are other galaxy clusters, and there is at least one of the major ones whose brightest members can be seen in a 6-inch telescope. This is the Coma Berenices Galaxy Cluster (not to be confused with the Coma Berenices star cluster, nor with the name Coma–Virgo Galaxy Cluster which is sometimes given to the Virgo Galaxy Cluster). The Coma Berenices Galaxy Cluster is located somewhere between about 250 to 400 million light-years away. When you see a galaxy of the Virgo Cluster, you are looking at that galaxy as it was 40 million years ago, almost as far back as the last days of the dinosaurs. But when you see a galaxy of the Coma Berenices Galaxy Cluster, you are looking back to the early days of the dinosaurs, perhaps even further back. The cluster contains maybe 1,000 galaxies, of which only two are easy targets for fairly small telescopes. The two galaxies are NGC 4889 and 4874. The brighter, with a photographic magnitude of about 13 but a visual magnitude apparently much brighter, is NGC 4889 and it is located about 2.3°W of Beta Comae. (For a list of slightly brighter galaxies at distances ranging from that of the Virgo to that of the Coma Berenices Galaxy Cluster, see "The Outer Limits: How Far Can You See?" by Alan Mac-Robert, *Sky & Telescope,* April 1983.)

The next of the really great galaxy clusters, perhaps fitting to be called a supergalaxy, is the Corona Borealis Galaxy Cluster. But its brightest members are only sixteenth magnitude. Therefore, this is a sight for only the most ambitious amateur astronomers with the largest amateur telescopes. How far is this cluster? Apparently somewhat over 1 billion (that is, 1 thousand million) light-years distant.

But there is a more distant sight in this universe that can be glimpsed with much smaller telescopes. To even hope to begin to understand it, however, we must pause to consider how astronomers have been able to learn the distances to the farther galaxies and what all this has to do with the famous cosmological theory of the origin of the universe, the Big Bang theory.

One of the great scientific advancements of this century now drawing to a close was the discovery of the red shifts of the galaxies and the significance of this to our understanding of the origins of the universe. Earlier in this book, we saw how the spectrum of the light of receding objects was red-shifted—a "pitch" of light itself changed by the Doppler effect even as the pitch of sound changes when a car or train rushes past us and away. The great discovery about the galaxies was that in all of them but the huddled-together Local Group the spectrum was red-shifted by enormous amounts. The galaxies were receding at tremendous speeds away from us.

The powerful explanation was that we must be seeing an expansion of the entire universe, all galaxies (except those closely bunched together) flying away from all others. The farther a galaxy is from us, the greater is its red shift. And by calculating back the separations of the galaxies, astronomers reached the conclusion that all of them must have been at one common origin point something like (very roughly) 15 billion years ago. The galaxies, and with them all that we know of in the universe, must have resulted from a "Big Bang" explosion.

Decades later, there are still stirs from those who believe in other theories. But the Big Bang still reigns. The Big Bang theory itself has been modified, with the first and most popular variation on the idea of an infinite expansion being the *oscillatory universe* in which there is enough matter for gravity to eventually halt the expansion and send all the galaxies falling back to a single point—setting off the next Big Bang and expansion, then contraction, and so on. In the last decade or two, an incredible proliferation of ideas has arisen to enrich (hopefully not choke with its extravagant growth) the field of cosmology. You can almost feel in the air that some breakthrough is imminent—but possibly of a nature which none of today's cleverest people in the field have anticipated at all. There certainly are some puzzling things to account for. One mystery lies in how the universe developed the large-scale structure we are starting to glimpse—the largest structure yet identified, called the Great Wall, and other indications that there are vast bubble-like cells along whose edges galaxies have formed.

Tremendous uncertainties exist in our understanding of the universe at large. Even the distances we have been quoting are highly approximate because they are subject to our determining correctly the figure in the red shift–distance equation that is known as *the Hubble constant*. The distance to the "edge of the universe" depends on that constant. The edge we refer to is actually the distance at which the red shift becomes so great that no light or other electromagnetic radiation of any kind can reach us—for at that distance, the combined speed of our recession and another object's would begin to exceed the speed of light itself.

How far is this *Hubble distance*? Perhaps something on the order of 14 billion light-years away (depending on the correct value for the Hubble constant). And astronomers have detected objects almost that far away—objects we are seeing as they were when the universe was just a small fraction of the age it now is. But those objects are not galaxies.

They are *quasars*. Just 30 years ago, astronomers realized that the spectra of strange *quasi-stellar objects* could be explained if the spectral lines were familiar ones that had been red-shifted by enormous amounts. But the objects in question must be hundreds of times more luminous than galaxies to appear so bright at the distances their red shifts indicate. And these objects appeared to be not thousands of light-years across but more comparable to the size of a solar system! A minority of astronomers has continued to maintain that the quasars cannot be so distant, that there is another cause for the red shift in their spectra. Most have accepted the great distances and attempted to offer some kind of explanation—however speculative and vague—about how quasars could produce so much energy. There is evidence that quasars might be intense centers of galaxies (a far more extreme version of Seyfert galaxies)—but at distances across which the outer regions of the galaxies are far too dim to see. If so, then perhaps it is the most massive black holes in the universe which somehow provide the energy for these beacons from the youth of the universe.

And so we at last return to the observational, and to the telescopes we have right at hand. There is one quasar that is bright enough to be seen in 6-inch telescopes. 3C 273 looks like a bluish star of about magnitude 12.7, though it varies from about the twelfth to the thirteenth magnitude. It is located, coincidentally, in that galactic treasure house Virgo, at precisely $12^h29^m06.7^s$ and $+2°03'07''$ (for a finder chart, see the article mentioned below). The distance of 3C 273 is probably about 2 billion light-years, though it could be considerably farther.

Remarkably, the quasars are so luminous that even some of the most distant are sixteenth magnitude and within the range of the largest amateur telescopes. A superb article ("The Outer Limits: How Far Can You See?") on observing these and other distant objects, complete with finder charts and precise positions, was authored by Alan MacRobert in the April 1983 issue of *Sky & Telescope*. If you observe 3C 273, you are seeing light which glimmered before life left the waters of our planet—perhaps even before life itself. But, as MacRobert says, if you observe some of the farther quasars—fifteenth- and sixteenth-magnitude quasars which are roughly 7 to 12 billion light-years away—you are seeing "presolar light." That light shining through your telescope set out on its journey to you before the Earth and Sun were born. When you behold it, you are—astronomers think—seeing light from the early days and almost the farthest accessible ends of the universe.

Questions

1. How many of the galaxies on our chart of the central region of the Virgo Galaxy Cluster can you find? What is the greatest number you can observe the shapes of, or at least the nonstellar nature of, in one field of view? What are some of the particularly beautiful combinations of various spiral and elliptical galaxies that you see?

2. Can you observe the brightest member of the Coma Berenices Galaxy Group? Can you make out its shape?

3. Can you glimpse the quasar 3C 273 and thus behold light from before the time life came upon the lands of Earth? Can you glimpse the even further quasars and look upon sights from the early days of time and space?

APPENDIXES

Note that much of the information that some astronomy books give in an appendix, this book gives in the tables that appear in the text (for instance, Table 2 is a listing of the nearest stars).

Note also that a few of the statistics in these appendixes may differ (usually slightly) from figures given in the tables or text. This is not an error, but rather a reflection of the different opinions of different authorities about what these values are.

The data in this appendix are derived from the manuscript of Richard Dibon-Smith's book *StarList 2000* with his kind permission.

Name	App. Mag.	Abs. Mag.	Lum.	Dist.	Ann. P.M.	Dir.	Rad. V.	Space V.	Spect.	Diam.
Sirius	−1.46	1.4	22	8.6	1.328	204	−8	18	A1Vm	1.4
Canopus	−0.72	−2.4	720	70	0.034	50	+21	22	F0II	17
Alpha Centauri	−0.27									
A	−0.01	4.35	1.4	4.39	3.678	281	−25	34	G2V	1.2
B	1.33	5.69	0.4	4.39	3.678	281	−21	31	K1V	0.9
Arcturus	−0.04	−0.2	100	35	2.28	209	−5	118	K2III	15
Vega	0.03v	0.50	50	25	0.348	35	−14	19	A0Va	2
Capella	0.08	0.09	70	45	0.430	169	+30	40	G8III (G6III + G2III)	9.5
Rigel	0.12	−7.1	55,000	910	0.004	236	+21	21	B8Iac	44
Procyon	0.38	2.64	7	11.4	1.248	214	−3	20	F5IV	2.1
Achernar	0.46	−1.6	345	85	0.108	105	+16	25	B3Vpe	1.8
Betelgeuse	0.50v	−5.6	14,000	540	0.027	68	+21	33	M1Iab	290v
Beta Centauri	0.61v	−5.1	8,600	450	0.030	221	+6	17	B1III	5.3
Alpha Crucis	0.76									
A	1.58	−3.9	2,900	405	0.030	236	−11	21	B0.5IV	2.5
B	2.09	−3.4	1,800	410(?)	0.031	248	−1	18	B1V	2.4
Altair	0.77	2.24	10	16.5	0.662	54	−26	30	A7IV–V	1.5
Aldebaran	0.85v	−0.6	135	65	0.200	161	+54	57	K5III	20
Antares	0.96v	−4.7	6,000	440	0.024	197	−3	5.6	M1I	190v
Spica	0.98v	−3.5	2,000	255	0.054	232	+1	11	B1III	2.6
Pollux	1.14	0.98	30	35	0.629	265	+3	32	K0IIIb	6.9
Fomalhaut	1.16	2.03	12	21.9	0.373	116	+7	14	A3V	1.6
Beta Crucis	1.25v	−5.0	7,900	580	0.042	246	+16	37	B0.5III	4
Deneb	1.25	−7.5	80,000	1,800	0.005	11	−5	6.4	A2Ia	105
Regulus	1.35	−0.6	135	70	0.249	271	+4	27	B7V	1.9
Adhara (ε CMa)	1.50	−4.4	4,500	495	0.002	27	+27	29	B2II	4.6
Castor	1.58	1.14	30	45	0.198	239	+6	15	A1V (and A2V)	1.7

The columns are, respectively: name, apparent magnitude, absolute magnitude, luminosity (Sun = 1), distance (in light-years), annual proper motion (in arc-seconds), direction of proper motion (in degrees—0° = due north, 90° = due east, and so on), radial velocity (in km/s), space velocity (in km/s), spectral and luminosity class, and diameter (Sun = 1).

Appendix 2
The Constellations

Name	Genitive	Abbreviation	Area (square degrees)	Order of Size
Andromeda	Andromedae	And	722	19
Antlia	Antliae	Ant	239	62
Apus	Apodis	Aps	206	67
Aquarius	Aquarii	Aqr	980	10
Aquila	Aquilae	Aql	652	22
Ara	Arae	Ara	237	63
Aries	Arietis	Ari	441	39
Auriga	Aurigae	Aur	657	21
Boötes	Boötis	Boo	907	13
Caelum	Caeli	Cae	125	81
Camelopardalis	Camelopardalis	Cam	757	18
Cancer	Cancri	Cnc	506	31
Canes Venatici	Canum Venaticorum	CVn	465	38
Canis Major	Canis Majoris	CMa	380	43
Canis Minor	Canis Minoris	CMi	183	71
Capricornus	Capricorni	Cap	414	40
Carina	Carinae	Car	494	34
Cassiopeia	Cassiopeiae	Cas	598	25
Centaurus	Centauri	Cen	1,060	9
Cepheus	Cephei	Cep	588	27
Cetus	Ceti	Cet	1,231	4
Chamaeleon	Chamaeleontis	Cha	132	79
Circinus	Circini	Cir	93	85
Columba	Columbae	Col	270	54
Coma Berenices	Comae Berenices	Com	386	42
Corona Australis	Coronae Australis	CrA	128	80
Corona Borealis	Coronae Borealis	CrB	179	73
Corvus	Corvi	Crv	184	70
Crater	Crateris	Crt	282	53
Crux	Crucis	Cru	68	88
Cygnus	Cygni	Cyg	804	16
Delphinus	Delphini	Del	189	69
Dorado	Doradus	Dor	179	72
Draco	Draconis	Dra	1,083	8
Equuleus	Equulei	Equ	72	87
Eridanus	Eridani	Eri	1,138	6
Fornax	Fornacis	For	398	41
Gemini	Geminorum	Gem	514	30
Grus	Gruis	Gru	366	45
Hercules	Herculis	Her	1,225	5
Horologium	Horologii	Hor	249	58
Hydra	Hydrae	Hya	1,303	1
Hydrus	Hydri	Hyi	243	61
Indus	Indi	Ind	294	49
Lacerta	Lacertae	Lac	201	68
Leo	Leonis	Leo	947	12
Leo Minor	Leonis Minoris	LMi	232	64

(continued)

Appendix 2 (continued)

Name	Genitive	Abbreviation	Area (square degrees)	Order of Size
Lepus	Leporis	Lep	290	51
Libra	Librae	Lib	538	29
Lupus	Lupi	Lup	334	46
Lynx	Lyncis	Lyn	545	28
Lyra	Lyrae	Lyr	286	52
Mensa	Mensae	Men	153	75
Microsopium	Microscopii	Mic	210	66
Monoceros	Monocerotis	Mon	482	35
Musca	Muscae	Mus	138	77
Norma	Normae	Nor	165	74
Octans	Octantis	Oct	291	50
Ophiuchus	Ophiuchi	Oph	948	11
Orion	Orionis	Ori	594	26
Pavo	Pavonis	Pav	378	44
Pegasus	Pegasi	Peg	1,121	7
Perseus	Persei	Per	615	24
Phoenix	Phoenicis	Phe	469	37
Pictor	Pictoris	Pic	247	59
Pisces	Piscium	Psc	889	14
Piscis Austrinus	Piscis Austrini	PsA	245	60
Puppis	Puppis	Pup	673	20
Pyxis	Pyxidis	Pyx	221	65
Reticulum	Reticuli	Ret	114	82
Sagitta	Sagittae	Sge	80	86
Sagittarius	Sagittarii	Sgr	867	15
Scorpius	Scorpii	Sco	497	33
Sculptor	Sculptoris	Scl	475	36
Scutum	Scuti	Sct	109	84
Serpens	Serpentis	Ser	637	23
Sextans	Sextantis	Sex	314	47
Taurus	Tauri	Tau	797	17
Telescopium	Telescopii	Tel	252	57
Triangulum	Trianguli	Tri	132	78
Triangulum Australe	Trianguli Australis	TrA	110	83
Tucana	Tucanae	Tuc	295	48
Ursa Major	Ursae Majoris	UMa	1,280	3
Ursa Minor	Ursae Minoris	UMi	256	56
Vela	Velorum	Vel	500	32
Virgo	Virginis	Vir	1,294	2
Volans	Volantis	Vol	141	76
Vulpecula	Vulpeculae	Vul	268	55

APPENDIXES

Appendix 3
The Greek Alphabet

A	α	Alpha	H	η	Eta	N	ν	Nu	T	τ	Tau
B	β	Beta	Θ	θ	Theta	Ξ	ξ	Xi	Υ	υ	Upsilon
Γ	γ	Gamma	I	ι	Iota	O	o	Omicron	Φ	φ	Phi
Δ	δ	Delta	K	κ	Kappa	Π	π	Pi	X	χ	Chi
E	ε	Epsilon	Λ	λ	Lambda	P	ρ	Rho	Ψ	ψ	Psi
Z	ζ	Zeta	M	μ	Mu	Σ	σ	Sigma	Ω	ω	Omega

Appendix 4
The Messier Objects

M	NGC	RA 2000.0 h m	Dec. ° '	Constellation	Size* '	Integrated Magnitude	Description
1	1952	05 34.5	+22 01	Tau	6 × 4	c. 8.4	Supernova remnant
2	7089	21 33.5	−00 49	Aqr	13	6.5	Globular Cluster
3	5272	13 42.2	+28 23	CVn	16	6.4	Globular Cluster
4	6121	16 23.6	−26 32	Sco	26	5.9	Globular Cluster
5	5904	15 18.6	+02 05	Ser	17	5.8	Globular Cluster
6	6405	17 40.1	−32 13	Sco	15	4.2	Open Cluster
7	6475	17 53.9	−34 49	Sco	80	3.3	Open Cluster
8	6523	18 03.8	−24 23	Sgr	90 × 40	c. 5.8	Diffuse Nebula
9	6333	17 19.2	−18 31	Oph	9	c. 7.9	Globular Cluster
10	6254	16 57.1	−04 06	Oph	15	6.6	Globular Cluster
11	6705	18 51.1	−06 16	Sct	14	5.8	Open Cluster
12	6218	16 47.2	−01 57	Oph	14	6.6	Globular Cluster
13	6205	16 41.7	+36 28	Her	17	5.9	Globular Cluster
14	6402	17 37.6	−03 15	Oph	12	7.6	Globular Cluster
15	7078	21 30.0	+12 10	Peg	12	6.4	Globular Cluster
16	6611	18 18.8	−13 47	Ser	7	6.0	Open Cluster
17	6618	18 20.8	−16 11	Sgr	46 × 37	7	Diffuse Nebula
18	6613	18 19.9	−17 08	Sgr	9	6.9	Open Cluster
19	6273	17 02.6	−26 16	Oph	14	7.2	Globular Cluster
20	6514	18 02.6	−23 02	Sgr	29 × 27	c. 8.5	Diffuse Nebula
21	6531	18 04.6	−22 30	Sgr	13	5.9	Open Cluster
22	6656	18 36.4	−23 54	Sgr	24	5.1	Globular Cluster
23	6494	17 56.8	−19 01	Sgr	27	5.5	Open Cluster
24		18 16.9	−18 29	Sgr	90	c. 4.5	See notes
25	IC 4725	18 31.6	−19 15	Sgr	32	4.6	Open Cluster
26	6694	18 45.2	−09 24	Sct	15	8.0	Open Cluster
27	6853	19 59.6	+22 43	Vul	8 × 4	c. 8.1	Planetary Nebula
28	6626	18 24.5	−24 52	Sgr	11	c. 6.9	Globular Cluster
29	6913	20 23.9	+38 32	Cyg	7	6.6	Open Cluster

M	NGC	RA	Dec	Con	Size	Mag	Type
30	7099	21 40.4	−23 11	Cap	11	7.5	Globular Cluster
31	224	00 42.7	+41 16	And	178×63	3.4	Spiral Galaxy
32	221	00 42.7	+40 52	And	8×6	8.2	Elliptical Galaxy
33	598	01 33.9	+30 39	Tri	62×39	5.7	Spiral Galaxy
34	1039	02 42.0	+42 47	Per	35	5.2	Open Cluster
35	2168	06 08.9	+24 20	Gem	28	5.1	Open Cluster
36	1960	05 36.1	+34 08	Aur	12	6.0	Open Cluster
37	2099	05 52.4	+32 33	Aur	24	5.6	Open Cluster
38	1912	05 28.7	+35 50	Aur	21	6.4	Open Cluster
39	7092	21 32.2	+48 26	Cyg	32	4.6	Open Cluster
40		12 22.4	+58 05	UMa		8	*See notes*
41	2287	06 47.0	−20 44	CMa	38	4.5	Open Cluster
42	1976	05 35.4	−05 27	Ori	66×60	4	Diffuse Nebula
43	1982	05 35.6	−05 16	Ori	20×15	9	Diffuse Nebula
44	2632	08 40.1	+19 59	Cnc	95	3.1	Open Cluster
45		03 47.0	+24 07	Tau	110	1.2	Open Cluster
46	2437	07 41.8	−14 49	Pup	27	6.1	Open Cluster
47	2422	07 36.6	−14 30	Pup	30	4.4	Open Cluster
48	2548	08 13.8	−05 48	Hya	54	5.8	Open Cluster
49	4472	12 29.8	+08 00	Vir	9×7	8.4	Elliptical Galaxy
50	2323	07 03.2	−08 20	Mon	16	5.9	Open Cluster
51	5194–5	13 29.9	+47 12	CVn	11×8	8.1	Spiral Galaxy
52	7654	23 24.2	+61 35	Cas	13	6.9	Open Cluster
53	5024	13 12.9	+18 10	Com	13	7.7	Globular Cluster
54	6715	18 55.1	−30 29	Sgr	9	7.7	Globular Cluster
55	6809	19 40.0	−30 58	Sgr	19	7.0	Globular Cluster
56	6779	19 16.6	+30 11	Lyr	7	8.2	Globular Cluster
57	6720	18 53.6	+33 02	Lyr	1	c. 9.0	Planetary Nebula
58	4579	12 37.7	+11 49	Vir	5×4	9.8	Spiral Galaxy
59	4621	12 42.0	+11 39	Vir	5×3	9.8	Elliptical Galaxy
60	4649	12 43.7	+11 33	Vir	7×6	8.8	Elliptical Galaxy
61	4303	12 21.9	+04 28	Vir	6×5	9.7	Spiral Galaxy
62	6266	17 01.2	−30 07	Oph	14	6.6	Globular Cluster
63	5055	13 15.8	+42 02	CVn	12×8	8.6	Spiral Galaxy
64	4826	12 56.7	+21 41	Com	9×5	8.5	Spiral Galaxy
65	3623	11 18.9	+13 05	Leo	10×3	9.3	Spiral Galaxy

Appendix 4 (continued)

M	NGC	RA h	m 2000.0	Dec. °	'	Constellation	Size* '	Integrated Magnitude	Description
66	3627	11	20.2	+12	59	Leo	9×4	9.0	Spiral Galaxy
67	2682	08	50.4	+11	49	Cnc	30	6.9	Open Cluster
68	4590	12	39.5	−26	45	Hya	12	8.2	Globular Cluster
69	6637	18	31.4	−32	21	Sgr	7	7.7	Globular Cluster
70	6681	18	43.2	−32	18	Sgr	8	8.1	Globular Cluster
71	6838	19	53.8	+18	47	Sge	7	8.3	Globular Cluster
72	6981	20	53.5	−12	32	Aqr	6	9.4	Globular Cluster
73	6994	20	58.9	−12	38	Aqr			See notes
74	628	01	36.7	+15	47	Psc	10×9	9.2	Spiral Galaxy
75	6864	20	06.1	−21	55	Sgr	6	8.6	Globular Cluster
76	650−1	01	42.4	+51	34	Per	2×1	c. 11.5	Planetary Nebula
77	1068	02	42.7	−00	01	Cet	7×6	8.8	Spiral Galaxy
78	2068	05	46.7	+00	03	Ori	8×6	8	Diffuse Nebula
79	1904	05	24.5	−24	33	Lep	9	8.0	Globular Cluster
80	6093	16	17.0	−22	59	Sco	9	7.2	Globular Cluster
81	3031	09	55.6	+69	04	UMa	26×14	6.8	Spiral Galaxy
82	3034	09	55.8	+69	41	UMa	11×5	8.4	Irregular Galaxy
83	5236	13	37.0	−29	52	Hya	11×10	c. 7.6	Spiral Galaxy
84	4374	12	25.1	+12	53	Vir	5×4	9.3	Elliptical Galaxy
85	4382	12	25.4	+18	11	Com	7×5	9.2	Elliptical Galaxy
86	4406	12	26.2	+12	57	Vir	7×6	9.2	Elliptical Galaxy
87	4486	12	30.8	+12	24	Vir	7	8.6	Elliptical Galaxy
88	4501	12	32.0	+14	25	Com	7×4	9.5	Spiral Galaxy
89	4552	12	35.7	+12	33	Vir	4	9.8	Elliptical Galaxy
90	4569	12	36.8	+13	10	Vir	10×5	9.5	Spiral Galaxy
91	4548	12	35.4	+14	30	Com	5×4	10.2	Spiral Galaxy
92	6341	17	17.1	+43	08	Her	11	6.5	Globular Cluster
93	2447	07	44.6	−23	52	Pup	22	c. 6.2	Open Cluster
94	4736	12	50.9	+41	07	CVn	11×9	8.1	Spiral Galaxy
95	3351	10	44.0	+11	42	Leo	7×5	9.7	Spiral Galaxy

M	NGC	RA	Dec	Con	Dimensions	Mag	Type
96	3368	10 46.8	+11 49	Leo	7×5	9.2	Spiral Galaxy
97	3587	11 14.8	+55 01	UMa	3	*c.* 11.2	Planetary Nebula
98	4192	12 13.8	+14 54	Com	10×3	10.1	Spiral Galaxy
99	4254	12 18.8	+14 25	Com	5	9.8	Spiral Galaxy
100	4321	12 22.9	+15 49	Com	7×6	9.4	Spiral Galaxy
101	5457	14 03.2	+54 21	UMa	27×26	7.7	Spiral Galaxy
102							*See notes*
103	581	01 33.2	+60 42	Cas	6	*c.* 7.4	Open Cluster
104	4594	12 40.0	−11 37	Vir	9×4	8.3	Spiral Galaxy
105	3379	10 47.8	+12 35	Leo	4×4	9.3	Elliptical Galaxy
106	4258	12 19.0	+47 18	CVn	18×8	8.3	Spiral Galaxy
107	6171	16 32.5	−13 03	Oph	10	8.1	Globular Cluster
108	3556	11 11.5	+55 40	UMa	8×2	10.0	Spiral Galaxy
109	3992	11 57.6	+53 23	UMa	8×5	9.8	Spiral Galaxy
110	205	00 40.4	+41 41	And	17×10	8.0	Elliptical Galaxy

Source: A. Hirshfeld and R. W. Sinnott (eds.), *Sky Catalogue 2000.0,* Vol 2 (Sky Publishing Corp./Cambridge University Press, 1985).

*The dimensions given are as seen on long-exposure photographs and, for galaxies in particular, are larger than the sizes that will be seen visually.

M1   Crab Nebula
M8   Lagoon Nebula; contains a star cluster
M11   Wild Duck Cluster
M16   Surrounded by the Eagle Nebula
M17   Omega Nebula
M20   Trifid Nebula
M24   Star field in Sagittarius, containing the open cluster NGC 6603
M27   Dumbbell Nebula
M31   Andromeda Galaxy
M40   Faint double star Winnecke 4, mags. 9.0 and 9.6
M42, M43 Orion Nebula
M44   Praesepe, the Beehive Cluster
M45   The Pleiades; no NGC or IC number
M51   Whirlpool Galaxy
M57   Ring Nebula
M64   Black-Eye Galaxy
M73   Small group of four faint stars
M97   Owl Nebula
M102   Duplicate of M101
M104   Sombrero Galaxy

Glossary

The entries that state "*See* Fundamental . . ." refer to the Fundamental Measurements in Astronomy section in the beginning of this book.

Absolute Magnitude: The magnitude of brightness a star would have if it were seen at a standard distance of 10 parsecs (about 32.6 light-years).

Altazimuth (System): System for indicating the position of a celestial object in altitude and azimuth.

Altitude: Apparent angular height in the sky.

Antapex (of the Sun's Way): The point on the celestial sphere that the Sun appears to be moving away from as judged by the motions of stars in its neighborhood of the galaxy (*see also* apex). Also called "the Sun's Quit."

Apastron: The farthest point in the orbit of a companion star from its primary in a double star system (*see also* periastron).

Apex (of the Sun's Way): The point on the celestial sphere that the Sun appears to be moving toward as judged by the motions of stars in its neighborhood of the galaxy (*see also* antapex).

Apparent Magnitude: The magnitude of brightness a star appears to have in our sky.

Association, Stellar: A confederation of stars—usually the hot, young stars of O and B associations—moving through space together but more loosely bound than a star cluster.

Asterism: A visually noticeable pattern of stars which is neither an official constellation in the sky nor necessarily a true cluster, association, or moving group in space.

Atmospheric Extinction: Dimming of the light of celestial objects due to absorption by the Earth's atmosphere.

Averted Vision: Technique of looking just to the side where a faint object is in order to see it better because its light falls on the most sensitive area of the retina.

Azimuth: Angular measure around the horizon or parallel to it in the sky. (0° is usually considered north, 90°, east, and so on to complete a 360° circle).

Big Bang: An "explosion" thought to have brought the universe into being, hypothesized to account for the red shifts of galaxies which seem to indicate an expanding universe.

Binary (Star): A double star system consisting of members which are thought to orbit each other.

Black Hole: An object, thought to be the result of a massive star's collapse, whose gravity has become so intense as to prevent even light (and other electromagnetic radiation) from escaping it.

Blue Giant: A massive, large, and very luminous star of spectral type O or B which radiates at high temperature and therefore with blue–white color.

Bolometric Magnitude: The magnitude of an astronomical object measured at all wavelengths of the electromagnetic spectrum.

Celestial Sphere: The imaginary sphere surrounding Earth whose inner surface is the sky above and below one's horizon.

Cepheid Variable: A major class of variable star (containing such individual kinds as classical Cepheids and RR Lyrae stars) in which changes in the star itself (perhaps cyclic ionization and recombination of helium in the star's atmosphere) give rise to precisely regular brightness variations (variations that can be employed to estimate these stars' distances by use of *the period–luminosity relation*).

Circumpolar: Close enough to a celestial pole so as never to set as seen from certain latitudes on Earth.

Collimation: The alignment of optical elements in a telescope or other optical instrument.

Comes: The companion (less bright star) in a double star system. The plural is *comites*.

Constellation: An official pattern of stars, or, more strictly, the officially demarcated section of sky in which that pattern lies.

Cosmology: The study of the origin and evolution of the universe.

Culmination: The highest point a celestial object reaches in its nightly (or daily) journey across the sky occurs when it comes to the *meridian.*

Dark Adaptation: The increase in the sensitivity of the eyes to dim light that occurs when they are kept away from bright light for a while.

Dark Nebula: A nebula that does not shine by either emitted or reflected light and is therefore visible only in silhouette against a more distant bright nebula or starry background.

Dawes' Limit: Limit to resolving ability (and thus ability to split double stars) for a telescope of a given aperture, as determined by an empirical formula of the nineteenth-century astronomer W. R. Dawes.

Declination: *See* Fundamental. . . ."

Deep-Sky Object: An astronomical object beyond our solar system (usually refers to star clusters, nebulae, and galaxies, less often to double stars or variable stars).

Diffuse Nebula: A luminous nebula that reflects the light of nearby stars (*reflection nebula*) or is heated enough by very hot stars to glow on its own (*emission nebula*). From such nebulae are stars born, in contrast to *planetary nebulae,* which are the ejected gas of dying stars.

Double Star: A star that, upon closer or further observation, turns out to consist of two or more component stars.

Eclipsing Variable: A variable star in which the brightness changes are caused by periodic eclipses of one star by the other, or both stars by each other.

Emission Nebula: Type of, or area of a, diffuse nebula that is lit by very hot stars so that it begins to emit light (*see also* reflection nebula).

Flare Star: A dwarf star that exhibits brief and sometimes large brightness changes due to an outbreak of activity on a localized area of its surface.

Galactic Cluster: *See* Open Cluster.

Galaxy: A vast congregation of many millions or billions of stars in elliptical, spiral, or irregular formation.

Galaxy Cluster: A grouping of galaxies in space.

Globular Cluster: An approximately round and rather densely populated cluster containing hundreds of thousands or even a few million stars, and forming part of a spherical halo of such clusters centered on the core of the galaxy (other kind of cluster: *galactic,* or *open, cluster).*

Hertzsprung–Russell Diagram (H–R Diagram): A tremendously revealing diagram that plots the true brightness (in terms of absolute magnitude or luminosity) of a star versus its spectral class or surface temperature.

Hubble Constant: A still imprecisely known quantity that relates the galaxies' velocity of recession to their distance.

Light Pollution: Excessive or misdirected artificial lighting.

Limiting Magnitude: The faintest magnitude (level of brightness) at which celestial objects (usually stars) can be seen with a given set of sky conditions and optical instruments (including the naked eye).

Luminosity: The true brightness of a star, independent of its distance from us, measured in units of the Sun's true brightness (a star twice as luminous as the Sun has a luminosity of 2, the Sun itself has a luminosity of 1).

Magnitude (as a Measure of Brightness): *See* "Fundamental . . ." and the glossary entries on *apparent magnitude, absolute magnitude,* and *bolometric magnitude.*

Main Sequence: The heavily populated section of the Hertzsprung–Russell diagram occupied by stars more or less like the Sun which are not in the various *dwarf* or *giant* classes.

Meridian: The imaginary line from due north to overhead to due south in the sky.

Messier Objects (M Objects): The prominent clusters, nebulae, and galaxies originally cataloged or noted by the eighteenth-century astronomer Charles Messier (MESS-ee-yay).

Minutes of Arc: *See* "Fundamental. . . ."

Moving Group: A confederation of stars too loosely bound to one another to be a cluster, and generally consisting of stars fairly advanced in age (as opposed to the stars of O and B association stars, which are young). Even more loosely connected are the stars of a *stream* (at whose center may still exist a moving group).

Multiple Star: A double star system consisting of more than two member stars.

Nebula: A cloud of gas or dust in space among or around the stars (the major kinds are: diffuse, planetary, and dark).

Neutron Star: The collapsed, ultra-dense core of a star left after a supernova formed from an original star not massive enough to collapse all the way into becoming a *black hole*.

Nova: A star that undergoes a far lesser explosion than a supernova, perhaps due to material from another star in its system falling upon its hot white dwarf surface.

Occultation: The hiding of one celestial object by another (a *grazing occultation* is one in which the uneven edge of one body alternately hides and reveals the other).

Open Cluster: A fairly sparsely populated cluster of stars, found chiefly in the spiral arms of galaxies (other kind of cluster: *globular cluster*). Also called *galactic cluster*.

Parallax: The change in a star's position caused by our change in viewpoint (usually our change from one side of Earth's orbit to the opposite side).

Parsec: A portmanteau word for "parallax-second," the distance at which the views from opposite sides of Earth's orbit would cause an object to have an apparent position change (a *parallax*) of 1 arc-second (1 parsec is equal to about 3.26 light-years).

Periastron: The nearest point in the orbit of a companion star to its primary in a double star system (*see also* apastron).

Period–Luminosity Relation: A relation between the period of brightness variations and the true brightness of Cepheid variables which enables their distances to be calculated.

Planetary Nebula: A nebula formed from the ejected gas of a dying, very hot star (the other major kinds of nebula are: diffuse and dark).

Population I Stars: The younger stars found mostly in the spiral arms and equatorial disk of a galaxy, formed in part from several previous generations of stars which have lived and exploded (*see also* Population II stars).

Population II Stars: The older stars found mostly in the central bulge and the globular clusters of a galaxy, and belonging to the original generation of stars in the galaxy (*see also* Population I stars).

Position Angle (PA): The direction angle (0° is north, 90° is east, and so on through 360° back to north) in a field of view—in stellar astronomy, a measurement of the direction of a companion star from its primary.

Primary: In double stars (and other pairs of bodies orbiting each other), the more massive (and typically brighter) star of the system.

Proper Motion: The movement of a star relative to the Sun as projected on the celestial sphere—in other words, the change in a star's position on the celestial sphere produced by the component of its *space velocity* (motion through space) which is transverse (neither toward nor away from us).

Pulsar: A neutron star whose emissions of radio waves or visible light are detectable, though only in pulses, by us because they are oriented so as to be sent in our direction each time the star rapidly rotates the emitting area around to point toward us.

Quasar (Quasi-Stellar Object): An object that appears as pointlike as a star but that must emit many times more light and other radiation than entire galaxies if its great red shift does in fact indicate it is one of the universe's most distant objects.

Radial Velocity: The component of a star's motion which is either toward or away from us.

Red Dwarf: A small star far less massive than the Sun which radiates relatively little light and mostly in the red due to its comparatively low surface temperature.

Red Giant: A huge and fairly massive star of extremely low density which radiates mostly in the red due to its low surface temperature and which represents the next stage in life for stars like the sun when they leave the *main sequence.*

Red Shift: The shifting of spectral lines toward the red end of the spectrum caused (usually) by the object's moving away from us.

Reflection Nebula: A type of *diffuse nebula,* or part of one, which shines only by the light reflected off it from stars in or near it (*see also* Emission Nebula).

Relfix: A double star system in which the members' positions appear to be fixed (no significant change in position angle) in relation to each other.

Right Ascension (RA): *See* Fundamental. . . ."

Schwarzschild Radius: The radius to which a star of a particular mass must contract before its gravity prevents the escape of all radiation and it becomes a *black hole.*

Seconds of Arc: *See* Fundamental. . . ."

Seeing: The sharpness of astronomical images as a function of atmospheric turbulence.

Skyglow: Illumination of the sky by terrestrial sources (almost always artificial sources, usually cities).

SNR: *See* Supernova Remnant.

Space Velocity: The velocity of a star through space, sometimes called its *true* velocity, although it has to be really the velocity relative to a certain chosen frame of reference (in this case, that of stars in our general *neighborhood* of space).

Spectral Class: The subcategory of spectral type in which a star belongs (*see* spectral type)—for example, O5, G2, M3, in which the letter denotes the type and together with the number indicates the class.

Spectral Type: The category—ranging from O (the hottest normal stars) to M (coolest normal star), with some alternative unusual types—into which a star is placed according to the appearance (including position of chemically produced *spectral lines*) of its light's spectrum.

Supernova: A very massive star that explodes to a brightness tremendously greater than novae, in fact sometimes brighter than entire galaxies, probably due to the collapse of its core and the consequent blasting off of its outer layers.

Supernova Remnant (SNR): The cloud of material ejected by a supernova explosion and sometimes visible for many thousands of years afterwards.

Transparency: The quality of the atmosphere's ability to pass light (in other words, clarity of the air).

Variable Star: A star that changes brightness periodically (whether the period is regular or not).

Wolf–Rayet Stars: Stars of a special spectral type, characterized by extremely high temperatures and broad, intense emission lines in their spectra.

White Dwarf: A hot, extremely small but fairly massive and therefore very dense star that represents the last luminous stage in many stars' lives.

Zenith: The overhead point in the sky.

Zodiac: The band of constellations in which the Sun, Moon, and planets are found and whose midline is the *ecliptic*.

Sources of Information

Handbook

Burnham, Jr., Robert. *Burnham's Celestial Handbook* (three volumes). New York: Dover Publications. There's no doubt about it: If you could only have one work to go along with your atlas and telescope, this is the one you should pick for stellar and deep-sky observations. Although some of the information is becoming outdated, this handbook contains almost all the data you would need to observe a majority of the interesting deep-sky objects visible in telescopes up to about 8 or 10 inches—plus thorough, rich, and elegant discussions of the physical nature and the lore of the objects.

Column

Houston, Walter Scott. "Deep-Sky Wonders," monthly for over 40 years in *Sky & Telescope* (see address in Periodicals below). Houston might be called the first and still the best of modern deep-sky observers and writers. Whatever you call him, his column remains as full of shrewd wisdom, exuberant enthusiasm (and the challenges that such enthusiasm calls for), and effortless, beautiful writing as you will find anywhere in all of astronomy.

Books

Ferris, Timothy. *Galaxies.* New York: Crown. This huge book is not an observer's guide, but a lucid and sumptuously illustrated account of the physical nature of galaxies and the large-scale structure of the universe.

Harrington, Philip S. *Touring the Universe through Binoculars*. New York: John Wiley & Sons. Much information also good for wide-field telescopes.

Hartmann, William K., and Ron Miller (with Pamela Lee and Tom Miller). *Cycles of Fire*. New York: Workman. A collection of many dozens of fine paintings of imagined views out among the stars and galaxies and a fascinating text concerning the nature and evolution of stars and galaxies.

Levy, David. *Observing Variable Stars*. New York: Cambridge University Press.

Mallas, John, and Evered Kreimer. *The Messier Album*. Cambridge, MA: Sky Publishing Corporation.

Manzel, Donald, and Jay Pasachoff. *Field Guide to the Stars and Planets*. Boston: Houghton Mifflin.

Mitton, Simon, ed. *The Cambridge Encyclopedia of Astronomy*. New York: Crown.

Muirden, James. *The Amateur Astronomer's Handbook*. New York: Harper & Row.

Ottewell, Guy. *The Astronomical Companion*. Illuminating diagrams and explanations of stars in general, their spectral types, double stars, variable stars, galaxies, and the three-dimensional layout of the universe from our Earth–Moon system out to the vastest spread of the cosmos. Astronomical Workshop, Furman University, Greenville, SC 29613.

Ottewell, Guy. *The Thousand-Yard Model*. Booklet with instructions for making a marvelous model of the Solar System with common objects. Available from same address as Ottewell above.

Sanford, Jack. *Observing the Constellations*. New York: Simon & Schuster. Star maps to naked-eye limit, tables, and descriptions of many objects not in Norton's lists, and dramatic color astrophotos, all in one handy volume.

Schaaf, Fred. *Seeing the Sky*. New York: John Wiley & Sons. First in the trilogy of which the book you are holding in your hands is the third. This first volume in the trilogy contains many naked-eye projects concerning topics like deep-sky objects and light pollution.

Star Atlases (in Order of Increasing Faintness Covered)

Norton's 2000.0 Star Atlas and Reference Handbook. Ian Ridpath, ed. New York: Longman Scientific & Technical and John Wiley & Sons. Limiting star magnitude: 6.5.

Sky Atlas 2000.0. By Wil Tirion. Cambridge, MA: Sky Publishing Corporation. Limiting star magnitude: 8.0.

Uranometria 2000.0 (two volumes). By Wil Tirion, Barry Rappaport, and George Lovi. Willmann-Bell, Inc., P.O. Box 3125, Richmond, VA 23235. Limiting star magnitude: 9.0.

Star Catalog

Sky Catalogue 2000.0 (two volumes). Alan Hirshfeld and Roger Sinnott, eds. Limiting star magnitude: 8.0 (companion to *Sky Atlas 2000.0*).

Telescopes

Brown, Sam. *All About Telescopes.* Edmund Scientific Company, 101 East Gloucester Pike, Barrington, NJ 08007. Outdated in places but very user-friendly with clear text and innumerable diagrams.

Muirden, James. *How to Use an Astronomical Telescope.* New York: Simon & Schuster.

Rutten, H., and M. van Venrooij. *Telescope Optics—Evaluation and Design.* Willmann-Bell, Inc. (see address for *Uranometria* above).

Periodicals

Astronomy. Kalmbach Publishing Co., 21027 Crossroads Circle, P.O. Box 1612, Waukesha, WI 53187. General astronomy magazine.

Deep Sky. Same address as for *Astronomy.* Devoted especially to deep-sky observing.

Mercury. Publication of the Astronomical Society of the Pacific, 390 Ashton Avenue, San Francisco, CA 94112. The title does not mean the magazine is only devoted to the planet Mercury—the full range of astronomy topics is covered.

Sky & Telescope. Sky Publishing Corporation, P.O. Box 9111, Belmont, MA 02178. General astronomy magazine.

Sky Calendar. Abrams Planetarium, Michigan State University, East Lansing, MI 48824.

News Service

Skyline. Recorded telephone message, updated weekly (sometimes more often), by *Sky & Telescope* (see address above). Gives nova discoveries and positions, and much else. Phone number: 617-497-4168

Annuals

Astronomical Almanac. U.S. Naval Observatory, 34th and Massachusetts Avenue, NW, Washington, DC 20392. The standard reference of this kind.

Astronomical Calendar. See address of Ottewell book above.

Observer's Handbook. Toronto: Royal Astronomical Society of Canada.

Maps, Audiovisual Aids, and Other Educational Materials

Astronomical Society of the Pacific. For address, see *Mercury* above. This organization offers photographs, slide sets, video- and audiotapes, plus books and more.

Sky Publishing Corporation. For address, see *Sky & Telescope* above. Among many other publications, ESSCO classroom publications (including Laboratory Exercises in Astronomy).

Organizations

American Association of Variable Star Observers (AAVSO). 25 Birch Street, Cambridge, MA 02138.

Association of Binary Star Observers. 306 Reynolds Drive, Saugus, MA 01906.

National Deep-Sky Observers Society. 3123 Radiance Road, Louisville, KY 40220.

Webb Society (North American Division). 1440 South Marmora Avenue, Tucson, AZ 85713.

Indexes

GENERAL INDEX

The following index cannot cite all of the celestial objects mentioned in the text. For objects that do not appear in this listing, seek out the activity that deals with that type of body. Listed here are deep-sky objects with proper names, including bright stars (listed by proper name, usually not by Bayer letter designation unless such has virtually become the proper name). Two following indexes list Messier objects by number and NGC objects by number. Terms given in this main index are generally just the major ones (see glossary for a fuller listing and definition), and the pages cited the key or first important ones on which they are discussed. References to objects or terms in the paragraphs stating the goal of each activity, and in the question section at the end of each activity are generally not given (the objects are discussed more fully in the activity text itself which is referenced in this index). People are indexed for more substantial contributions than a minor appraisal of a star's color.

MESSIER OBJECT INDEX

NGC OBJECT INDEX

This index does not include the NGC listing of most of the Messier objects, objects which appear in their own index (preceding this one).